Ada⁹⁵

for
C *and* C++
Programmers

INTERNATIONAL COMPUTER SCIENCE SERIES

Consulting Editor **A D McGettrick** University of Strathclyde

SELECTED TITLES IN THE SERIES

Programming in Ada95 *John Barnes*

Software Development with Z *J B Wordsworth*

Program Verification *N Francez*

Performance Modelling of Communication Networks *P G Harrison and N M Patel*

Concurrent Systems: An Integrated Approach to Operating Systems, Database, and Distributed Systems *J Bacon*

Introduction to Parallel Processing *B Codenotti and M Leoncini*

Concurrent Programming *A Burns and G Davies*

Comparative Programming Languages (2nd Edn) *L B Wilson and R G Clark*

Functional Programming and Parallel Graph Rewriting *R Plasmeijer and M van Eekelen*

Object-Oriented Database Systems: Concepts and Architectures *E Bertino and L D Martino*

Software Design *D Budgen*

Ada from the Beginning (2nd Edn) *J Skansholm*

Programming Language Essentials *H E Bal and D Grune*

Human-Computer Interaction *J Preece et al.*

Distributed Systems: Concepts and Design (2nd Edn) *G Coulouris, J Dollimore and T Kindberg*

Fortran 90 Programming *T M R Ellis, I R Philips and T M Lahey*

Parallel Processing: The Transputer and its Applications *M E C Hull, D Crookes and P J Sweeney*

Foundations of Computing: System Development with Set Theory and Logic *T Scheurer*

Principles of Object Oriented Engineering *A Eliëns*

Object-Oriented Programming in Eiffel *P Thomas and R Weedon*

Compiler Design *R Wilhelm and D Maurer*

Miranda: The Craft of Functional Programming *S Thompson*

Ada 95

for C and C++ Programmers

Simon Johnston

ADDISON-WESLEY

Harlow, England • Reading, Massachusetts • Menlo Park, California
New York • Don Mills, Ontario • Amsterdam • Bonn • Sydney • Singapore
Tokyo • Madrid • San Juan • Milan • Mexico City • Seoul • Taipei

© Addison Wesley Longman 1997

Addison Wesley Longman Limited
Edinburgh Gate
Harlow
Essex CM20 2JE
England

and Associated Companies throughout the World.

Cover designed by Designers and Partners Ltd, Oxford
and printed by The Riverside Printing Co. (Reading) Ltd
Illustrations by PanTek Arts, Maidstone
Typeset by 34
Typeset in 10/12 Times NR MT
Printed and bound by Biddles of Guildford

First printed 1997

ISBN 0-201-40363-3

British Library Cataloguing in Publication Data

A catalogue record for this book is available from the British Library

Contents

Trademark Notice

Windows NT is a trademark of Microsoft Corporation; Windows 95 is a trademark of
Microsoft Corporation; ObjectAda is a trademark of Aonix; AppletMagic is a trademark of
Intermetrics Inc.; Java is a trademark of Sun Microsystems Inc.; OS/2 is a trademark of
International Business Machines Corporation; Solaris is a trademark of Sun Microsystems
Inc.; Aonix is a trademark of Aonix (a company of Thomson/CSF Group); UNIX is a
trademark of X/Open Company Ltd; *Simula is a trademark of Simula AS; Smalltalk is a
trademark of Xerox Corporation; Occam is a trademark of INMOS Group of Companies;
Microsoft Word is a trademark of Microsoft Corporation; Win32 is a trademark of
Intermetrics Inc.; PL/1 is a trademark of Oracle Corporation UK Ltd.

Foreword

Ada95 was adopted as a language standard by ISO and ANSI early in 1995. To the Ada83 standard, which already embodied strong and stable support for encapsulation, generic templates, exception definition and handling, and active-object concurrent programming, Ada95 adds full support for inheritance and dynamic polymorphism, hierarchically structured program libraries, and a rich collection of standard library packages.

Since early 1995, we have seen the appearance in print of a dozen or so well-written and effective Ada95-related texts. As author of two of these, and as chair of the ACM SIGAda Education Working Group, and as an active teacher and user of Ada, I have followed the development and emergence of these books with great interest.

There is remarkably little duplication in this set of books. Each has its intended target audience; each author lends a different perspective and viewpoint to the discussion. Simon Johnston's work makes an important contribution to this text collection. Its target audience is the large number of programmers with experience in the C and C++ languages. Johnston's perspective is that of an active software developer fluent in all these languages; his goal is to show readers how Ada95 helps them to do what they already know how to do in C and C++.

Johnston has shown considerable bravery by putting early versions of this text on the World Wide Web. He has revealed his ideas to the eyes of many thousands of critical readers, and this courageous approach has benefited both readers and author. The result is a very polished piece of work.

Three features of Johnston's book are especially useful. First, his prose and code are cogent and clear. Second, throughout the book the author develops and follows through one major case study, introducing Ada95 capabilities through refinement of the design and alternative strategies. Finally, Johnston introduces and carefully explains the richness of the standard libraries, presenting these in a systematic fashion without merely paraphrasing the Reference Manual.

During the first few years of Ada83, C++ was scarcely known. Indeed, Stroustrup's landmark text on C++ appeared only late in 1985. Since then, C++ has attracted huge numbers of programmers across the industry. Ada has been widely used in the safety-critical sector, especially in real-time systems like air traffic control, satellite communication, avionics, and high speed ground transportation, but has been relatively little known outside this sector.

One can speculate at length on the reasons why C++ became so rapidly and widely popular while Ada did not. This is unproductive debate; the facts 'on the ground' are that the Ada95 standard is causing many C and C++ programmers to want to take a second look (or perhaps even a first look) at Ada.

A number of Ada95 software development systems – GNU Ada95 (GNAT), ObjectAda, AppletMagic, and others – have entered the market with strong capabilities, remarkable stability, and very moderate price tags. Nearly every popular computing 'platform' is supported by one or more of these systems, and it is even possible to produce Java applets directly from Ada95 source. The emergence of this software makes Ada95 accessible to all.

For the C or C++ programmer, Johnston's text, aided by one of these nice development systems, will go far in making the Ada95 experience a pleasant and rewarding one.

Michael B. Feldman
The George Washington University

Preface

You are a professional programmer using C and C++ to get a job done; you know the strengths and weaknesses of the language you use. What if I were to offer you a tool that could almost eradicate all those pointer problems for you (memory leaks, dangling pointers), solve all those array bounds problems for you (running off the end of arrays), and eradicate all those header file inconsistency problems for you? You have seen, as I have, a number of tools you can use to improve the safety and reliability of your code, you run them periodically to report on a file or two. This tool will work on your whole project, it runs every time you compile (at no extra cost!), and will guarantee that you cannot proceed until you have fixed problems. What is this new tool? An Ada compiler: start writing your next project in Ada95 and reap the benefits of static safe typing backed up with dynamic run-time checking and you have a programming environment that will improve the reliability of your software and your faith in it.

Why Ada?

Ada, as a programming language, has had something of a bad press; its detractors claim it is overly verbose, too complex, and technically dated. Ada has, however, always been a powerful force in the computing community: it was specifically developed to support software engineering principles with safety and reliability as prime concerns. Ada proved that object-based software could be developed in a performance-critical environment at a time when object oriented programming was being criticized for being too resource-hungry. Ada also pioneered the mainstream use of generic programming long before C++ introduced templates.

With the revision process that has provided us with the Ada95 programming language, Ada has come of age. The addition of true object oriented programming techniques, interfaces to other programming languages and a wealth of other important alterations has given us a language that allows us to get our work done with the minimum of fuss and the maximum confidence in the resulting applications. Ada has come out of its traditional military embedded systems and has hit the high street!

To sum up the philosophy of those working on the revision process I have included below the first paragraph from the introduction of the *Ada95 Reference Manual* [1]:

> 'Ada was originally designed with three overriding concerns: program reliability and maintenance, programming as a human activity, and efficiency. This revision to the language was designed to provide greater flexibility and extensibility, additional control over storage management and synchronization, and standardized packages oriented toward supporting important application areas, while at the same time retaining the original emphasis on reliability, maintainability and efficiency.'

Why this book?

The development of this book has progressed through three distinct phases. Firstly it was a simple collecting of e-mails and Internet news items that discussed C++ and Ada95. These discussions covered areas such as comparisons of language features and interfacing Ada and C/C++ code. I tried to organize this collection into some form of frequently asked question list with my own questions and answers as well. Before I completed the list it dawned on me that this might be of use to other C++ programmers hoping to benefit from using Ada, so I rewrote it as a tutorial and published it on the World Wide Web. Since making it available I have received a number of requests and comments, including one that suggested that I consider writing a book.

The result of a lot of work and even more questions is a book that will help professional C++ programmers to understand the Ada95 programming language and see where it will benefit them as software engineers. It is important to remember that Ada95 is just a programming language; it is not a cure-all and does not do your work for you. The course of this book expects that the reader is familiar with programming complex systems, usually in C or C++, and has some experience in object oriented programming, possibly some systems programming, and possibly some experience with a multi-threaded environment.

New topics will be introduced wherever possible in C++ terminology and then using the Ada terms and semantics so that not only is the programming language taught, but also the culture and background.

Structure

The book is in two parts: the first covers the core language with its structures, types, and organization; the second part focuses on the library and the Ada95 specialized needs annexes, sections which provide optional support for certain specialist application areas.

Part 1   The core language

Chapter 1   Introduction

This brief chapter includes the history of the Ada programming language and a short tour of language features. It also introduces and examines the examples and the ongoing case study used in the text.

Chapter 2   Language building blocks

We start our tour of Ada with the control structures and operators provided by the language. This section should hold no great surprises; at the level of simple statements, the two languages are very similar.

Chapter 3   Strong typing for solid programs

This chapter provides a description of the standard types and more importantly the general type model which underpins Ada's mechanisms supporting abstract data types and object oriented programming. C++ has brought strong typing to C programmers but the type checking in Ada is far stricter.

Chapter 4   Packages for structured programming

Packages are a feature found in a number of languages such as Modula-2, Modula-3 [18] and Oberon [17] (in these languages they are called modules). They provide name spaces and are an important feature for designing Abstract Data Types (ADTs) and object-based designs.

Chapter 5   Generics for reusable programming

Like templates in C++ Ada provides a method for producing parameterized subprograms which can then be instantiated for a number of argument types. Ada also allows us to develop generic packages for parameterized types. This all leads to the provision of more general types and algorithms to support a high level of reuse.

Chapter 6   Tagged types for objected oriented programming

Ada has always allowed object-based design and programming (based around abstract data types). Tagged types are the Ada95 facility for true object oriented programming. Tagged types provide inheritance and polymorphism and are as powerful as classes in C++, though their different implementation can be frustrating for C++ programmers new to Ada.

Chapter 7   Tasking for concurrent programming

Ada provides portable language features for concurrent processing within a single program. This facility is similar to the facilities called threads or lightweight processes found in many modern operating systems such as OS/2, Windows 95, Windows NT, or Solaris.

Ada95 has extended some of these features and added a passive thread-safe component called a protected type.

Part 2   The Ada library and language annexes

Chapter 8   A standard library for portable programming

The standard library defined for Ada83 and Ada95 is vast. A number of common topics are covered, including input/output and mathematical operations. One very strong feature of the Ada95 library is its string handling. Although introduced in the section on the string type itself a more detailed tour will be presented here.

Chapter 9   Language annexes

The annexes contain additional features which, in some cases, may be left unimplemented by compiler vendors. The exception is the annex describing features to interface Ada to code written in other languages; this annex is required.

The description of the core language will attempt to cover as much common ground as possible to start with so that change is brought in as slowly as possible. However, this does not mean that I have shied away from introducing Ada features for which there is no C++ equivalent; this is not a comparison of the two languages. Many modern operating systems, for example, contain constructs known either as *lightweight processes* or as *threads* which allow programmers to have multiple threads of execution within the same address space. Ada has a model of concurrency in the core language itself which means that you can write applications using multiple threads that will operate even on operating systems which do not directly support threads. The tour of the standard library and annexes provides further knowledge allowing you to apply the language to complex problems with the minimum of development by introducing extensive string handling, file and text input/output, mathematics libraries, systems programming support, and real-time systems support amongst others.

Style

I have used the standard Ada documentation conventions; code will be in Courier font, like this with keywords in bold, like **this**. The C++ code will also appear in the Courier font,but no keyword highlighting will be done; this is usual in C++ documentation.

Some topics, however, may not be covered as fully here as in other texts, especially [6] and [7], because I hope to present a book that will help to convert your professional skill and knowledge of one high-level language, C++, into marketable skills in Ada95. I will attempt to avoid getting into detailed language design issues and focus on the information required to perform everyday tasks. This has led to a somewhat terse style because I am assuming that my readers have already learned the science and art of software design and implementation and are more interested in solving problems than the pseudo-religion of programming language design. I will also include as many references to the *Ada Reference Manual* [1] as possible so that you may read over a topic in more detail if you want.

Why one case study?

As we go through the book we will be working on fragments of a single case study, though in many cases smaller stand-alone examples will have to suffice in the earlier chapters since we will not have covered enough to work with real code. We may have to re-implement the work two or three times, but such re-implementation of code using more appropriate techniques is part of our everyday existence as programmers. The case study itself is taken from work I have done with ICL Retail Systems, although it is not based directly on any work made commercially available by them. The completed example is available on the companion CD or from my web site, and contains more than I managed to get into this book. If you have comments, queries, or improvements to the application, write and I will maintain an *extended* copy as well!

Companion CD-ROM

The companion CD-ROM contains a complete Ada95 compiler environment for the Windows NT and the Windows 95 operating systems, kindly provided by Aonix. Aonix have also provided a number of useful resources other than the compiler and its tutorial.

- The Ada95 Language Reference Manual. This text is the official language definition document for the Ada programming language. It is clear, concise and as part of the open development process of the Ada language printable copies are made freely available. This free access promotes the use of the text, where for example the C++ equivalent is expensive and rarely used by programmers.
- The Ada95 Rationale. This is a document which accompanies the language reference manual and describes why the language is the way it is, some of the decisions involved in the language design and more in the way of examples than the reference manual. Again you will find nearly all Ada programmers have access to the Rationale as it is also distributed free.
- All the examples are provided in source form on the CD, and should compile with any version of the GNAT compiler, though some packages may contain

operating system dependent code. I have also committed to keeping an up-to-date copy on my web site at `http://www.acm.org/~skj/CppToAda/examples.html`. All examples have been compiled using the Aonix compiler and also the GNAT Ada95 compiler for Win32 from LabTek at Yale University.

Other Internet resources which are useful to all Ada programmers include the *Home of the Brave Ada Programmers* World Wide Web site at `http://www.adahome.com/` which will contain many of the resources from this CD and is also one of the best places to start looking for general Ada information. The Usenet news group `comp.lang.ada` is alive with debate on the language itself, helps with common problems and is frequented by most of the acknowledged experts on the language.

Simon K. Johnston
`http://www.acm.org/~skj/`
`skj@acm.org`

Acknowledgments

The author would like to thank the following people:

Tucker Taft (Intermetrics) for the initial idea for a WWW page and constant help since. Magnus Kempe (EPFL) for maintaining the Home of the Brave Ada Programmers WWW site and checking my initial WWW pages. Michael Bartz (University of Memphis), David Wheeler (IDA), Kevin Nash (Bournemouth University), Laurent Guerby (student at Télécom Bretagne), and Bill Wagner (Hazeltine) for comments on the WWW pages. Jono Powell (ICL) for comments on the WWW page and proof reading early work on the book. Finally Keith Burton (ICL) for his honest and constructive comments on the first draft.

Mike Feldman (GWU) for comments, encouragement, guidance, and the initial contact with Addison Wesley Longman. LabTek for the Windows NT version of GNAT used to develop the code in this book and Tom Griest in particular for fielding my queries and gripes. Mitch Gart (Intermetrics) for the Ada95 binding to the Win32 API used in the example. The compiler vendor Aonix also provided a Windows NT compiler for me to develop my code with (ObjectAda 7.0) and to David Wood, who organized it, my thanks.

Kit Lester (University of Portsmouth) for teaching me Ada in the first place, and as one of those who inspired me to enjoy what I do.

Finally the people at Addison Wesley Longman, Simon Plumtree, Fiona Kinnear and specifically Sally Mortimore.

Addison Wesley Longman Ltd and the author gratefully acknowledge Aonix Software for providing the ObjectAda compiler on which the examples were tested. The publisher wishes to thank the following for permission to reproduce material in this book: quotation from M. Ellis & B. Stroustrup, *The Annotated C++ Reference Manual*, (extract from p.165) © 1990 At & T Bell Telephone Laboratories Inc., reprinted by permission of Addison Wesley Longman Inc., Reading, MA; quotations from the *Ada Reference Manual*, taken from the Intermetrics Inc. printed copy.

Aonix international offices are located at:

United States
10251 Vista Sorrento Parkway
San Diego, CA 92121
1-800-97-AONIX
Tel: (619) 457-2700
Fax: (619) 452-2117
email: info@aonix.com

European Headquarters – France
Batiment H
66–68 Avenue Pierre Brossolette
92247 MALAKOFF Cedex
France
Tel: +33 1 41 48 10 00
Fax: +33 1 41 48 10 20

UK
Partridge House
Newton Road
Henley On Thames, OXON, RG9 1EN
United Kingdom
Tel: +44 1 491 57 90 90
Fax: +44 1 491 57 18 66

Germany
Kleinoberfeld 7
D-76135 KARLSRUHE
Germany
Tel: +49 721 98 65 30
Fax: +49 721 98 65 398
email: info@aonix.de

Sweden
Martinens Vag 30
S-13640 Haninge
Sweden
Tel: +46 8 707 30 60
Fax: +46 8 707 30 80

Part 1

The core language

The following chapters cover the language itself; the syntax and semantics. The core language as covered by the ISO (International Organization for Standardization) standard should be implemented by all compilers, although some embedded systems may, for instance, not have tasking support.

Wherever possible, the text will build upon only features introduced before; however, the Ada language is intricate and many features are supportive, for example packages and tagged types are bound up very closely and so if I do have to refer forward please bear with me.

These chapters act as the foundation for the rest of the book; they will give you a brief introduction to Ada basics, such as types and statements. Once you have an understanding of these you will be able to read quite a lot of Ada source without difficulty. We start with the Ada operators, arithmetic, relational logical and bitwise (C++ classification). Section 2.3 covers the statements available in Ada and compares them directly with their C++ counterparts. The following section on types is possibly the most challenging and may require some attention; Ada is very strongly typed but provides a very wide set of predefined or library types and allows you an unprecedented level of control over defining your own types. Chapter 2 ends with a view of the safety features of Ada and some of the *unsafe* features.

Introduction

1.1   Ada95: a short history

We can trace the roots of the Ada language back to attempts by each of the US armed services to implement a common, high-level programming language. Each service did, and still does, develop large amounts of mission and safety-critical real-time systems frequently based around embedded systems. These are often developed by more than one contractor, each with their own favourite languages/systems. The United States Department of Defense decided that the definition of the language should also be a common project and so the individual service projects were brought together in 1975 under the title 'High-Order Language Working Group' (HOLWG).

This group then met once a month to attempt to establish a set of common (existing) programming languages that could be used across service projects. It was realized that one common language was preferable and so each language was in turn measured against the working group's requirements which became known as 'Strawman'.

The Strawman was a loose document which included general requirements in the areas of reliability, maintainability, efficiency, and implementability. You will notice that none of these requirements is easily measured and some are very subjective. The group had to be careful not to get too detailed and to preclude any of their identified languages this early in the process. Up until this time there had been no funding or official direction in these proceedings until political support was gained from the Department of Defense for Research and Engineering and initial financial support was gained from the Navy. With this backing the Strawman was reviewed and refined into a complete set of requirements, the Woodenman.

This document was ordered into required language characteristics and secondary 'welcome' characteristics. At this point Woodenman was reviewed, not only by the services and Department of Defense, but also by the general academic and commercial community across the world.

The next issue of these requirements, Tinman, removed a number of requirements and formalized the remainder into a document which in January 1976 was accepted by the Assistant Secretary of Defense for Research and Engineering. This acceptance led to a further round of comments leading to a workshop held at Cornell University which looked at the technical feasibility of each of the requirements.

It was about this time that the scope for the language was widened, the focus on real-time embedded systems was expanded to include the problems of large-scale, multi-contractor software engineering projects. The request was now for a truly wide-reaching, general-purpose programming language.

Before the next release, Ironman, a number of groups set about comparing current programming languages (including Algol 68 and PL/1) against the Tinman requirements and found that not one of the 23 languages under study could act as a single, common development language. Thus Ironman (January 1977) was in effect a requirement specification for a new high-order language.

Ironman already had a different feel to its predecessors; rather than being a discussion document based around a set of general topics, it was written as a specification for, or description of, the required language. It became clear that it was from Ironman that someone would be developing a new, common high-order language.

The design of this language was put out to tender, with 4 groups (selected from an initial entry of 17) competing to develop the language. The teams were Cii-Honeywell Bull, Intermetrics, SofTech, and SRI International, which were all given a colour code to keep judging impartial (Green, Red, Blue, and Yellow, respectively). In 1978 the four teams were reduced to two by a review which included evaluation by no fewer than 125 panels across the world.

On 2 May 1979 it was announced to the world that the selection was Green; the result of a review by now 900 panels had selected the Cii-Honeywell Bull team led by Jean Ichbiah.

1.1.1 The name 'Ada'

The name 'Ada' was proposed by Commander John D. Cooper from the Navy. Up until this point the language had been known as DoD-1, a designator that was both unfriendly and might adversely influence its acceptance in the commercial world. Ada, Countess of Lovelace, was arguably the world's first computer programmer, helping Charles Babbage work out some of the principles of the Analytical Engine and how to program it.

It was very important that the Ada language was quickly standardized so that the idea of a common language was a reality. The initial standard was developed by the Department of Defense as MIL-STD-1815 (the number 1815 was chosen as it was the year of birth of Ada Lovelace). This standard was then developed by the American National Standards Institute (ANSI) standards group who published the Language Reference Manual in 1983. In 1987 the International Organization for Standardization (ISO) published standard 8652 for the Ada programming language.

1.1.2   Validation

As another approach to standardization the Department of Defense held the trademark Ada, which was only granted to a compiler implementation when it had passed a set of standard, independent, validation tests. These tests ensured that no vendor could supply a subset or superset of the language and ensured portability and customer confidence in the language. Since this time, however, the Department of Defense has dropped ownership of the Ada trademark, but still continues to validate compilers offering compiler vendors a (currently pentagon shaped) validation certification sticker.

1.1.3   Ada 9X Project

In 1988 it was decided that the language specification could benefit from a review in the light of new requirements, new technology, and new environments. The Ada 9X project was started and in 1990 the initial requirements proposal was published. Again the Department of Defense sent out an invitation to tender to a number of teams and this time the job of design went to a team at Intermetrics (led by S. Tucker Taft) who developed the new standard.

In February 1995 Ada95 was born as ISO-8652: 1995. The standard has been developed in a flexible manner and contains a mandatory section on the core language that must still be fully implemented to pass validation. Added to this are seven annexes (six of which are optional in a compiler implementation) which address industry-specific areas such as real-time, systems programming, and information systems. One of the major enhancements to the language was the provision of language features for object oriented programming, bringing Ada into line with its more modern counterparts such as C++.

Ada83 did not provide what many people term **true object oriented** features, although object-based, and even object oriented programming can be accomplished in the language with some thought. Ada83 was statically provable, which means that you could follow the route the code would take given certain inputs from the source code alone. This has been a great benefit and provided Ada programmers with a great deal of confidence in the code they wrote.

Ada95 has introduced new features covering what most people saw as deficiencies in Ada83, object oriented programming through tagged types, a better model for access types (pointers), including access to subprograms which make it more difficult to prove an Ada95 program statically, but the language designers decided that such features merited their inclusion in the language to further another goal, that of high reuse.

Many firms use Ada with its reputation for reliability, maintainability, and cost effectiveness; many universities use Ada with its ability to support many software engineering principles and its safety. Now that it has been brought up to date I think Ada95 can only do well: cheaper, more accessible compilers and tools are coming to market every day and it will be a foolish manager who does not consider Ada as a core technology when setting out development requirements today.

Table 1.1 compares the timelines of the Ada95 programming language and C++ (taken from [15]).

1.2 A brief tour of the language

The Ada programming language is a seemingly large and complex language, although, as we progress, you will realize that underpinning it is a relatively small set of values that have been selected to provide support for many types of programming tasks.

Ada was designed to support the development of large, sometimes very large, and complex reliable systems. To this end it has many features which promote the development of reusable software which includes a typing model with compile-time checks that protect the developer of one component from its misuse elsewhere. To assist in the decomposition of software into components for either design or development reasons Ada provides the package mechanism which provides a way to describe the interface for a component and its dependencies.

This section will introduce a few brief examples so that we can refer forward to some features introduced later in the text. The reason for this is two-fold: firstly to give you a flavour for the things we will cover during the remainder of the text and secondly to allow us to use some later features to make earlier examples a little more accessible.

To start our tour let us consider the now ubiquitous *Hello World* program and how we would tend to implement it in C:

```
#include <stdio.h>

void main (void)
{
    puts ("Hello World");
}
```

This is nice and simple; the only point worth noting is that you have to include the header file for `stdio` so that the `main` function has a prototype available for the `puts` function. If we were now to re-implement this using C++ we could simply use the code above (most valid C code is also valid C++) or we could decide to use some more C++ specific features:

```
#include <iostream.h>

void main (void)
{
    const char* message = "Hello World";
    cout << message << nl;
}
```

Table 1.1   Development of Ada95 and C++.

1974	Department of Defense starts looking at its spending on software projects.
1975	Department of Defense initiates High-Order Language Working Group. The first document from this group, Strawman, is published.
1976	Tinman accepted by the Assistant Secretary of Defense for Research and Engineering and the Cornell workshop was held.
1977	Ironman, the requirement specification for the new common programming language, published and the Department of Defense begins the competition to design the new language.
1978	The final two teams were reviewed by the 125 panels world-wide. Steelman published.
1979	The Green team led by Jean Ichbiah was announced the winner. Bjarne Stroustrup begins work on C with Classes and first implementation completed.
1980	The High-Order Language Working Group becomes the Ada Joint Program Office.
1982	First public paper on C with Classes published by Stroustrup. Ada named by Commander John Cooper.
1983	The language reference manual for MIL-STD-1815, the *Ada Programming Language*, is published. C++ is named and the first implementation is in use.
1984	First C++ language manual.
1985	First commercial release of C++, Cfront release 1.0 and the book *The C++ Programming Language* available.
1987	Cfront 1.2 released as is the first GNU C++ compiler. ISO publishes ISO-8652, the international standard for the Ada programming language.
1988	The Ada 9X project is started.
1989	ANSI X3J16 committee first meets to discuss an ANSI C++ standard.
1990	The initial requirements proposal for Ada 9X is published as is *The Annotated C++ Reference Manual*. Two new features, templates and exceptions, are accepted into the C++ language.
1991	The first meeting of ISO WG21, the C++ working group.
1993	Two new features, run-time type identification and namespaces, are accepted into the C++ language.
1994	First public release of GNAT at the Paris Ada Europe conference.
1995	The first draft of the proposed ISO C++ standard. ISO publishes ISO-8652:1995, the new Ada95 standard, the first international standard object oriented programming language.
1996	First validated compiler available from Intermetrics, followed closely by GNAT compilers for Silicon Graphics machines.

This is a slightly better piece of code since it also defines the text as a constant called message, making it easier to change at a later date. It also uses the C++ streams library denoted by the include file `iostream.h` instead of `stdio.h` and then uses the stream operators `<<` to the standard stream `cout`.

1.2.1 Examples

We can now look at how we might write the message 'Hello World' in Ada. The following example is our first look at real code so we will describe it in some detail below.

This text relies heavily on the examples included, and the full text of these can be found on the CD. I have classified the examples into the following three types:

- 'Snippets' – short extracts which illustrate a certain point. They are not compilable on their own and are not included on the companion CD.

- Full code examples – still small, these can be taken, compiled, and used elsewhere. Each such example can be found on the CD and will also include descriptive comments and headers, not shown in the text for brevity.

- Extracts from the case study below. These extracts will not in general appear on the CD, although the complete solution will. In some cases, however, where an alternative to the final solution is explored in the text it may appear in the chapter's example directory.

The CD contains an examples directory with a subdirectory for each chapter. Example 1.1 shown above is therefore in the `Chapt01` subdirectory held as `Hello_World.adb` and is ready to compile and run.

Note that I have not included the C/C++ example code.

Example 1.1   The simplest input/output example _____

```
--  **************************************************************
--  *                     Hello_World.adb
--  * Copyright (c) Simon Johnston & Addison Wesley Longman 1996.
--  *
--  * Chapter: 01  Example 01
--  * Description: This is an example of what an example looks
--  *    like, taken from the introduction chapter.
--  * Inputs:     None.
--  * Outputs:    will write the contents of the constant string
--  *             "Message" to the standard output stream.
--  **************************************************************

--  Note that in the rest of the examples in the book the header
--  shown above will not be present, for brevity. The comment below
--  naming the file in which the example exists will be present.
```

```
-- file: Hello_World.adb
with Ada.Text_IO;
use  Ada.Text_IO;

procedure Hello_World is
   Message : constant String := "Hello World";
begin

   Put_Line(Item=> Message);
end Hello_World;
```

1.2.2   Case

Before we look into this example too deeply we should note one major difference between C/C++ and Ada; Ada is case-insensitive. This means that **begin BEGIN Begin** are all the same. This can be a problem when porting case-sensitive C code into Ada. The standard convention used in this book for writing Ada code is that keywords are written in lower case and will appear in the text in bold (as above). Identifiers are capitalized with names separated with underscores, for example An_Integer, A_Function.

The example itself starts with a comment block describing the example using the Ada comment sequence – similar to the C++ comment //. The code itself starts with the two lines

```
with Ada.Text_IO;
use  Ada.Text_IO;
```

which fulfils a similar need to either #include <stdio.h> or #include <iostream.h> in that it makes available the library operations for input/output (I/O). In Ada terms we have used the package called Ada.Text _IO. For a complete description of packages and the differences between packages in Ada and header files in C/C++ see Chapter 4.

The next block of code is the equivalent to the main function in the above examples and uses the Put_Line procedure to write the string message out to the console. The usage of the Put_Line procedure illustrates another syntactic difference, the use of named parameters.

```
Put_Line(Item => Message);
```

The identifier Item is the name of the parameter in the procedure specification in the library package. This syntax can be used for functions that take a number of arguments, or overloaded functions to identify which parameters are being passed.

Note that in Ada there is no special name for the procedure which acts as the starting point for an application; any parameterless procedure can be named as start point at link time.

The following example demonstrates some more I/O functions, using another library package to output numeric values.

Example 1.2   Another simple I/O example ————————————————————

```
-- file: Simple_Math.adb
with Ada.Text_IO;
use  Ada.Text_IO;
with Ada.Integer_Text_IO;
use  Ada.Integer_Text_IO;

procedure Simple_Math is

   Result : Integer;
begin

   Result := 2 + 2;
   Put (Item => "The result of 2 + 2 is ");
   Put (Item => Result);
   New_Line;
end Simple_Math;
```

Obviously we would expect to see the result 4; try it for yourself.

1.3   A case study: Point of Sale systems

To assist in our understanding of the Ada 95 programming language I felt that as well as the small examples included in the text a more substantial case study should be followed through the course of the text. This case study will allow us to consider design as well as programming issues and will demonstrate how many of the features of the language interact and support large-scale programming efforts.

The case study itself is the development of a Point of Sale (PoS) system for a small store, not a supermarket, which will replace some simple cash registers currently in use. Our customer has seen a catalog of peripherals he or she can attach to a standard personal computer, via standard serial ports, which will transform it into an all-singing, all-dancing PoS Terminal (PoST).

This section will outline the requirements for this system which we will add to as we progress through the text.

1.3.1   Analysis

During discussion with our customer we have covered the functionality required of the software system to control the Point of Sale:

- When started the application must detect if it is a valid time to be running, valid times being called the trading time. If it is not a valid trading time then the application will not continue.

- Allow for multiple users, so the user must enter his or her user ID and password before commencing a transaction so that the proprietor can then see which transactions were performed by which member of staff.

- Also allow for the possibility of more than one terminal; therefore each terminal must have a unique identifier.

- Keep a database of sale items, each with a price, description, and department code (department codes are used to denote taxable items).

- To accept and log a sale transaction. A sale transaction must consist of one or more items sold, and one or more payments totalling the value of the goods sold, or if in excess then change must be given.

- Payment types are cash, cheque, and credit cards, though more may be introduced at a later date, such as gift vouchers, so the system must be able to cope with possible extensions.

- The log must consist of all transactions, each item in the transaction and each payment type. The log will also consist of other important information such as users signing on or off and application events such as starting and stopping.

- Manage a standard set of peripheral devices, connected via the PC's serial or parallel port. The peripherals identified so far are:

  - Customer display (2×20 character LED (light-emitting diode) line display).
  - Cashier display (2×20 character LED line display). The cashier might have the PC monitor on, so it is possible to reflect the cashier display in the text window where the application is running.
  - Receipt printer (simple 40-column printer on continuous paper).
  - Cash drawer.
  - Bar-code scanner.

- Manage a simple user interface which allows the operator a complete view of the transaction.

The initial platform will be Windows NT, because the proprietor is already running it for other applications. However the system should be designed in an operating system neutral manner so the customer can run it on a different system if required.

1.3.2 Design

The overall design criteria are as follows:

- The bulk of the system should consist of a set of object oriented abstractions which cover the major elements of the system.

- These abstractions should be considered as part of a library which is then used by the separate applications.
- The abstractions can be backed up by data files to store information between
    - items – the things sold by the store,
    - departments – each item is part of a department which denotes some additional properties,
    - tenders – the type of money used to pay for items,
    - users – each user has some details stored about them, and
    - configuration – a set of values used to configure each terminal in the system.
- The data files are to use a common data access system. This can be written as part of the system or third party libraries can be used.
- The system should be made as customer-independent as possible, since we might like to sell it to someone else one day. This means that the customer-dependent parts of the application itself should be written in one place to facilitate easy customization.

1.3.3 Implementation

Abstractions

Analysis of the previous requirements led us to identify the following sets of abstractions:

- A set of common types: currency, quantity, descriptions.
- The system-wide abstractions: users, terminals, departments, and items.
- Trading application abstractions: tender types, transactions, promotions, and the peripheral abstractions.
- Logging: this is to be provided as a set of abstractions that describe events to be logged.
- A set of support abstractions: lists and file handling, for instance.

As we continue we will start to implement some of these abstractions, demonstrating how we can separate these sets into distinct libraries (using child packages) and how we can employ object oriented techniques to build hierarchies of classes (using tagged types).

For example, Figure 1.1 is an object model diagram, using the object modeling technique (OMT) notation described in [20], of the hierarchy used to describe the peripheral objects. Some support utilities are provided to the customer. These include:

- `Create_Database` which sets up default entries in the user, item, and department data files. This must be done first to make sure that the data is available for the trading application.
- `View_Log` which reads the log file and displays all activities. It is configurable from the command line to view only data for a given station, or starting from a given time.

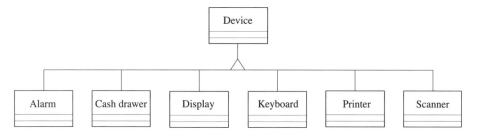

Figure 1.1   Object model.

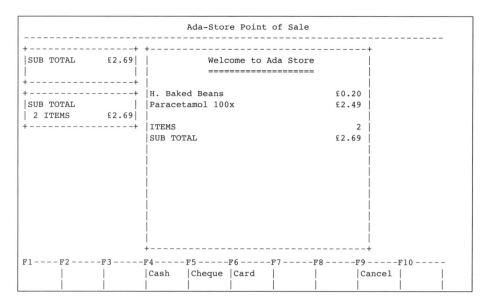

Figure 1.2   Screen shot of the application.

- `View_Basket` which reads the log and produces on the screen a complete representation of a basket. It is like a receipt but can be run from the command line to view a previous basket.

Figure 1.2 is a screen shot of the application in action. It shows the point where two lines have been sold and the subtotal calculated. The user is now waiting for the customer to pay.

1.3.4   Implementation deficiencies

The implementation provided has a number of known deficiencies and the list below presents some of these, which you may like to treat as exercises:

- The system, although expected to work in an environment with more than one terminal, has no central resource for sharing information between running applications. One possible implementation is to use the distributed systems annex (see Section 9.4) to provide shared information.

- The data files implemented all have their own file-handling code. It would be better if we could factor out this code. Possible implementations include a generic (Chapter 5) database package or a tagged type (Chapter 6) that can be derived from.

- It would be nice to provide some reporting statistics from the log file, such as transactions per day, items sold, etc.

2 Language building blocks

This chapter introduces the very heart of the language, its statements, control structures, and subprogram syntax. This is the first step on the road to understanding Ada and provides our first set of full examples. It is important that you have read this section fully before moving on since the text has been constructed as far as possible in a linear fashion. Having said this, the chapter may be read in less detail by readers familiar with the Pascal family of languages including Algol, Modula-2, Modula-3, and Oberon.

2.1 Reserved words

It is always worth reviewing the keywords (section 2.9 of the reference manual) in a programming language; Figure 2.1 shows the Ada95 set; those with an asterisk have been added since the Ada83 standard. One of the common, though misguided, ways of measuring the *complexity* of a programming language is to measure the number of key or reserved words. As you can see Ada does have a large set, although with the recent extensions to the C++ programming language there is now quite a similarity in the number of words in these two languages.

```
abort        else         new          return
abs          elsif        not          reverse
abstract*    end          null
accept       entry                     select
access       exception                 separate
aliased*     exit         of           subtype
all                       or
and          for          others       tagged*
array        function     out          task
at                                     terminate
             generic      package      then
begin        goto         pragma       type
body                      private
             if           procedure
case         in           protected*   until*
constant     is                        use
                          raise
declare                   range        when
delay        limited      record       with
delta        loop         rem
digits                    renames
do           mod          requeue*     xor
```

Figure 2.1   Ada95 keywords.

2.2   Operators

The set of C++ and Ada operators are similar, though frequently different in detail. Tables 2.1–2.7 compare the C++ and Ada operators, presented by category.

Table 2.1   Arithmetic operators.

Operator	C++	Ada
Addition	+	+
Subtraction	−	−
Multiplication	*	*
Division	/	/
Increment	++	
Decrement	−−	
Modulo division		mod
Remainder	%	rem
Absolute value		abs
Exponentiation		**

Table 2.2   Relational operators.

Operator	C++	Ada
Equality test	==	=
Non Equality test	!=	/=
Less Than	<	<
Less Than or Equal	<=	<=
Greater Than	>	>
Greater Than or Equal	>=	>=
Membership		in

Table 2.3   Assignment operation.

Operation	C++	Ada
Assignment	=	:=

One operation which does not fit into any category is the assignment operation, shown in Table 2.3. The differences in assignment (:=in Ada) and equality (simply = in Ada) are very important as they tend to be one of the common typing errors made by C/C++ programmers coding Ada programs. The following two code snippets are therefore identical:

```
if (an_int == 0)
{
    an_int = 1;
}
if An_Int = 0 then
    An_Int := 1;
end if;
```

Table 2.4   Logical operators.

Operator	C++	Ada
And	&&	and
Or	||	or
Not	!	not
Xor		xor

Table 2.5 Bitwise operators.

Operator	C++	Ada
And	&	and
Or	|	or
Xor	^	xor
Shift left	<<	
Shift right	>>	

Note that in the library package `Interfaces`, the operations `Shift_Left`, `Shift_Right`, `Rotate_Left`, and `Rotate_Right` are defined. These library procedures act on special unsigned integer types declared in the same package and described in the language reference manual, section B.2.

Table 2.6 Special operators.

Operator	C++	Ada
Stream in	>>	`'Read` `'Input`
Stream out	<<	`'Write` `'Output`
Address of	&	`'Address`
Pointer de-reference	*	
Ternary	? :	
Array concatenation		&
Range specification		..

In Table 2.6 the stream operators << and >> in C++ are overloaded versions of the shift operators. They are used for streaming as a convention, not because of any special meaning; they are active if one of the operands is of a stream type. Section 8.2.3 discusses Ada's approach to streams based around the attributes listed in the table.

The two operators & and * and their relation to the Ada `'Access` attribute will be discussed in Section 3.5 when we reach the subject of access types.

Table 2.7 C's combined operators.

Type					
Arithmetic	+=	-=	*=	/=	%=
Bitwise	&=	|=	^=		

In C and C++ a set of *combined operators* are available: Table 2.7. Combined operators allow you to combine either an arithmetic operation or a bitwise operation with an assignment. This makes the following two lines identical in operation:

```
an_int   = an_int + 2;  // longhand.
an_int += 2;            // using combined operator.
```

There are no combined operators in Ada; the long-hand version of assignment must always be used.

2.3   C++ statements to Ada

There are few examples in this section. I am assuming that your background will be in C and C++ programming (possibly you have already met Ada before) but in any case I will assume you have some programming experience. The only major difference between Ada and C++ at this level is syntax and so I will simply map a C++ construct to its Ada equivalent.

   Note: comments in Ada start with two minus signs, ––, and continue to the end of line. This is equivalent to the C++ // comment. No equivalent to /* ... */ exists in Ada.

2.3.1   The null statement

In C and C++ if we do not want to do anything, a simple semicolon on its own indicates a null statement, or *no-op*. In Ada we must be a little more explicit and use the statement **null**.

   Null statements are often used to specify logic in a readable manner or to mark a place holder for code to be added later, as in the examples below:

```
if ( thing_is_true )
{
    ;
} else
{
    do_something();
}

void empty_function (void)
{
    ; // add code later
}
```

The code below, although using constructs we have not covered yet, should be still readable:

```
if Thing_Is_True then
    null;
```

```
else
    Do_Something;
end if;
procedure Empty is
begin
    null;
end Empty;
```

2.3.2 Compound statement

A compound statement (known as a block in Ada and described in section 5.6 of the
reference manual) in C allows you to define variables local to that block; in C++ variables can be defined anywhere. In Ada objects are declared as part of the block, but
must appear in the declaration part which appears before the **begin** keyword.

```
{
    declarations

    statements
}
block_name:
    declare
        declarations
    begin
        statements
    end block_name;
```

Block naming

The block name and the declaration part are optional, simply **begin statements end**
is required. The declaration part is used to introduce new variables into a block of code:

```
begin -- simplified form.
    statements
end;
```

Ada loops can also be qualified by a name, which will be discussed further in
Section 2.3.5 on looping constructs; however, it can be used to improve readability.

Example 2.1   Ada block structure ─────────────────────────────

```
A_Block:
    begin
        Init_Code:
            begin
                Some—Code;
```

```
        end Init_Code;

    Main_Loop:
        loop
            if Some_Value then
                exit loop Main_Loop;
            end if;
        end loop Main_Loop;

    Term_Code:
        begin
            Some_Code;
        end Term_Code;
end A_Block;
```

You can readily see the position and use of block names, as a means of identifying code and increasing readability. We will cover the use of block names and looping constructs in Section 2.3.5 below.

2.3.3   if **statement**

The if statement (section 5.3 of the reference manual) is the primary selection tool available to programmers. The Ada **if** statement also has the **elsif** construct (which can be used more than once in any if statement), which is very useful for large complex selections where a switch/case statement is not possible.

   Note: Ada does not require brackets around the expressions used in **if, case** or **loop** statements.

```
if (expression)
{
    statements
} else if (expression)
{
    statements
} else
{
    statements
}

if expression then
    statements
elsif expression then
    statements
else
    statements
end if;
```

Short cuts

Have you ever had to code nested `if` statements such as the following in C++ to get around the problem of null pointers?

```
if (device != NULL)
{
    if (device->messages_available())
    {
        Message a_message = device->next_message();
    }
}
```

The reason for such nested code is that before the ANSI standard for C we had to test the `device` pointer before de-referencing it, since the language specification did not guarantee the order of evaluation. This meant the following code could not be used (a common mistake for inexperienced programmers):

```
if ((device) &&
      (device->messages_available()))
{
    a_message = device->next_message();
}
```

The Ada designers understood this mistake, and realized that the example above is a common programming requirement and one that you would logically like to group together. Consider the following:

```
if Device /= null and then
      Messages_Available(Device) = TRUE then

      A_Message = Next_Message(Device);
end if;
```

The **and then** construct forces the compiler to evaluate the first expression, and only evaluates the second if the first is true. This then behaves as we expect, the de-reference of the pointer `Device` cannot fail in the second test because the first check failed.

As you might expect the **and then** construct has a matching **or else** construct:

```
if Device = null or else
      Handler = null then

      Ada.Text_IO.Put_Line("Oops, dont know what next");
end if;
```

2.3.4   `switch` **statement**

The `switch` or `case` statement (section 5.4 of the reference manual) is a very useful tool where the number of possible values is large, and the selection expression is of a constant scalar type.

```
switch (expression)
{
    case value: statements
    default:    statements
}
```

```
case expression is
    when value  => statements
    when others => statements
end case;
```

In Ada the `default:` clause is represented by **when others** (**others** as a keyword is frequently used in this catch-all manner). There is another point worth noting here. In C the end of the statement block between case statements is a `break` statement, otherwise we drop through into the next case. In Ada such a statement is not required as the end of a clause is signified by either the **when** of the next clause or the **end** of the case statement itself.

   This lack of a `break` statement in Ada is more important than the simple syntactic difference. It is not uncommon to find a switch statement in C which looks like this:

```
switch (integer_value)
{
    case 1:
    case 2:
    case 3:
    case 4:
       value_ok = 1;
       break;
    case 5:
    case 6:
    case 7:
       break;
}
```

This allows us to perform a single action for a given set of values. Ada also allows us to combine values together in two ways. Consider the following:

```
case integer_value is
    when 1 .. 4     => value_ok := 1;
    when 5 | 6 | 7 => null;
end case;
```

This example uses the Ada syntax representing a range of values (see Section 3.3) to signify *1 through 4* and the selection syntax to represent *5 or 6 or 7*. You will also note that in the Ada example there must be a statement for each case, so we have used the Ada **null** statement as the operation of the second selection.

   Note: If all the **when** clauses do not cover all possibilities then a **when others** clause must be added; a **case** statement must cope with all possible values in Ada. A failure to cover all possible values results in a compilation error. The example above should therefore have been written as:

```
case integer_value is
    when 1 .. 4      => value_ok := 1;
    when others      => null;
end case;
```

2.3.5   Ada loops

All Ada loops (section 5.5 of the reference manual) are built around the simple **loop** **... end loop** construct:

```
loop
    statements
end loop;
```

The simple form above is a continuous loop that never ends.

while loop

The **while** loop is common in code and has a very direct Ada equivalent:

```
while (expression)
{
    statement
}
while expression loop
    statements
end loop;
```

do loop

The **do** loop has no direct Ada equivalent, though how to synthesize one is shown below in the section on **break** and **continue**.

```
do
{
    statements
} while (expression)
```

for *loop*

The `for` loop is used extensively in most languages to iterate over a known set of values. Ada has nothing corresponding directly to the C `for` loop (the most frighteningly overloaded statement in almost any language) but does allow you to iterate over a range, the most common use of this type of loop.

The general form of the C `for` statement is shown below:

```
for (init-statement ; expression-1 ; loop-statement)
{
    statements
}
```

The Ada **for** loop is equivalent to a restricted definition of the C `for` loop which iterates over a given discrete range, like this:

```
int ident;

for (ident = low; ident < high; ident++)
{
    statements
}
```

The Ada loop uses discrete range syntax (a discrete range is specified in Ada with the syntax `low .. high`; ranges will be discussed further in Section 3.3) to specify the lower and upper bound of the range.

```
for ident in range loop
    statements
end loop;
```

Unlike the C example `ident` is a local object which is only valid within the scope of the loop body; however, we do not have to specify the type as the compiler detects the type required to support the specified range.

```
for Count in 1 .. 10 loop
    Func_Call(Count);
end loop;
```

Reverse loops

But what if you want to loop from 10 down to 1? In Ada it would be wrong to specify a range of 10 .. 1 as this is defined as a 'null range.' It is legal to write such a piece of code but it would not execute as passing a null range to a **for** loop causes it to exit immediately. The code to iterate over a descending range is:

```
for Count in reverse 1 .. 10 loop
    Func_Call(Count);
end loop;
```

break *and* continue

In C and C++ we have two useful statements break and continue which may be used to add fine control to loops. Consider the following C code:

```
while (expression)
{
    if (expression1)
    {
        continue;
    }
    if (expression2)
    {
        break;
    }
}
```

The code above shows how break and continue are used. First you have a loop which takes an expression to determine general termination procedure. Now let us assume that during execution of the loop you decide that you have completed what you wanted to do and may leave the loop early; the break forces a 'jump' to the next statement after the end of the loop. A continue is similar but it takes you to the top of the loop.

In Ada there is no continue, and break is now called exit.

```
while expression loop
    if expression2 then
        exit;
    end if;
end loop;
```

The Ada **exit** statement, however, can combine the expression used to decide that it is required, and so the code below is often found:

```
while expression loop
   exit when expression2;
end loop;
```

do while

This leads us on to the do loop, which can now be coded as:

```
loop
   statements
   exit when expression;
end loop;
```

The problem with the break statement comes when used in complex code with nested loops.

Example 2.2   Control of nested loops ——————————————————————

The following example code is quite common in style. An inner loop spots the termination condition and has to signal this back to the outer loop. C has no way to use the break statement to exit from an inner loop.

```
{
   int percent_found = 0;
   fgets(file_handle, buffer);
   while (!feof(file_handle) && !percent_found)
   {
      for (char_index = 0;
           buffer[char_index] != '\n';
           char_index++)
      {
         if (buffer[char_index] == '%')
         {
            percent_found = 1;
            break;
         }
         // some other code, including get next line.
      }

      fgets(file_handle, buffer);

   }
}
```

Now consider the example below in Ada (note that in both examples code before and after has been omitted for clarity; the Ada example below is more complete in the accompanying source).

```
-- file: Complex_Loops.adb
begin
   Get_Line(File => File_Handle,
            Item => Input_Line,
            Last => Last_Char);

   Main_Loop:
      while not End_Of_File(File => File_Handle) loop

         for Char_Index in 1 .. Last_Char loop
            exit when Input_Line(Char_Index) = Null_Char;
            exit Main_Loop
               when Input_Line(Char_Index) = Percent_Char;
         end loop;

         Get_Line(File => File_Handle,
                  Item => Input_Line,
                  Last => Last_Char);

      end loop Main_Loop;

end Complex_Loops;
```

As you can see we have now used the loop name `Main_Loop` with the nested **exit** statement to allow us to *break* out of the inner loop. This level of control, without the use of additional Boolean flags, can minimize the complexity of nested loop management and increase the ease with which it is read, understood, and maintained.

2.3.6 return statement

Here again there is a direct equivalence between the C and Ada statements:

```
return value;     // C/C++ return from typed function
return ;          // C/C++ return from void function

return value;     -- Ada return from function
return ;          -- Ada return from procedure
```

In Ada the **return** statement (section 6.5 of the reference manual) is almost identical to the C statement. We have used the terminology relevant to each language and the difference between functions and procedures in Ada will be discussed in Section 2.4 below.

2.3.7 labels and goto

The `goto` statement (Section 5.8 of the reference manual) in the two languages is also identical; what is very different is the identification of the `label` to go to. Another similarity between the languages is the restriction that the `goto` and the `label` must exist within the same outer block, i.e. you cannot go to a `label` in one function from inside another.

```
label:
    goto label;
<<label>>;
    goto label;
```

In C one of the uses of the `goto` is in getting around the problem with nested loops described above, leading to code like that below:

```
while (!feof(file_handle))
{
    for (char_index = 0;
            buffer[char_index] !='\n';
            char_index++
    {
        if (buffer[char_index] == '%')
        {
            goto loop_end;
        }
        // some other code, including get next line.
    }
}
loop_end:
```

We have already seen how to work around these problems with Ada's **exit when** construct.

2.3.8   Exception handling

Ada and the newer versions of C++ support a feature termed exception handling (section 11.2 of the reference manual) for run-time errors. Exception handling consists of three components, the exception, raising the exception, and handling the exception.

In C++ there is no exception type; when you raise an exception you pass out any sort of type, and selection of the exception is done on its type. In Ada there is an exception type which will be discussed later.

Raising

Having deferred discussion of the exception type we must cover the next element, raising the exception:

```
throw (const char*)"an exception object";
raise Invalid_Operator;
```

In C++ we use the keyword `throw` and its operand is any object. In Ada we use the keyword **raise** and the operand is an exception name.

Catching

Firstly let us see how you catch an exception. The code below shows the basic structure used to protect `statements-1`, and execute `statements-2` or `statements-3` on detection of the specified exception:

```
try
{
    statements-1
} catch (declaration)
{
    statements-2
}

begin
    statements-1
exception
    when object : ident => statements-2
    when object : others => statements-3
end;
```

Note: in C++ the `catch` clause must contain a complete type-object declaration; in the Ada clause the object is optional. This will become more clear when we discuss the library package `Ada.Exceptions` in Section 8.1.5.

In the example below we call a function `function_call` which we know may raise a particular exception, but it may also raise exceptions we do not know about which we will pass back up to whoever called them. Both languages use the `throw`/**raise** statement with no operand to specify that within an exception handler we should reraise the current exception.

```
try
{
    function_call();
} catch (const char* string_exception)
{
    if (!strcmp(string_exception, "the_one_we_want"))
    {
        handle_it();
    } else
    {
        throw;
    }
}
```

```
} catch (...)
{
    throw;
}
```

Now the same in Ada:

```
begin
    Function_Call;
exception
    when The_One_We_Want => Handle_It;
    when others             => raise;
end;
```

This shows how much simpler the Ada version is; we know exactly what we are waiting for and can immediately process it. In the C++ case all we know is that an exception of type const char* has been raised; we must then check it still further before we can handle it. This flexibility means you can supply more information with an exception in C++ than you can in Ada.

You will also notice the similarity between the Ada exception catching code and the Ada **case** statement. This also extends to the fact that the **when** statement can catch multiple exceptions (though not ranges of exceptions):

```
begin
    Function_Call;
exception
    when The_One_We_Want |
         Another_Possibility => Handle_It;
    when others               => raise;
end;
```

This common syntax style is a feature used by Ada to maximize the readability of the resulting code.

Example 2.3   A suite of simple tests _____

```
-- file: Simple_Tests.adb
with Ada.Text_IO;
use  Ada.Text_IO;
with Ada.Integer_Text_IO;
use  Ada.Integer_Text_IO;
with Ada.Exceptions;
use  Ada.Exceptions;
```

```
procedure Simple_Tests is

    -- please ignore these declarations, see Chapter 3.
    Test_1, Test_2, Test_3 : Boolean;
    Test_4 : Integer;
    -- end of declarations.

begin

    pragma Page;
    Assignment_Tests:
        begin
            Put_Line("Assignment_Tests:");

            Test_1 := True;
            Test_2 := True;
            Test_3 := False;
            Test_4 := 1;
        end Assignment_Tests;

    pragma Page;
    Conditional_Statement_Tests:
        begin
            Put_Line("Conditional_Statement_Tests:");

            if Test_1 then
                Put_Line("condition 1");
            elsif Test_2 then
                Put_Line("condition 2");
            else
                Put_Line("condition 3");
            end if;

            if Test_1 and Test_2 then
                Put_Line("condition 4");
            end if;

            if Test_1 and then Test_2 then
                Put_Line("condition 5");
            end if;

            case Test_4 is
                when 0 =>
                    Put_Line("condition 6");
                when 1 =>
                    Put_Line("condition 7");
                when 2 | 3 | 4 =>
                    Put_Line("condition 8");
                when 5 .. 10 =>
```

```
              Put_Line("condition 9");
           when others =>
              Put_Line("condition 10");
        end case;

   end Conditional_Statement_Tests;

pragma Page;
Loop_Statement_Tests:
   begin
      Put_Line("Loop_Statement_Tests:");

      loop
         Put_Line("never ending loop ...")
      end loop;

      while Test_2 loop
         Test_2 := False;
      end loop;

      for New_Variable in 1 .. 10 loop
         Put_Line("You should see 10 of these");
      end loop;

      for New_Variable_2 in reverse 1 .. 10 loop
         Put_Line("You should see 10 of these as well");
      end loop;

      Test_2 := True;

      Outer_Loop:
         while Test_1 loop
            while Test_2 loop
               exit Outer_Loop when Test_4 > 0;
            end loop;
         end loop Outer_Loop;
   end Loop_Statement_Tests;

pragma Page;
Goto_Test:
   begin
      Put_Line("Goto_Test:");

      goto Goto_Target;
      Put_Line("You should never see this");

      <<Goto_Target>>
      null;
   end Goto_Test;
```

```
pragma Page;
Exception_Tests:
   begin
      Put_Line("Exception_Tests:");

      begin
         raise Program_Error;
      exception
         when Constraint_Error =>
            Put_Line("caught Constraint_Error");
         when Program_Error =>
            Put_Line("caught Program_Error");
         when The_Exception : others =>
            Put_Line("caught " &
                     Exception_Name(The_Exception));
      end ;
   end Exception_Tests;

Put_Line("Tests Complete");

end Simple_Tests;
```

This example demonstrates many of the features covered above. It is included in the source examples as a simple *cut and paste* reference when you begin to write Ada code yourself.

2.4   Subprograms

Subroutines, functions, methods, or procedures: whatever the name this method for partitioning code was the first attempt at software reuse.

In C++ we are used to writing functions; in Ada there are a number of topics to consider before rewriting all your C functions as Ada functions.

2.4.1   Declaring subprograms

Functions

The following piece of code shows how C++ and Ada both declare and define a function. Declaration is the process of telling everyone that the function exists and what its type and parameters are. The definitions are where you actually write out the function itself (in Ada terms the function specification and function body).

```
return_type func_name (parameters);
return_type func_name (parameters)
{
```

```
     declarations
     statements
}
```
function func_name(parameters) **return** return_type;

function func_name(parameters) **return** return_type **is**
```
     declarations
```
begin
```
     statements
```
end func_name;

A quick look at a simple function, to return the smaller of two integers. Firstly the C version (and I know how many shortcut versions of this can be written, but for now we will write it out in full):

```
// min.h
int min(int a, int b);
```

```
// min.c
int min(int a, int b)
{
    if (a < b)
    {
        return a;
    }
    return b;
}
```

Now let us look at the function as it might be written in Ada:

```
-- min specification
function min(a, b : in Integer) return Integer;
```

```
-- min body
function min(a, b : in Integer) return Integer is
begin
    if a < b then
        return a;
    end if;
    return b;
end min;
```

As an aside, consider the next piece of C code, a function declaration with no return type:

```
int func_name(void);
    func_name(void);   // int return type implied !!
```

C and C++ assume a return type of `int`, but in Ada you must specify the return type of all functions:

```
function func_name return Integer;
```

Procedures

Let us now consider a special kind of function, one that does not return a value. In C++ it is declared as a function returning a `void`, in Ada (or Pascal, Modula, and so on) it is declared as a procedure:

```
void func_name(parameters);

procedure func_name(parameters);
```

Our quick example this time is a function to swap two integers. I will only present the Ada version. This also demonstrates use of the declaration part of a subprogram where a temporary variable is defined:

```
-- swap specification
procedure swap(a, b : in out Integer);

-- swap body
procedure swap(a, b : in out Integer) is
    Temp : Integer := a;
begin
    a    := b;
    b    := Temp;
end swap;
```

This distinction between **function** and **procedure** may seem a little pointless but consider the following:

```
typedef int ERROR_CODE;

ERROR_CODE a_function(void);

{
    ..
    a_function();
    ..
}
```

The function `a_function` returns an error code which the caller should check; in this case it has not. In Ada when calling a function the returned value must be catered for which would make the above code illegal. The provision of the procedure in Ada allows us to write subprograms that have no need to return values.

2.4.2 Parameters

Parameter modes

Ada provides two keywords to specify how parameters are passed, **in** and **out**. These are used like this:

```
procedure proc(Parameter : in      Integer);
procedure proc(Parameter :     out Integer);
procedure proc(Parameter : in out Integer);
procedure proc(Parameter :         Integer);
```

These keywords should be used so that the compiler can protect you even more. If you have an **out** parameter it *may* warn you if you use it before it has been set. The compiler will *definitely not* let you assign to an **in** parameter, in fact an object passed as an **in** parameter cannot then be passed to another function as an **in out** parameter and so on. The final case where neither **in** nor **out** is specified defaults to simply **in**. Note that you cannot mark function parameters as **out** or **in out**, as functions are used to return values and such side effects are disallowed.

Next we must consider how we pass arguments to functions. C++ allows three parameter passing modes, by value, by pointer, and by reference:

```
void func1(int  by_value);
void func2(int* by_address);
void func3(int& by_reference); // C++ only.

procedure func1(param : in      Integer);
procedure func2(param : in out Integer);
procedure func3(param : in out Integer);
```

We will return to the passing of addresses to C and C++ functions later when we discuss access types; for now we can consider the above as equivalent results.

Default values

Ada (and C++) allow you to decide default values for parameters (section 6.4.1 of the reference manual). This means that when you call the function you can omit such a parameter from the call since the compiler knows what value to use:

```
procedure Create
    (File : in out File_Type;
    Mode : in       File_Mode := Inout_File;
    Name : in       String    := "";
    Form : in       String    := "");
```

This example is to be found in each of the Ada file-based IO packages. It opens a file, given the file 'handle', the mode, name of the file, and a system-independent 'form' for the file. You can see that the simplest invocation of `Create` is `Create(File_Handle);` which simply provides the handle and all other parameters are defaulted (in the Ada library a file name of `""` implies opening a temporary file). Now suppose that we wish to provide the name of the file also, would we have to write `Create(File_Handle, Inout_File, "text.file")`?

The Ada answer is no: by using **named notation** we could use the form:

```
Create(File => File_Handle,
       Name => "text.file");
```

We can now omit `Mode` and `Form` which take their default values. This feature can make code easier to understand where little-used functions are called by documenting what the parameters are expected to be.

Parameterless

A subprogram which takes no parameters can be written in two ways in C++, though only one in Ada:

```
void func_name(void);
void func_name();    // void is implied

procedure func_name;
```

The reason for this is less obvious with procedures, though the following example presents a function which returns a value depending on some internal state:

```
function Some_Constant return Integer is
begin
   if Some_Condition then
      return Value_1;
   end if;

   return Value_2;
end Some_Constant;
```

No parameters are required when calling `Some_Constant` and the resulting code below actually looks as if we are declaring the object `Temp` and initializing it to a constant value. There is no visible sign of the function call.

```
declare
   Temp : Integer := Some_Constant;
begin
   ..
end;
```

This is a feature of Ada that allows `Some_Constant` to be an object, constant, or function call by changing its definition and not having to change all uses of it.

2.4.3 Overloading

Ada allows more than one function/procedure with the same name as long as they can be uniquely identified by their profile (a combination of their parameter and return types):

```
function Day return Integer;
function Day(A_Date : in Date_Type) return Integer;
```

The first returns you the day of week, of today, the second the day of week from a given date. They are both allowed, and both visible. The compiler decides which one to use by looking at the types given to it when you call it.

    Note: you can get in a mess with both C++ and Ada when mixing overloading and defaults. For example:

```
procedure increment(A_Value : A_Type);
procedure increment(A_Value : in out A_Type;
                    By      : in     Integer := 1);
```

If we call `increment` with one parameter which of the two above is called? Now the compiler will show such things up, but it does mean you have to think carefully and make sure you use defaults carefully.

Operator overloading

As in C++ you can redefine the standard operators in Ada (section 6.6 of the reference manual); unlike C++ you can do this for any operator, with any types (C++ restricts operator overloading so that at least one formal parameter is of a class type).

    The syntax for this is to replace the name of the function (operators are always functions) with the operator name in quotes:

```
function "+"(Left, Right : in Integer) return Integer;
```

Operator overloading is a very useful mechanism for building abstract data types, and for completing the semantics for a user defined type.

    Operators that may be overloaded (see Section 2.2) are shown in Figure 2.2. In Ada83 it was illegal to overload the /= operator as this is defined to provide the logical not of the equality operator. Therefore, if you overload the equality operator it will be called for both equality and non-equality tests. In Ada95 it is legal to provide an overloaded non-equality operator as long as it *does not* return a `Boolean`. This ensures that the rule above still applies, but if you have need of the /= operator for some semantic purpose other than non-equality it is available.

=	/=			
<	<=	>	>=	
+	-	&	abs	not
*	/	mod	rem	**
and	or	xor		

Figure 2.2   Operators that may be overloaded.

new	delete							
+	-	*	/	%	^	&	|	~
!	=	<	>	+=	-=	*=	/=	%=
^=	&=	|=	<<	>>	>>=	<<=	==	!=
<=	>=	&&	||	++	--	,	->*	->
()	[]							

Figure 2.3   Operators that C++ allows to be overloaded.

Operators that C++ allows to be overloaded are shown in Figure 2.3. As you can see, the set of available operators (including the combined operators) is much larger for C++ and can aid in building complete abstractions.

For example the Standard Template Library [13, 15] for C++ uses a number of these additional operators to build complex container and iterator classes. Container classes that act like arrays can be made to look just like arrays by overloading the [] operator. The fact that the pointer dereference operators can be overloaded allows iterators to be built which behave in the same way as pointers.

In Ada it is not possible to overload the assignment, pointer dereference, or array element selection which makes the creation of similar abstractions more difficult (see the paper on implementing the C++ standard template library in Ada [26]).

2.4.4   Nesting subprograms

You can define any number of subprograms within the declaration part of another. This reduces clutter in the global name space; in C you will often find a source module littered with private functions which are only used by one public function.

```
procedure Sort(Sort_This : in out An_Array) is

   An_Object : A_Type;
```

```
   procedure Swap(Item1, Item2 : in out Element_Type) is
   begin
     ..
   end Swap;
begin
  ..
   Swap(Sort_This(1), Sort_This(10));
   ..
end Sort;
```

The nested subprograms also have access to other objects in the same declaration part
which means that statements in the body of Swap may access the object An_Object.

Example 2.4   A suite of simple subprogram tests _____

```
   -- file: Subprogram_Tests.adb
with Ada.Text_IO;
use  Ada.Text_IO;
with Ada.Integer_Text_IO;
use  Ada.Integer_Text_IO;

procedure Subprogram_Tests is

     -- the following subprograms are dealt with later on.
     function Min(A, B : Integer) return Integer;
     procedure Swap(A, B : in out Integer);
     procedure Say_Boo(To_Who : in String := "to a goose");

     function Min(A, B : Integer) return Integer is
     begin
        if A < B then
           return A;
        else
           return B;
        end if;
     end Min;

     procedure Swap(A, B : in out Integer) is
        Temp : Integer := A;
     begin
        A := B;
        B := Temp;
     end Swap;

     procedure Say_Boo(To_Who : in String := "to a goose") is
     begin
        Put_Line("Saying boo " & To_Who);;
     end Say_Boo;
     -- end of test subprograms.
```

```
    -- please ignore these declarations, see Chapter 3.
    Test_1, Test_2, Test_3 : Integer;
    -- end of declarations.
begin
  pragma Page;
  Function_Tests:
     begin
          Test_1 := 1;
          Test_2 := 10;

          Test_3 := Min(Test_1, Test_2);
          Put("Min is ");
          Put(Test_3);
          End_Line;

          Test_3 := Min(A => Test_1, B => Test_2);
          Put("Min is ");
          Put(Test_3);
          End_Line;
     end Function_Tests;

  pragma Page;
  Procedure_Tests:
     begin
          Swap(Test_1, Test_2);
          Swap(A => Test_1, B => Test_2);
          Put(Test_1);
          Put(Test_2);
          End_Line;

          Say Boo(To_Who => "the reader");
          Say_Boo;
     end Procedure_Tests;

  end Subprogram_Tests;
```

As with Example 2.3 this is provided in the accompanying source as a reference.

2.5 Pragmas

In C and C++ a number of compilers use the pre-processor directive #pragma to introduce special commands into the compilation stream. Examples are:

```
#pragma page              // new page in listing file
#pragma title ""          // page title for listing file
```

```
#pragma optimize options    // turn compiler option on or off
#pragma pack option         // turn structure packing on or off
```

In Ada there is a **pragma** keyword which is used to introduce special directives, except that the most common pragmas are defined by the language itself and so you can rely on their existence on more than one compiler. The language standard does allow additional pragmas to exist for platform-dependent implementations.

Example language-defined Ada pragmas are:

```
pragma Page;                    -- new page in listing file

pragma Optimize(identifier);    -- turn compiler option on or off
pragma Pack(type);              -- pack the given type.

pragma Import(C, C_String_Copy, "strcpy");
                                -- import a C function.
```

One very important pragma is **pragma** `Restrictions` `(..)` which allows programmers to restrict the set of features they wish to use. More pragmas will be introduced where they are important; in general an exhaustive coverage is not required and individual pragmas can be looked up in the language reference manual.

2.6 Summary

This chapter should have provided no nasty surprises. If you had been given a piece of real Ada code before we started you should have been able to pick out the control structures, for example, without too many problems.

The following list extracts the statement definitions from the above section and acts as a quick reference to the syntax introduced so far. Italic items are optional in the syntax.

```
-- Null Statement
null;

-- Compound Statement
block_name:
    declare
        declarations
    begin
        statements
    exception
        exception_handler
    end block_name;

-- If Statement
if expression then
    statements
```

```
elsif expression_1 and then
      expression_2 or else
      expression_3 then
   statements
else
   statements
end if;

-- Case Statement
case expression is
   when value =>
      statements
   when value_1 .. value_2 =>
      statements
   when value_1 | value_2 =>
      statements
   when others =>
      statements
end case;

-- Loop Statement
Loop_Name:
   loop
      statements
   end loop Loop_Name;

-- While Loop
Loop_Name:
   while expression loop
      statements
   end loop;

-- For Loop
Loop_Name:
   for ident in reverse range loop
      statements
   end loop;

-- Exit Statement
Loop_Name:
   loop
      exit Loop_Name when expression;
   end loop;

-- Return Statement;
return value;

-- Label and Goto
```

```ada
<<label>>

goto label;

-- Raise an exception
raise Invalid_Operator;

-- Subprogram Specification
function func_name(parameters) return return_type;
function "+"(parameters) return Integer;
procedure proc_name(parameters);
procedure proc_name;

-- Parameter types
procedure proc_name(Param_1 : in      Integer;
                    Param_2 :     out Integer;
                    Param_3 : in out Integer;
                    Param_4 : in      Integer := 1);

-- Subprogram body
function func_name(parameters) return return_type is
   declarations
begin
   statements
exception
   when ident =>
      statements
   when ident | ident =>
      statements
   when others =>
      statements
end func_name;
```

What I have attempted to provide in this chapter is a basic grounding in Ada syntax and an insight into some of the language style. The goal of readability is helped by the provision of block naming and parameter naming and the use of keywords such as **begin** and **end** instead of { and }. Safety and predictability are enhanced with a simple and well-understood exception mechanism, which although not as flexible as its C++ counterpart can be used as effectively.

Parameter modes specified by **in** and **out** are preferable to relying on convention and passing of pointers.

Example 2.5 Some C++/Ada mixed code ─────────────────────────

```ada
-- file: Fix_This.adb
procedure Fix_This is
```

```
      int a;
begin

    if a == 1 then
        a = 2;
    end if;
end Fix_This;
```

This example shows the common errors made by programmers working with C/C++ and Ada. They are simply typing errors which make sense to a C compiler. See if you can spot them all (answers in the file `Fixed.adb` in the CD).

At this point it is not worth reviewing progress on our example as we do not know enough to write any Ada code, even though we should be able to read it quite well.

3 Strong typing for solid programs

Ada, like C++, is a statically typed language which means any object has to be declared with a specific type, unlike languages such as Basic. However, Ada is also a strongly typed language which means that the rules on how and when an object can be changed from one type to another are very strict. To be able to place such restrictions on the use of types, Ada ensures that a rich set of fundamental types is available to choose from in the first place.

The following diagram (section 3.2 of the reference manual) shows the relationship between types in Ada95:

```
all types
     elementary
          scalar
               discrete
                    enumeration
                         character
                         boolean
                         other enumeration
                    integer
                         signed integer
                         modular integer
```

```
                real
                       floating point
                       fixed point
                                ordinary fixed point
                                decimal fixed point

        access
                access-to-object
                access-to-subprogram

    composite
          array
                 string
                 other array
          untagged record
          tagged
          task
          protected
```

The rest of this chapter is devoted to the description of those types not in italics. In many cases Ada types appear to be directly equivalent to C++ types such as `Integer` to `int` but look again and you will find much safer types with greater flexibility than anything provided by C or C++.

Attributes

It is now time to introduce another thing to watch for in Ada source: the use of an apostrophe ' which in Ada is called a *tick*. The tick is used to access attributes for an object; for instance, the following code is used to assign to value `Integer_Size` the size in bits of an integer:

```
{
   int int_size = sizeof(int) * 8;
   ..

declare
   Integer_Size : constant Integer := Integer'Size;
   ..
```

The tick acts as a mechanism to select a system-defined function specific to a type, so in effect the above calls a function `Size` specific to the type `Integer`. Sometimes the attribute functions may take an object as a parameter, such as:

```
declare
   A : constant Integer := 1;
   B : constant Integer := 2;
   C : constant Integer := Integer'Max(A, B);
```

We will see a lot more uses of the tick as we continue!

3.1 Declarations

Before we start we need to understand some Ada terms. In Ada all variables, constants, exceptions, arrays, tasks, and so on are termed 'objects'. This is somewhat confusing when in C++ the term object is usually used to describe an instance of a class. Also in C and C++ the distinction is made between the definition of something and its declaration; in Ada we simply talk about declarations.

These terms will become clearer as we move through examples.

3.1.1 Object declarations

The following C++ code might be found in any code fragment and simply declares a set of integer variables:

```
int i;
int a, b, c;
int j = 0;
int k, l = 1;
```

Below is the Ada equivalent. Note that objects are declared in reverse order to C++: the object name is first, then the type of the object.

As in C++ you can declare lists of objects by separating them with commas:

```
i        : Integer;       -- see Simple_Tests.adb
a, b, c  : Integer;
j        : Integer := 0;
k, l     : Integer := 1;
```

The first three declarations are identical to the C++ code above, they create the same objects, and the third line assigns j the value 0 in both cases. However, the fourth example in C leaves k undefined and creates l with the value 1. In the Ada example it should be clear that both k and l are initialized with the value 1.

3.1.2 Constant declarations

The way Ada and C++ declare constants is also subtly different, for example:

```
// C++ constant
const int days_per_week = 7;

-- Ada constant (see Simple_Tests.adb)
days_per_week : constant Integer := 7;
days_per_week : constant := 7;
```

In the example above the second declaration of **days_per_week** does not specify a type and so the constant does not have a type. In effect it becomes simply a **named number**; like a C #define it is equivalent to an integer literal.

In C++ objects declared as const are not truly constant; const is known as a type modifier and can be cast away. Consider:

```
const unsigned Lines = 10;

unsigned* nonconst_Lines = (unsigned*)Lines;

*nonconst_Line = 2;
```

The new object nonconst_Lines points to the contents of Lines and by use of the cast we have made a way to change the contents of the constant.

The rules governing pointers, or access types, in Ada do not permit such a redefinition of a constant.

3.1.3 Type declarations

Before we delve into descriptions of the predefined Ada types it is important to show you how to declare new types in Ada.

Ada is a static and strongly typed language, in fact possibly the strongest. Its type model is therefore strict and absolutely stated. In C the use of typedef introduces a synonym which can be used as a new type. Consider:

```
typedef int transaction_id;

transaction_id  a_trans;
int             an_int;

an_int = a_trans; // works, no problem
```

The compiler knows that they are both integers. Now consider:

```
-- file: Type_Subtype.adb
declare
   type Transaction_ID is new Integer;

   A_Trans     : Transaction_ID;
   An_Integer  : Integer;
begin
   An_Integer := A_Trans; -- fails.
```

The important keyword is **new**, which really sums up the way Ada is treating that line. It can be read as 'a new type Transaction_ID has been created from the type Integer', whereas the C line may be interpreted as 'a new name Transaction_ID has been introduced as a synonym for int'. In language design terminology C and C++ demonstrate structural equivalence of types: if they are built the same, they are the same. Ada, on the other hand, is built around name equivalence: if they are named the same, they are the same.

3.1.4   Subtype declarations

This strong typing can be a problem, and so Ada also provides a feature for reducing the distance between the new type and the base type. Consider the following:

```
-- file: Type_Subtype.adb
declare
   subtype Transaction_ID is Integer;

   A_Trans     : Transaction_ID;
   An_Integer : Integer;
begin
   An_Integer := A_Trans;   __ works.
```

The most common usage of a subtype is to constrain the parent type in some way, for example to place an upper or lower boundary for an integer value (see section below on ranges).

Synonyms in Ada

Using the **subtype** declaration it is possible to create a synonym for a given type. The example above allows `Transaction_ID` to be viewed as a synonym for `Integer`. This is not the primary use of `subtype`, however, as we will come to see.

Type conversion

As you might expect from what we have seen so far, Ada must allow us some way to relax the strong typing it enforces. In C the cast allows us to make anything look like something else, in Ada *type conversion* can allow you to convert between two similar types; for example:

```
declare
   type Thing is new Integer;

   an_Integer : Integer;
   a_Thing     : Thing;
begin
   an_Integer := a_Thing;                -- illegal
   an_Integer := Integer (a_Thing); -- legal
```

This can only be done between similar types; the compiler will not allow such conversion between very different types (far too often done in C and C++). For this you need the standard library's generic function `Unchecked_Conversion` (see

Section 5.5.1) which takes an object of one type, and returns an object of another type.

One other point about the use of type conversion in C and C++ is that the compiler frequently converts types on its own without explicit casts. The most common form of implicit cast is during calculations:

```
{
    int    int_value;
    short short_value;

    short_value = int_value;        // 1

    short_value = short_value + 10 // 2
}
```

The above example illustrates the problem well. We might expect the first assignment to fail at compile-time as you are assigning a large object to a smaller object. In Ada this would be an error, but in C++ it would usually be a warning and in most C compilers it would pass through without comment. The second example is more subtle: why do many C++ compilers warn that you cannot assign an int to a short in this line? The answer is that during calculations the compiler *promotes* (casts) values to the largest size, in this case the size of the int literal 10. To get around this you must explicitly cast the 10 to be a short or cast the result of the calculation.

3.2   Primitive operations

The title for this section is an Ada term best described by example, so consider the following:

```
-- file Primitive_Ops.adb
declare
   A_Trans : Integer;
begin
   A_Trans := A_Trans + 1;
```

The addition operator is a primitive operation of the type Integer, and is defined as follows:

```
function "+"(Left, Right : Integer) return Integer;
```

Now let us consider the type Transaction_ID. We might want to increment one, but we do not have an addition operator defined – or do we?

```
declare
   type Transaction_ID is new Integer;
   A_Trans : Transaction_ID
begin
   A_Trans := A_Trans + 1;
```

When you create a new type it inherits all its parents' primitive operations and rede-
fines them, so that in effect a new primitive operation exists which looks like:

```
function "+"(Left, Right: Transaction_ID) return Transaction_ID;
```

If you were to create your own version of the function above, then any new types
derived from `Transaction_ID` would inherit your new addition operator, not the
standard one.

Note: this is not inheritance as we know it in C++ with classes, but is an Ada-
specific interpretation which has been very useful in Ada83 for developing abstract data
types before the introduction of full object oriented features in Ada95.

3.3   Scalar types

Scalar types have the property that they are ordered: they have upper and lower bounds
and some order between. This also implies that relational operators such as <, >, <=,
>= exist for all scalar types.

The exact classification of all types in Ada is not necessary for day-to-day programming in the language; more information can be found in Chapter 3 of the language reference manual.

3.3.1   Discrete types

Discrete types are a subset of scalar types, defined in the reference manual, section 3.5,
with the statement 'each value of a discrete type has a *position number* which is an
integer number.'

The easiest way to describe discrete types, and a good place to start describing
Ada types, in general, is the range. Ranges are not types in themselves but are essential
in understanding types.

Ranges

You have already seen a range in use (in the `for` loop). It is expressed as `low ..
high` and can be one of the most useful ways of expressing simple discrete types, for
example:

```
-- file: Data_Time.adb
declare
    type Hours24 is new Integer range 0 .. 23;
    type Hours    is range 1 .. 12;
    type Minutes is range 1 .. 60;
```

Note: for `Hours` and `Minutes` we have not specified a base type, therefore the compiler is at liberty to provide the most appropriate base type. You can of course query to see what base type the compiler has provided by using the `'Base` and `'Range` attributes.

Considering `Hours` and `Minutes` again, it is more usual to use subtypes for related types, however. Here is a more *complete* example:

```
declare
    type     Hours24 is new Integer range 0 .. 23;
    subtype Hours    is Hours24        range 1 .. 12;
    type     Minutes is new Integer range 1 .. 60;
```

It is now possible for the compiler and run-time to detect out of range values and any such violations either stop compilation or will result in a `Constraint_Error` exception being raised at run-time.

Consider the code below. We have reversed the order of declaration so that `Hours24` is a subtype of `Hours`. Unfortunately `Hours24` is going to be a problem as it is declared with a range outside that of its parent type.

```
declare
    type     Hours    is new Integer range 0 .. 12;
    subtype Hours24 is Hours          range 0 .. 24;
```

Another problem is having an assignment from a type which supports a large range into a type with a smaller supported range.

```
declare
    type     Hours24 is new Integer range 0 .. 23;
    subtype Hours    is Hours24        range 1 .. 12;

    End_Of_Day : Hours24;
    Hour_Now   : Hours;

begin

    End_Of_Day := 17;
    Hour_Now := End_Of_Day; -- raise Constraint_Error
```

This range checking is performed for all discrete types, so we have to be very careful when mixing types in arithmetic operations.

'`in`' *operator*

To assist us in this case Ada provides an operator to check for range inclusion, so we could rewrite the example above as:

```
declare
    type     Hours24 is new Integer range 0 .. 23;
    subtype Hours    is Hours24      range 1 .. 12;

    End_of_Day : Hours24;
    Hour_Now   : Hours;
begin
    End_Of_Day := 17;

    if End_Of_Day in 1 .. 12 then
        Hour_Now := End_Of_Day;
    else
        Put_Line ("End_Of_Day not in 1 .. 12");
    end if;
```

This guards some code, and makes sure that the assignment from `End_Of_Day` to `Hour_Now` is legal before attempting it.

Scalar attributes

Ada provides some very useful attributes for all scalar types, discussed below. These will be used later to build some very powerful code which is independent of the type of data passed to it because these attributes can be used to acquire details about the type. The descriptions here are a little terse, but you will see examples of them used throughout the rest of the book, so do not be alarmed.

Consider the following type declarations when working through the examples below:

```
declare
    subtype Max_Temp     is Integer   range −273 .. +100_000;
    subtype Working_Temp is Max_Temp range 10 .. 80;
```

- `subtype'Base` This attribute will return a type which indicates the base type of `Type_Name`, so the result of `Week_Day'Base` is `Day`. This is important as it is often used as the argument to type-independent functions, almost as a base class is used as the argument to a virtual function in a C++ class. Consider the following:

  ```
  Working_Temp'First    is 10

  Working_Temp'Base'First    is −273
  ```

  This attribute is often used to denote parameter types. It acts like specifying a base class pointer; values of any derived type can be passed.

- `subtype'First` This attribute returns the first value of the type, so:

  `Max_Temp'First`   `is -273`

  `Working_Temp'First`   `is 10`

- `subtype'Last` This attribute returns the last value of the type, so:

  `Max_Temp'Last`   `is 100000`

  `Working_Temp'Last`   `is 80`

- `subtype'Length` This attribute returns the number of values held by the type, so:

  `Max_Temp'Length`   `is 100274`

  `Working_Temp'Length` `is 70`

- `subtype'Range` This type returns the range of values, so:

  `Max_Temp'Range`   `is -273 .. +100000`

  `Working_Temp'Range`   `is 10 .. 80`

  It can also be used to simplify the example used above to describe the `in` operator.

  ```
  begin
      End_Of_Day := 17;

      if End_Of_Day in Hours'Range then
          Hour_Now := End_Of_Day;
      else
          Put_Line("End_Of_Day not in the range of Hours");
      end if;
  ```

- `subtype'Succ(Arg : subtype'Base)` This supplies the 'successor' to the current value, so that:

  `Max_Temp'Succ(1)`   `is 2`

  `Max_Temp'Succ(Max_Temp'Last)` `-- exception`

  Note: if the value of the object is the last allowable then a `Constraint_Error` exception is raised; you cannot call `Succ` with the last value of a type. This rule is also applicable to the following attribute:

- `subtype'Pred(Arg : subtype'Base)` This attribute provides the 'predecessor' of a given value, so that:

  `Max_Temp'Pred(2)`   `is 1`

  `Max_Temp'Pred(Max_Temp'Succ(1))` `is 1`

  `Max_Temp'Pred(-273)`   `-- exception`

- `subtype'Max(L,R : subtype'Base)`   This attribute returns the larger of the two passed values:

    `Max_Temp'Max(2, 10)     is 10`

- `subtype'Min(L,R : subtype'Base)`   This attribute returns the smaller of the two passed values:

    `Max_Temp'Min(2, 10)     is 2`

These two attributes are required as it would be impossible in Ada to define a library function that would act on all possible discrete types.

- `subtype'Image(Arg : subtype'Base)`   If you have ever had to use the C functions `itoa`, `ltoa`, and so on then you will have had to write some pretty unpleasant code, such as

    ```
    {
        char string[20];
        int   value = 1;
        int   decimal_radix = 10;
        itoa(value, string, decimal_radix);
    }
    ```

This has two major drawbacks: you do not know how big a string you will need (and there is no standard for which functions are supplied) and in many cases, for instance, there is no equivalent function for floating point values.

   In Ada we use the `Image` attribute to return the string representation of a scalar, so

    ```
    declare
        Value : Max_Temp  := 20;
        Text  : String    := Integer'Image(Value);
    ```

The resulting string is " 20" where the leading space is used to denote a positive number, so if `Value` had been set to −20 then the string would have been "−20".

- `subtype'Value(Arg :  String)`   This is the opposite to the `Image` attribute in that it returns a value from a string, so it is the equivalent of C's `atoi` functions. Note that this attribute could raise a `Constraint_Error` if the value of the string supplied cannot be represented in the object on the left of the assignment.

    ```
    declare
        Text  : String    := "−20";
        Value : Max_Temp  := Integer'Value(Text);
    ```

- `subtype'Width`   In the `Image` and `Value` examples we have not said how long a string we require because the assignment from the attributes sets their size (see Section 3.4.2), but what if we will assign to the string in the body of the code? How can we create a big enough string?

We could take the C approach and create a string big enough to hold the largest possible value, or use the `Width` attribute which returns the maximum number of characters required for a type. For `Max_Width` the width would be enough to hold -100000, or 7:

```
declare
    Text  : String(1 .. Max_Temp'Width);
    Value : Max_Temp;
begin
    :
    Text  := Integer'Image(Value);
```

Wide characters   We will meet wide characters below, characters which hold Unicode 16-bit values. To support wide characters the last three attributes also come in the following forms:

```
subtype'Wide_Image(Arg : subtype'Base)
subtype'Wide_Value(Arg : Wide_String)
subtype'Wide_Width
```

Discrete attributes   There are also two additional attributes defined for discrete types:

- `subtype'Pos(Arg : subtype'Base)`   This attribute returns the integer position of the argument in the range of the type. This seems a little pointless for integer types as it will return the value we gave it, but it will become more meaningful when we talk of non-integer types later on. Thus:

  ```
  Max_Temp'Pos(-273) = -273
  ```

- `subtype'Val(Arg : Universal_Integer)`   Given the integer position, return the value of the discrete type at that position, thus:

  ```
  Max_Temp'Val(-273) = -273
  ```

- `object'Valid`   This attribute can be used to make sure that the value of the object denoted is valid. An invalid value may be stored if the object has been read from a file or has been passed to a routine in another language.

  ```
  if A_Value'Valid then
     ..
  end if;
  ```

Integers

Any Ada compiler must provide the type `Integer`, a signed integer, which must be at least 16 bits wide. The compiler is also at liberty to provide `Long_Integer`, `Short_Integer`, `Long_Long_Integer`, and so on as needed.

Ada also provides the integer subtypes `Positive` and `Natural` within the library package `Standard`.

```
subtype Positive is Integer range 1 .. Integer'Last;
subtype Natural  is Integer range 0 .. Integer'Last;
```

Modular types

Ada95 has added an unsigned integer type, the so-called modular type to the set of discrete types available.

Modular types have the feature that arithmetic is cyclic, underflow and overflow cannot occur, which means that if you have a modular type capable of holding values from 0 to 255, and its current value is 255, then incrementing it wraps it around to zero; contrast this with range types above. A modular type is defined in the form:

```
type BYTE is mod 256;
type BYTE is mod 2 ** 8;
```

Modular type declarations consist of any positive, static, integer value that denotes the maximum value plus 1 (all modular types start at 0).

Because these types are often used to represent low-level or system types you will frequently see declarations like the second above. The declaration uses an expression which in effect denotes the number of bits used to store the values. This is very important and allows us to declare unsigned types corresponding to the standard integer types, for example:

```
type Unsigned_Integer is mod 2 ** Integer'Size;
```

Enumerations (including Boolean)

First, let us consider enumerated types in C++, for example:

```
enum day { monday, tuesday, wednesday, thursday, friday,
           saturday, sunday };

day today     = tuesday;
int day_off   = sunday;

day tomorrow  = 2;      // illegal, type mismatch
day yesterday = (day)20;
```

In the example we have defined a new type called `day` as an enumeration, and then declared four objects. The first is of type `day` and is assigned a value of type `day`, all of which is perfectly reasonable. The second is of an integer type, but is assigned a value of type `day`; this is allowed as the type is promoted to an integer. The third is of type `day` and is assigned a value of type `int`, which (although legal in C) is illegal as you cannot directly convert from an integer to an enumeration. The fourth object, however, is a day and is assigned an integer value, but that value is cast to the type day and is therefore legal even though it is not a legal value for the type day.

If you were to try to compile the above with a C compiler you would find that you would get very different results from your compiler. First, an enum is not an integral type in C and so a typedef must be used, and, second, because of this the illegal assignment above is now legal. In effect in a C-only environment enumerated types act very much like named numbers. The C version of the above code follows:

```
typedef enum { monday, tuesday, wednesday, thursday, friday,
               saturday, sunday } day;

day today      = tuesday;
int day_off    = sunday;

day tomorrow   = 2;     /* now legal */
day yesterday  = (day)20;
```

The code below shows how we might accomplish the same in Ada, a type called Day, with similar objects Today, Tomorrow, and Yesterday. You will notice that we cannot simply assign an integer to an object of an enumeration type: this is a type mismatch, as is the assignment of an enumeration value to an integer type.

```
declare
    type Day is (Monday, Tuesday, Wednesday, Thursday, Friday,
                 Saturday, Sunday);

Today      : Day       := Tuesday;
Day_Off    : Integer := Sunday;        -- type mismatch error.

Tomorrow   : Day       := 2;            -- type mismatch error.

Day_Off2   : Integer := Day'Pos(Sunday);
Tomorrow2  : Day       := Day'Val(2);

Day_Off    : Day       := Day'Val(20); -- raise Constraint_Error
```

To accomplish what we did in the C example above we require the use of the attributes Val and Pos which allow us to convert between discrete types and integers. Note, however, that even using the Val attribute we cannot assign the value 20 to an enumeration as we could in the C++ code above.

Now if we combine enumerations and ranges, using the definition of Day from above, we might have:

```
declare
    type Day is (Monday, Tuesday, Wednesday, Thursday, Friday,
                 Saturday, Sunday);
```

```
   subtype Week_Day is Day range Monday .. Friday;
   subtype Weekend  is Day range Saturday .. Sunday;
```

We can now take a Day, and see if we want to go to work:

```
-- file: Enum_Tests.adb
declare
   Today : Day := A_Date_Function;

begin
   if Today in Week_Day then
      Ada.Text_IO.Put_Line("Go to work");
   else
      Ada.Text_IO.Put_Line("Stay in bed");
   end if;
```

Ada provides a predefined Boolean type (section 3.5.3 of the reference manual), which is defined in the package Standard as an enumerated type:

```
type Boolean is(False, True);
```

Returning quickly to the subject of attributes, then we can use 'Image and 'Value with enumerations to get string representations of the values. You can also use the library package Ada.Enumeration_IO; see Section 8.2.1.

```
declare
   True_Text  : String := Boolean'Image(True);
   False_Text : String := Boolean'Image(False);

   A_Boolean : Boolean := Boolean'Value(True_Text);
```

It is important to realize that to support the use of the 'Image attribute the compiler must store all the textual names for the enumeration. This can be a source of concern for developers who have restrictions on the size of applications so a pragma can be used to instruct the compiler not to store these names.

```
declare
   type Day is (Monday, Tuesday, Wednesday, Thursday, Friday,
                Saturday, Sunday);

   pragma Discard_Names (On => Day);
```

This means that if we apply the 'Image attribute to an object of type Day the result is implementation-defined (see reference manual C.2). Also note that this pragma can be applied to exceptions and tagged types, and can be used without a target object to discard names for all objects in the enclosing scope.

Characters

The Ada `Character` type (section 3.5.2 of the reference manual) is very similar to the C `char` type except that in C it is simply a special form of a numeric type, and in Ada it is a special form of an enumerated type:

```
declare
    Char_1 : Character;
    Char_2 : Character := 'h';
```

The type itself is actually defined in the package `Standard` (section A.1 of the reference manual), and as such is part of the implementation details.
    Ada95 uses the Latin-1 (ISO 8859-1) character set and a specific library package called `Ada.Characters.Latin_1` provides complete names for all 256 characters in the character set. So for example to declare a string containing the word 'Simon' we can write:

```
declare
    My_Name : String := ( 'S', LC_I, LC_M, LC_O, LC_N );
```

where `LC_I` means lower case 'I'.

Ada95 also defines a type `Wide_Character` for handling non-Latin-1 character sets. The `Wide_Character` type is based upon the ISO 16-bit standard (ISO 10646 or Basic Multilingual Plane, BMP) commonly called Unicode and will therefore be able to accommodate all current and (it is hoped) future character sets.

3.3.2   Real types

Ada has two non-integer numeric types, the floating point and fixed point types. The predefined floating point type is `Float` (which *should* support at least six digits of precision according to the language standard) and implementations may add new types such as `Long_Float` (supporting *at least* 11 digits of precision). These restrictions are specified by the language standard and so any implementation providing less than these recommended values must document the fact, and why.
    Note: a complete example, `Real_Types.adb`, builds upon the code presented below.

Floating point types

A new floating point (section 3.5.7 of the reference manual) type may be defined in one of two ways:

```
type FloatingPoint1 is new Float;
type FloatingPoint2 is digits 5;
```

The first simply makes a new floating point type, from the standard `Float`, with the precision and size of that type, regardless of what it is. The second line asks the compiler to create a new type, which is a floating point type 'of some kind' with a minimum of five digits of precision.

This level of precision in declaring types is invaluable when writing numeric-intensive programs.

The value supplied for **digits** above can be queried programmatically by use of an attribute `'Digits`.

```
declare
    type FloatingPoint2 is digits 5;

    number_of_digits : Integer := FloatingPoint2'Digits;
    base_digits      : Integer := FloatingPoint2'Base'Digits;
```

As you can see we can also check to see how many digits are used by the type we have derived from, so `number_of_digits` will hold 5, whereas the value of `base_digits` is implementation-dependent.

Fixed point types

Fixed point types (section 3.5.9 of the reference manual) are unusual; there is no pre-defined type 'Fixed' and such a type must be declared in the long form:

```
type Fixed is delta 0.1 range −1.0 .. 1.0;
```

This defines a type which ranges from −1.0 to 1.0 with an accuracy of 0.1. Each element, accuracy, low-bound, and high-bound must be defined as a static real expression.

Attributes

Fixed point types have a number of additional attributes:

- `subtype'Delta`   This returns the value specified for the **delta** keyword in the type declaration.
- `subtype'Fore`   The minimum number of characters required before the decimal place. This includes an addtional character which is either a space or minus sign:

    ```
    Fixed'Fore      is 2
    ```

- `subtype'Aft`   The number of characters required after the decimal place:

    ```
    Fixed'Aft       is 1
    ```

- subtype'Scale   This attribute is best described by the following example:

declare
```
    A_Value : Float := 1.3E8;
    A_Value'Scale is 8
subtype'Round(Arg : Universal_Real)
```

This rounds the value passed as follows:

declare
```
    Value_1 : Float := 10.3;
    Value_2 : Float := 10.8;

    Float'Round(Value_1) = 10.0
    Float'Round(Value_2) = 11.0
```

Decimal types

Ada95 has also added a specific form of fixed point types called decimal types. Decimal types themselves are part of the core language; however, they are of little use on their own without a compiler that supports the Information Systems Annex (see Section 9.5).

The decimal type and the Information Systems Annex are provided to support applications where types representing financial amounts are used. Such types must support very strictly controlled rules on rounding and truncation during arithmetic. The Ada95 decimal type does support such rules: all arithmetic operations on decimal objects truncate the result unless you explicitly use the 'Round attribute. The Information Systems Annex also provides other features, notably edited output of decimal values most usually associated with COBOL applications.

To declare a decimal type add a clause **digits** to a standard fixed point type:

```
type Decimal is delta 0.01 digits 10;
```

This specifies a fixed point type of 10 digits with two decimal places (note that the **range** clause is optional).

The number of digits includes the decimal part and so the maximum range of values becomes

```
−99,999,999.99 .. +99,999,999.99
```

For more information see Section 9.5 where the Information Systems Annex is described in more detail. As you might expect, decimal types are used within our Point of Sale case study; the main objects represented are monetary amounts and weights.

```
type Currency is delta 0.01  digits 10;
type Weight    is delta 0.001 digits 6;
```

These types therefore support values in the range:

```
Currency  -99,999,999.99 .. +99,999,999.99
Weight     -999.999 .. +999.999
```

3.4 Composite types

Composite types are types which have components, so an array is a composite type composed of a given number of identical components accessed by a discrete index. A record is a composite type where each component may be different and may be elementary or composite and is accessed by name.

3.4.1 Arrays

Arrays in Ada (section 3.6 of the reference manual) make use of the range syntax to define their bounds and can be arrays of any type.
      Some examples in C++ are as follows:

```
char name[31];
int  track[3];
int  dbla[3] [10];
int  init[3] = { 0, 1, 2 };

typedef char[31] name_type;
name_type name;

track[2]    = 1;
dbla[0] [3] = 2;
```

And their equivalent in Ada:

```
-- file: Array_Tests.adb
declare
   Name  : array (0 .. 30) of Character;
   Track : array (0 .. 2)  of Integer;
   DblA  : array (0 .. 2, 0 .. 9) of Integer;
   Init  : array (0 .. 2)  of Integer := (0, 1, 2);

   type Name_Type is array (0 .. 30) of Character;
   Name  : Name_Type;

begin
   track(2)    := 1;
   dbla(0, 3)  := 2;
```

Now try the following in C:

```
declare
    type Large_Array is array (0 .. 100) of Integer;

    a, b : Large_Array;
begin
    a := b; -- will copy all elements of b into a.
```

Multiple dimensions

You may have noticed that DblA is a multi-dimensional array. Ada distinguishes between multi-dimensional arrays, for example:

```
DblA_1 : array (0 .. 2, 0 .. 9) of Integer;
```

and arrays of arrays,

```
type SingleA is array (0 .. 9) of Integer;

DblA_2 : array (0 .. 2) of SingleA;
```

Note: you cannot accomplish the above array of array with a type declaration such as the following:

```
DblA : array (0 .. 2) of array (0 .. 9) of Integer;
```

In Ada the right hand side of the keyword **of** must be a type name, so in effect you are defining a type within another type, which is illegal. You must define a prior type for the second dimension, which is what we have introduced SingleA for.

There is also a difference in accessing components of multi-dimensional arrays and arrays of arrays:

```
DblA_1(1, 1)   := 0;

DblA_2(1) (1) := 0;
```

These accomplish the same thing; the difference is that the first is a single entity, and in effect the second is a composite type where each element is also a composite type. This also has another important effect. Consider the following C code:

```
int      entity_1[2];
int      entity_2[2] [2];

void take_array(int[] argument) { .. }

take_array(entity_1);
take_array(entity_2[1]);
```

Basically C only understands arrays of arrays so that the function which takes an array of integers can be passed either the complete `entity_1` or one dimension of `entity_2`.

Now consider the following Ada code. The function `Take_Array` can be passed a dimension from `DoubleA` because each dimension is a separate array. There is no way we can write a function that takes a dimension from a multi-dimensional array.

```
declare
    type SingleA is array (1 .. 2) of Integer;
    type DoubleA is array (1 .. 2) of Single_A;

    type DoubleB is array (1 .. 2, 1 .. 2) of Integer;

    Entity_A : DoubleA := ((1, 2), (1, 2));
    Entity_B : DoubleB := ((1, 2), (1, 2));

    procedure Take_Array(An_Array : SingleA) is
    begin
        ..
    end;
begin
    Take_Array(Entity_A(1));

    Take_Array(Entity_B(1)); -- illegal must specify each
    subscript.
```

Non-zero bases

Because Ada uses ranges to specify the bounds of an array then you can easily set the lower bound to anything you want. For example:

```
Example : array (-10 .. 10) of Integer;
```

For example a `String` is defined as having a range type `Positive` which starts at 1.

Non-integer ranges

In the examples above we have used the common abbreviation for range specifiers. The ranges above are all integer ranges, and so we did not need to use the general form which is:

```
array (type range low .. high)
```

which would make Example above **array** (`Integer` **range** -10 .. 10).

Now you can see where we are going – take an enumerated type, `Day`, and you can define an array:

```
Hours_Worked : array (Day range Monday .. Friday)
       of Integer;
```

Array attributes

Arrays as well as the elementary types have some attributes:

- `arraytype'First`   This attribute returns the value of the lower bound of the array; for arrays of arrays use `arraytype'First(dimension)`. So given the following types

  ```
  declare
      type Array_1 is array (1 .. 5) of Integer;
      type Array_2 is array (5 .. 6, 10 .. 20) of Integer;

      Instance_1 : Array_1 := (10, 20, 30, 40, 50);
      Instance_2 : Array_2 := ((11, 21), (12, 22));
  ```

  the following are therefore true:

  ```
  Instance_1'First                  is 1
  Instance_2'First(1)               is 5
  Instance_2'First(2)               is 20
  Instance_1(Instance_1'First)      is 10
  ```

- `arraytype'Last`   This attribute returns the upper bounds of the array.

- `arraytype'Range`   This attribute returns the range `arraytype'First .. arraytype'Last`.

- `arraytype'Length`   This attribute returns the number of values stored in an array.

Unconstrained types

The examples above demonstrated how to declare an array type. One of Ada's goals is reuse, and to have to define a function to deal with a 1 .. 10 array, and another for a 0 .. 1000 array is silly. Therefore Ada allows you to define unconstrained array types. An unconstrained type is defined in section 3.2 of the reference manual with the statement 'A subtype is called an unconstrained subtype if its type has unknown discriminant, or if its type allows range, index, or discriminant constraints, but the subtype does not impose such a constraint.'

   Therefore an unconstrained array type is one without a specified range. Such an unconstrained array can be used as a parameter type, but you cannot define a variable of an unconstrained array type. Consider:

```
declare
    type    Vector is array (Integer range <>) of Float;
    subtype SmallVector is Vector(0 .. 1);
```

```
Illegal_Variable  : Vector;
Legal_Variable    : Vector(1 .. 5);

Another_Legal     : SmallVector;
```

`Vector` is an unconstrained type, its range is left unspecified. This allows us great flex-ibility to define functions and procedures to work on arrays regardless of their size, so a call to `sort_vector` could take the `Legal_Variable` object or an object of type `SmallVector`, etc.

It is important to realize that the subtype `SmallVector` is a constrained type and so can be legally used to declare variables.

Array parameters

You can define formal parameters of array types including unconstrained types as long as, at run-time, the actual parameter is constrained. Consider the following example where we want to print all values in a given `Vector` of any length. In C we must pass the details of the array length, so the C function has to have the extra parameter `length`, thus:

```
void print_vector(float[] print_this, int length);
```

procedure Print_Vector(Print_This : **in** Vector);

If you are passed an object where the formal parameter is an unconstrained array and want to loop over its values then you need to know where it starts and how long it is. Unlike C programmers, who always know arrays start at 0, but have to be told how long they are, we can use the array attributes introduced above to iterate over a given array.

Example 3.1   Printing the contents of an array ────────────────────────

```
void print_vector(float[] print_this, int length)
{
    for (int item = 0; item < length; item++)
    {
        printf("Item %d = %f\n", item, print_this[item]);
    }
}
```

```
-- file: Print_Array.adb
procedure Print_Vector(Print_This : in Vector) is
begin
    for Item in Print_This'Range loop
        Put("Item ");
        Put(Integer'Image(Item));
        Put(" = ");
```

```
        Put(Float'Image(Print_This(Item)));
        New_Line;
    end loop;
end Print_Vector;
```

We will cover the rather messy output code in the Ada example later in this chapter.

Aggregates

When initializing an array you can use aggregates, as you can in C using the braces to construct the array. However, in Ada you can specify much more control over the initialization:

```
{
    int init[4] = {1, 1, 1, 1};
    ..
}
declare
    Init_1 : array (0 .. 3) of Integer := (1, 1, 1, 1);
    Init_2 : array (0 .. 3) of Integer;
    Init_3 : array (0 .. 3) of Integer;
begin

    Init_2 := (0 .. 3 => 1);
    Init_3 := (0 => 1, others => 0);
```

You will also have noticed that unlike C you can use aggregates to assign to an array in the body of the code. Note the use of the keyword **others** to set any elements not explicitly handled; again the syntax used in **case** statements and exception handling crops up again.

Named syntax

In the examples above we have used what we term named syntax in Ada, the specifying of the target for a parameter or aggregate component. In the examples above we have 0 => 1 and **others** => 0; this explicit naming of the component is very useful in improving the readability of code.

Slicing

Array slicing means to take a section out of one array and assign it into another. Where this is possible at all in C it is usually accomplished using the library routine memcpy, a highly unsafe operation.

```
declare
   Large : array (0 .. 100) of Integer;
   Small : array (0 .. 3)   of Integer;
begin
   -- extract section from one array into another.
   Small(0 .. 3) := Large(10 .. 13);

   Small(0 .. 3) := Large(0 .. 10);
   --                     ^^^^^^^^ range too big.
```

Note: both sides of the assignment must be of the same type, that is the same dimensions with each element the same.

Concatenation

The Ada concatenation operator & is defined for all array types, so in the next example we will swap the top and bottom halves of the array `Large` above by concatenating two array slices.

```
Large := Large(51 .. 100) & Large(1 .. 50);
```

3.4.2   Strings

As in C and C++ the basis for the string (section 3.6.3 of the reference manual) is an array of characters, so you can use standard array indexing syntax to address individual characters and define strings of set length as you do in C. In Ada you also get to use array slicing to extract and manipulate substrings. The definition of the type (in the package `Standard`) is an unconstrained array as follows:

```
type String is array (Positive range <>) of Character;
```

Note: because the range type is `Positive` it means that all string ranges have to be greater than or equal to 1. If we look back at the definition of the C character array name above we can represent it as a string, as below. Because in C and C++ all arrays start at 0, then name has elements at 0 .. 30; in Ada we have to define the range as 1 .. 31.

```
char name[31];

Name : String (1 .. 31);
```

Note: a C string is null-terminated, in Ada they are not. Because strings are based on arrays with given bounds the size of the string is denoted by the range given at declaration time. This makes strings much safer than in C where writing off the end of a character string like this is possible; in Ada it is not. However, this can lead to problems with strings which contain padding, or other values. We will discuss this later.

```
const char* name_const = "this is a very long name isnt it";
char name[11];

strcpy(name, name_const);
// if we are lucky this will crash now, if not it may
// crash much later and we won't know why!
```

In the example above we have also used another C type, pointer to character, to represent a string. In Ada we cannot use the string type without specifying a size: it would be an unconstrained array.

```
-- file: String_Tests.adb
Illegal : String;
Legal   : String(1 .. 20);
```

Another way to specify the size is by initialization, for example:

```
Name : String := "Simon";
```

is the same as defining Name as a String(1 .. 5) and assigning the value "Simon" to it separately.

You can also initialize with an aggregate, thus:

```
Name : String := ('S', 'i', 'm', 'o', 'n');
```

As we said before, because of the base type being an array we can perform array slicing and concatenation on a string:

```
declare
    String_1 : String    := "Hello World";
    String_2 : String    := "Universal Appeal";
    Char_1   : Character := 'e';

    String_3 : String    := String_1(1 .. 6) & -- "Hello "
                            String_2(1 .. 7) & -- "Univers"
                            Char_1;            -- "e";
began
    -- String_3 = "Hello Universe";
```

Of course you may not want this sort of behaviour, so if you just want to put hello at the beginning and clear the rest you might want to consider the string-handling packages in the standard library (see Section 8.1.3).

In our coverage of arrays we said we would revisit our Print_Vector example. Now we know about string slicing and concatenation and how to convert scalar values to strings we can rewrite that nasty output in a more elegant way. Some may argue that this is still not as simple to write and understand as printf, but it is a lot safer.

```
procedure Print_Vector(Print_This : in Vector) is
begin
    for Item in Print_This'Range loop
        Ada.Text_IO.Put_Line("Item " &
                             Integer'Image(Item) &
                             " = " &
                             Float'Image(Print_This(Item)));

    end loop;
end Print_Vector;
```

In fact this example is more directly comparable to C++'s stream IO facility where it might be written something like this:

```
#include <ostream.h>

void print_vector(float[] print_this, int length)
{
    for (int item = 0; item < length; item++)

    {
        cout << "Item "
             << item
             << " = "
             << print_this[item]
             << endl;

    }
}
```

The full details of Ada's input/output library can be found in Chapter 8.

3.4.3 Records

Basic Ada record syntax should be easy to read and understand; you can see an almost direct mapping from C structs to Ada **records** (section 3.8 of the reference manual) for simple structures. Note the example below does not try to convert type to type, thus the C char*, to hold a string, is converted to the Ada String type.

```
typedef struct {
    int    major_number;
    int    minor_number;
    char   name[20];
} Device;
```

```
-- file: Record_Tests.adb
type Device is
   record
      major_number : Integer;
      minor_number : Integer;
      name         : String(1 .. 21);
   end record;
```

Aggregates

Ada uses the same element reference syntax as C, so to access the minor_number element of an object lp1 of type Device we write lp1.minor_number. Ada allows, like C, the initialization of record components at declaration time and the use of aggregate assignment.

```
Device lp1 = {1,
              2,
              "lp1"}; // this may result in a compiler warning.

declare
   lp1 : Device := (1,
                    2,
                    "lp1                    ");

   lp2 : Device := (major_number => 1,
                    minor_number => 3,
                    name         => "lp2                    ");

   tmp1 : Device := (major_number => 255,
                     name         => "tmp                    ");
                     -- illegal, missing minor_number.

   tmp2 : Device;

begin
   tmp2 := (major_number => 255,
            minor_number => 1,
            name         => "tmp                    ");
```

Note: the comment on the C++ initializer is that some C++ compilers will warn that 'you may not assign a char[3] to a char[20]'; in Ada it is a type error – the full 20 characters must be supplied.

Specifying default values for record components improves readability, improves safety, imparts some information about the meaning and use of the record, and cuts maintenance costs. As C++ programmers we know the value of constructors for classes, producing a known initial state, and Ada provides this for its base record type:

```
type struct_device is
   record
      major_number : Integer            := 0;
      minor_number : Integer            := 0;
      name         : String(1 .. 19)   := (others => 0);
   end record;
```

Structures/records like this are simple, and there is little more to say. The more interesting problem for Ada is modelling C unions (see Section 3.8).

Discriminated records

Discriminant types (section 3.7 of the reference manual) are a way of parameterizing a composite type (such as a record, tagged, task, or protected type).

Consider the example of a system that is required to log some events that are generated by various parts of the system. The log is cyclic and has a fixed, relatively small, size so that old events are overwritten. We do not, however, know how many events are to be stored in the log until the program runs and we do not want to get into writing linked lists or other dynamic constructs.

```
declare
   type Event_Item is
      record
         Event_ID   : Integer;
         Event_Info : String(1 .. 80);
      end record;

   type Log_Index is mod 2 ** 8;

   type Event_Array array (Log_Index range <>) of Event_Item;

   type Cyclic_Event_Log(Max_Size : Log_Index) is
      record
         Opened_On  : Some_Date_Type := Some_Initial_Value;
         Last_Event : Log_Index        := 0;
         Events     : Event_Array(0 .. Max_Size);
      end record;
```

First we have to declare a record type to hold our event information in and an incomplete array type which can be used to hold an array of events.

We then declare a type which is a log of such events. This log has a discriminant that specifies the maximum size of the array, so we can write:

```
declare
   My_Event_Log : Cyclic_Event_Log(128);
```

If it is known that nearly all event logs are going to be 128 items in size, then you could make that a default value, so that the following code is identical to that above:

```
declare
    ..

    type Cyclic_Event_Log(Max_Size : Integer := 128) is
        ..

    My_Event_Log : Cyclic_Event_Log;
```

To query the value of the discriminant of an object is easy: it appears as an element of the record like any other, except that you cannot assign to the discriminant. Imagine declaring an event log with an initial value for `Max_Size` of 100, then changing `Max_Size` by hand to 2; what happens? You can change the discriminant as part of an aggregate assignment because you are changing the whole structure, so it is legal to do this:

```
declare
    My_Event_Log_2 : Cyclic_Event_Log_2(2);
begin
    My_Event_Log_2 := (Max_Size   => 3,
                       Opened_On  => Some_Date_Value;
                       Last_Event => (1,
                       Events     => (1 .. 3 => Empty_Event));
```

The rather complex aggregate resizes the array to three elements and then assigns to each component a safe initial value for the `Event_Info` record.

It is important at this point to realize what the compiler is generating for the definition of `Cyclic_Event_Log` above. The compiler has to support the possibility of the programmer wishing to resize the array as above and so most implementations will allocate the largest possible size when the object is first declared and so support the resizing of the array without further allocation. This means that even for `My_Event_Log_2` above which only requires two elements the compiler is likely to allocate `Log_Index'Last` elements, in this case 256. If we had therefore used another type, for example `Integer`, we could have ended up with a very large number of array elements indeed!

Variant records

Anyone who has worked in a Pascal language will recognize that the discriminant can be used for variant records (section 3.8.1 of the reference manual). They are conceptually similar to C unions except that they are safer, and have a very different implementation.

Ada variant records allow you to define a record that has two or more blocks of data (in Ada terms a variant part) of which only one is available at any time. The availability of any block is determined by the value of its discriminant. The following example illustrates a variant record, where the details held about a payment against a sale depend on how the payment was made:

```
-- file: Variant_Tests.adb
declare
   type Payment_Type is (Cash, Cheque, Credit);

   type Transaction(The_Type : Payment_Type) is
      record
         Transaction          : Transaction_ID;
         Amount               : Currency;
         case The_Type is
         when Cash =>
            null;

         when Cheque =>
            Cheque_Number      : Integer;
            Cheque_Card_Number : Card_ID;

         when Credit =>
            Credit_Card_Number : Card_ID;
            Expiry             : Date;
         end case;
   end record;
```

So if you declare `A_Trans : Transaction(Cash);` then you can ask for the number of the transaction, and the amount tendered, but you cannot ask for the cheque number, or what the credit card expiry date is.

Note: the `Cheque_Card_Number` and `Credit_Card_Number` components cannot both be simply called `Card_Number` as you might expect because it is illegal to have components with the same name even in different alternatives.

In the C union representation of `Transaction` above any block is visible regardless of what type of transaction it is; you can easily ask for the expiry date of a cheque payment and C will use the bit pattern of the available data to provide you with some erroneous value.

```
typedef int payment_type;

typedef struct {
   transaction_id transaction;
   currency       amount;
   payment_type   the_type;
   union {
```

```
    struct {
        int       cheque_number;
        card_id   card_number;
    } cheque;

    struct {
        card_id   card_number;
        date      expiry_date;
    } credit;
  } types;
} Transaction;
```

In C++ you might be more tempted to write this as a hierarchy of classes, though the example below using struct as a representation of the above assumes public members:

```
struct transaction {
    transaction_id transaction;
    currency       amount;
};

typedef transaction cash_ transaction;

struct cheque_ transaction : public transaction {
    int            cheque_number;
    card_id        card_number;
};

struct card_ transaction : public transaction {
    card_id        card_number;
    date           expiry_date;
};
```

In Ada you must specify the discriminant when you declare an object (unless it has a default value) so the relevant part of the variant record is always known, and cannot change. This means that if you declare an object as Transaction(Cash) it is not possible to access any item from the Cheque part. You can try but a Constraint_Error exception (Section 3.6.2) will be raised. This means that you *cannot* use a variant record to redefine a piece of memory from one type to another (as you can very easily, and sometimes by mistake, with a C union).

As we have said before, when considering discriminants above, you cannot assign to the discriminant alone, therefore it is illegal to do the following:

```
declare
    A_Trans : Transaction(Cash);
begin
    A_Trans.The_Type        := Cheque;
```

```
A_Trans.Transaction    := Next_Transaction;
A_Trans.Amount         := 10.99;
A_Trans.Cheque_Number := 10099;
```

It is, however, always legal to query the discriminant, thus:

```
begin
    case A_Trans.The_Type is
        when Cash =>
            Accept_Amount(A_Trans.Amount);

        when Cheque =>
            if Endorse_Cheque(A_Trans.Cheque_Number,
                              A_Trans.Cheque_Card_Number) then
                Accept_Amount(A_Trans.Amount);
            end if;

        when Credit =>
            if Authorize_Card(A_Trans.Amount,
                             A_Trans.Credit_Card_Number,
                             A_Trans.Expiry_Date) then
                Accept_Amount(A_Trans.Amount);
            end if;
    end case;
```

To simplify things you can declare subtypes of the variant record which define the variant; we will use name notation for clarity.

```
declare
    subtype Cash_Transaction    is Transaction(Cash);
    subtype Cheque_Transaction is Transaction(The_Type => Cheque);
    subtype Credit_Transaction is Transaction(The_Type => Credit);

    A_Trans : Cash_Transaction;
```

You can, however, use aggregate reassignment to redefine the discriminant of an object, under certain conditions:

```
declare
    A_Trans : Transaction(Cash);
begin
    A_Trans := (The_Type        => Cheque,
                Transaction     => Next_Transaction,
                Amount          => 10.99,
                Cheque_Number => 10099);
    -- illegal
```

The reason that the above is illegal is that the object `A_Trans` is a constrained type, and its discriminant is unchangeable. If we were to define `Transaction` as an unconstrained type by giving it a default discriminant then we could write:

```
declare
   type Transaction(The_Type : Payment_Type := Cash) is
   ..

   A_Trans : Transaction;  -- this is now legal
begin
   A_Trans := (The_Type        => Cheque,
               Transaction     => Next_Transaction,
               Amount          => 10.99,
               Cheque_Number => 10099);
   -- and so is the above.
```

3.5   Access types (pointers)

In C and C++ there are three types of objects, globally declared, stack data, and heap allocated. Global and stack objects are allocated, and if necessary de-allocated, by the code generated by the compiler. Heap objects are allocated by the programmer (with either the `malloc` function in C or the operator `new` in C++) and must also be de-allocated by the programmer.

Example 3.2   Types of data ————————————————————————

```
int global_data = 0;

void some_procedure(void)
{
   int stack_data;

   ;
}

int a_function(void)
{
   int* heap_data = new int;

   return *heap_data;
}
```

This example demonstrates what we mean by global, static, and heap data.

———

Heap-allocated memory in C and C++ is referenced by a pointer type (`int*` in the above example), and is then de-referenced with the `*` operator. Consider the following example:

```
int an_int;

int* pointer_1;
int* pointer_2;

pointer_1 = new int;
pointer_2 = &an_int;

an_int = *pointer_1;
```

What we see is that `pointer_1` is used to reference a piece of dynamically allocated memory; `pointer_2`, however, references a piece of static memory by using the address-of operator (`&`).

All of this is, I am sure, familiar to us all but is useful in understanding some of the features of Ada in respect to access types (section 3.10 of the reference manual). Firstly we will look at access type in Ada83 and then the extensions added in Ada95.

3.5.1 Ada83 access types

Ada83 is very strict on the use of access types: they can only be used to reference heap-allocated memory, and therefore there is no address-of operator. At the time of the design of Ada there was some concern about the overuse of pointers leading to complications in program design and to introducing bugs such as memory leaks or dangling pointers. Thus we will review here the use of access types to manage such heap-allocated memory.

One common use of heap-allocated memory is in the creation of so-called **dynamic data structures**, lists for example.

```
struct _element_holder {
    element_type            actual;
    struct _element_holder* next;
};

typedef struct _element_holder* list_ptr;

typedef struct _list {
    list_ptr head;
    list_ptr tail;
} list;
```

The following is the Ada equivalent to the code above:

```
declare
    type Element_Holder;
    type List_Ptr        is access Element_Holder;

    type Element_Holder is
```

```
      record
         Actual    : Element_Type;
         Next      : List_Ptr := null;
      end record;

   type List is
      record
         Head      : List_Ptr := null;
         Tail      : List_Ptr := null;
      end record;
```

Note: the need to forward declare the `Element_Holder` type before the access type `List_Ptr` is familiar to Pascal or Modula programmers, and does make the declaration of the component `Next` much easier to read.

Let us now consider creating a new list node on the head of the message list, firstly in C:

```
{
   list our_list;

   our_list.tail =
      (list_ptr)malloc(sizeof(struct _element_holder));

   memcpy(our_list.tail->actual,
          a_value,
          sizeof(element_type));

   our_list.tail->next = (list_ptr)0;
```

Allocators

When it comes to dynamically allocating memory in Ada we use what is termed an allocator which looks very similar to the operator new in C++:

```
   declare
      Our_List : List;
   begin
      Our_List.Tail          := new Element_Holder;
      Our_List.Tail.Actual := A_Value;
```

We have simplified the assignment of the components of the element holder because we can assign records directly and we have set up a default value for `Next`.

Allocator aggregate

We can simplify the assignment even further by using an aggregate with the allocator. The aggregate values are separated from the allocator itself by use of the tick again, so it looks like an attribute of the allocation – it is not.

```
declare
   Our_List : List;
begin
   Our_List.Tail := new Element_Holder'(A_Value, null);
   -- or, of course:
   Our_List.Tail := new Element_Holder'(Actual => A_Value,
                                        next   => null);
```

Note: there is no difference in syntax between access of elements of a statically allocated record and a dynamically allocated one. We use the `record.element` syntax
for both.

Example 3.3   Simple linked list handling ───────────────────────────

```
-- file: Access_Tests1.adb
procedure Access_Tests is

   type Element_Type is new Integer;

   type Element_Holder;
   type List_Ptr is access Element_Holder;

   type Element_Holder is
      record
         Actual : Element_Type;
         Next   : List_Ptr := null;
      end record;

   type List is
      record
         Head : List_Ptr := null;
         Tail : List_Ptr := null;
      end record;

   Actual_1 : Element_Type := 1;
   Actual_2 : Element_Type := 3;
   Actual_3 : Element_Type := 5;

   Temp_Ptr : List_Ptr;
   My_List  : List;
begin
   Temp_Ptr := new Element_Holder'(Actual => Actual_1,
                                   Next   => null);
   My_List.Tail := Temp_Ptr;
   My_List.Head := My_List.Tail;

   Temp_Ptr := new Element_Holder'(Actual => Actual_2,
                                   Next   => null);
```

```
   My_List.Tail.Next := Temp_Ptr;
   My_List.Tail := My_List.Tail.Next;

   Temp_Ptr := new Element_Holder'(Actual => Actual_3,
                                   Next   => null);
   My_List.Tail.Next := Temp_Ptr;
   My_List.Tail := My_List.Tail.Next;
end Access_Tests;
```

This is a complete example for creating a linked list and inserting some elements into it. It can be used as a starting point for more complete list handling which we will discuss in Chapter 5 on generics.

Ada allows you to assign between access types, and, as you would expect, it only changes what the access type points to, not the contents of what it points to. One thing to note again: Ada allows you to assign one structure to another if they are of the same type, and so a syntax is required to assign the contents of an access type. The following code compares the C and Ada approaches to this problem:

```
int* int_s1;                              // 1
int* int_s2;

int_s1 = new int;                         // 2
int_s2 = new int;

*int_s1 = 1;                              // 3
*int_s2 = 2;

int_s1 = int_s2;                          // 4

declare
   type Int_Star : access Integer;

   Int_s1 : access Integer;
   Int_s2 : Int_Star;                     -- 1
begin

   Int_s1 := new Integer;                 -- 2
   Int_s2 := new Integer;

   Int_s1.all := 1;                       -- 3
   Int_s2.all := 2;

   Int_s1 := Int_s2;                      -- 4
```

The keyword **all** is used to de-reference an access value, and is directly equivalent to the use of the de-reference operator in C and C++. Other than **.all** and the explicit declaration of an access type (Int_Star) there is very little difference between access types and pointers at this level.

Deallocator

What you may have noticed is that we have not discussed the operator to free the memory we have allocated, the equivalent of C's `free()` or C++'s `delete`. There is a good reason for this: Ada does not provide a simple statement-level support for one.

To digress for a while, Ada was designed as a language to support garbage collection, that is the run-time would manage deallocation of no longer required dynamic memory. However, at that time garbage collection was slow, required a large overhead in tracking dynamic memory and tended to make programs erratic in performance, slowing as the garbage collector takes control. The language specification (section 13.11 of the Reference Manual) therefore states 'An implementation need not support garbage collection . . ..' This means that you must, as in C++, manage your own memory deallocation.

Ada requires you to use the generic procedure `Unchecked_Deallocation` (see Section 5.5.2) to deallocate a dynamic object. This procedure must be instantiated for each dynamic type and should not (ideally) be declared on a public package spec, that is provide the client with a deallocation procedure which uses `Unchecked_Deallocation` internally.

3.5.2   Ada95 access types

Because of the inclusion of object oriented constructs in Ada95 and some other relaxations of the Ada83 rules it was decided to extend the scope and use of access types. All of the above discussion on Ada's handling of heap-allocated memory is still valid; in Ada95 such access values are termed **pool-specific access types** to denote the fact that the allocator allocates objects from a **storage-pool** (the Ada95 term for a heap).

In addition five topics have been added to the model for access types:

- General access types, the ability to assign to an access variable the address of a static variable, the equivalent of the C address-of operator &.
- Access parameters are used to add flexibility to parameter passing with new rules on object oriented programming.
- Access discriminants can be used to create self-referencing data structures.
- Access to subprogram types, the ability to pass pointers to functions as they are known in C, was added to enhance the ability to interface Ada code with systems written in other languages.
- Storage pool management is the Ada95 equivalent of C++'s ability to overload the operators new and `delete`.

Because of the possibility of an implementation providing garbage collection for access types, Ada also provides a pragma to instruct the compiler that objects of a given access type are not to be garbage collected. For example:

```
declare
    type Int_Ptr : access Integer;
    pragma Controlled(Int_Ptr);

    Ex_1 : access Integer;
```

General access types

We have mentioned above the lack of an equivalent to the C address-of operator (&)
in Ada83; we can now use the Ada95 attribute 'Access to assign to a valid access
type. The usage of general access types requires keywords to be added to both the
access type declaration and the declaration of the type to be accessed. The following
code (Access_Tests2.adb) demonstrates the use of the new features:

```
-- file: Access_Tests2.adb
declare
    type Integer_Ptr        is access all        Integer;
    type Const_Integer_Ptr is access constant Integer;

    Ptr_1         : Integer_Ptr;
    Const_Ptr_1 : Const_Integer_Ptr;

    Variable_1  : Integer;
    Constant_1  : constant Integer := 1;

    Variable_2  : aliased Integer;
    Constant_2  : aliased constant Integer := 1;
begin
    Ptr_1         := Variable_1'Access; -- illegal
    Const_Ptr_1 := Constant_1'Access; -- illegal

    Ptr_1         := Variable_2'Access; -- legal
    Const_Ptr_1 := Constant_2'Access; -- legal

    Ptr_1         := Constant_2'Access; -- illegal
    Const_Ptr_1 := Variable_2'Access; -- legal
```

You will notice the two keywords **all** and **constant** added to declaration of the
access types above. These designate that the object is a general access type and what
types of static data can be accessed. (The options are **all** – read–write or **constant**
– read only). The next declarations are a normal variable and constant and an aliased
variable and aliased constant; the aliasing allows us to use the 'Access attribute on
the object.

The body of the code demonstrates some assignment combinations, some legal,
some not. The first two are illegal because the variable is not marked as aliased and so
the 'Access attribute cannot be used. The following are legal: an aliased variable
assigned to an access all variable; the second is an aliased constant assigned to an access
constant variable – again fine.

Lastly we try to assign to an access all variable the result of 'Access applied to a constant. If this were to work we would provide read–write access to a read-only variable – illegal. We can, however, take a read–write variable and assign it to an access constant variable: we are narrowing its accessibility which is perfectly acceptable. Remember our example about casting away const in C and C++? You can now see how Ada's access type rules forbid such an operation.

Access levels

Because Ada is going to try to ensure that you cannot create either memory that no longer has references to it and therefore cannot be reclaimed (memory leaks) or pointers that point to memory which has been reclaimed (dangling pointers), you must be careful when using access types.

The language designers did not want to burden the programmer with a run-time overhead checking all access values, so a simple scheme has been produced which uses a static compile-time check that works on a principle called access levels or lifetimes.

```
-- file: Access_Tests3.adb
declare
   type Data_Ptr is access all Integer;

   procedure Test1(Data : Data_Ptr) is
   begin
      null;
   end Test1;

   procedure Test2 is
      Data : aliased Integer;
   begin
      Test1(Data'Access);  -- illegal
   end Test2;
begin
   null;
end;
```

The compiler will reject the noted line because it is at a *deeper access level* than the access type. This is the Ada95 jargon, which means that the lifetime of the access type Data_Ptr is longer than that of the data item Data.

There is one access level which extends from the **declare** to the very last **end**, and another which extends across Test1, from the **is** to its **end**, and another across Test2. These levels are a little like scopes and are logically nested, so that because we have entered a new level we cannot take the 'Access value of a data item.

This may seem a little prohibitive, but let us imagine what might happen if we remove this rule. Consider this familiar C++ problem:

```
int* get_data(void)
{
    int data;

    return &data;
}
int* a_ptr = get_data();
```

which might look like this in Ada95:

```
declare
    type Data_Ptr is access all Integer;

    function Get_Data return Data_Ptr is
        Data : aliased Integer;
    begin
        return Data'Access;
    end Get_Data;

    A_Ptr : Data_Ptr := Get_Data;
```

We now have an access value which is somewhere in the old stack, and could point to anything; writing to it would be disastrous, and frequently is. If we now apply the Ada95 access level rule we see that the **return** statement is illegal as the object Data is at a lower access level than the type Data_Ptr.

To get around this problem you have two choices, the correct one and the one you must be *very sure* of before you use!

The correct way to solve the problem is to promote the data item to the same access level as the access type:

```
declare
    type Data_Ptr is access all Integer;

    procedure Test1(Data : Data_Ptr) is
    begin
        null;
    end Test1;

    Data : aliased Integer;

    procedure Test2 is
    begin
        Test1(Data'Access); -- illegal
    end Test2;
```

Another perfectly legal way is to use the attribute 'Unchecked_Access instead of 'Access. This implies that you take responsibility for what happens to the data item, and if you know, for instance, that `Test1` does very little with the data you pass it then you might want to use `'Unchecked_Access` instead of promoting the data:

```
procedure Test2 is
   Data : aliased Integer;
begin
   Test1(Data'Unchecked_Access); -- now legal
end Test2;
```

One frequent use of `'Unchecked_Access` is when interfacing to C code which expects an access type simply so it can assign a value to it:

```
declare
   A_Value : aliased Integer;
begin
   A_C_Function(A_Value'Unchecked_Access);
   ..
```

The use of `'Unchecked_Access` is acceptable in this case because we know that the function we are calling does not do anything with the pointer provided except assign a value to it.

Access parameters

This new feature complements the theme of general access types and provides a safe, flexible way to pass access types to procedures. We might then rewrite our example as:

```
procedure Test1(Data : access Integer) is
begin
   null;
end Test1;

procedure Test2 is
   Data: aliased Integer;
begin
   Test1(Data'Access);
end Test2;
```

You will notice that we have no access type (`Data_Ptr`) and no problem with access levels. The reason for this is that the formal parameter for `Test1` is an access parameter and is distinct from a formal parameter which passes an object of an access type such as `Data_Ptr`. The actual type for `Data` within `Test1` is an 'anonymous access type', which means that the Ada compiler invents a new and unique type for `Data`, therefore you cannot declare any other object of the same type.

Note: all access parameters are passed as **in** parameters; in fact you are not allowed to specify either **in**, **out**, or **in out** for access parameters. This means that you cannot alter the value of Data itself although you may of course alter the object it accesses.

At this point, though, Ada has had to introduce a dynamic run-time check on access types. This is demonstrated well by the example below:

```
declare
    type Data_Ptr is access all Integer;

    procedure Test0(Data : Data_Ptr) is
    begin
        null;
    end Test0;

    procedure Test1(Data : access Integer) is
    begin
        Test0(Data_Ptr(Data));
    end Test1;

procedure Test2 is
        Data : aliased Integer;
    begin
        Test1(Data'Access);
    end Test2;
```

Test2 and Test1 are the same as before, except that Test1 now calls a new function Test0, converting its access parameter Data to be of type Data_Ptr. When run this will raise a **Program_Error** exception even though it compiled without problems.

The reason for this exception is that the language allows you to convert an access parameter to a corresponding access type, which we have done. However, in this example we have actually subverted the access level rules because the integer we are using in Test2 is at a deeper access level than the access type. To check for this case, however, we cannot statically analyze the access levels at compilation time, but must check each conversion inside Test1 to see if it is allowed. To do this each access type must carry details about the access level of the original object.

If we promote the integer in Test2 or use 'Unchecked_Access as we did above then the program runs with no exception.

Access discriminants

It is possible for the type of a discriminant to be an access type (usually, but not always, an anonymous access type); this allows us to declare an object with a reference to another object.

Note: an access discriminant is only allowed for limited types.

Example 3.4   Using access discriminants _____

```
-- file: Access_Test4.adb
procedure Access_Test is

    type Element_Holder;
    type List_Ptr is access Element_Holder;

    type Element_Holder(Actual : access Element_Type) is limited
        record
            Next        : List_Ptr := null;
        end record;

    type List is
        record
            Head        : List_Ptr :=null;
            Tail        : List_Ptr :=null;
        end record;

    A_Value : aliased Element_Type;

    List_Node : Element_Holder(A_value'Access);
```

We have now rewritten our linked list node using an access discriminant to hold the data.

_____

This feature can be used to create more general **self-referential structures**; consider the following example:

```
    type Device is limited private;

    type Device_Monitor(Owner : access Device) is limited
        record
            ..
        end record;

private
    type Device is limited
        record
            ..
            A_Message : Device_Monitor(Device'Access);
        end record;
```

This means that each object of type `Device` has a component of type `Device_Monitor` which also has a link back to the `Device` containing it. This structure means that subprograms that deal with the device monitor can also call functions that deal with the device itself.

Note: first, types that include access discriminants must be declared as limited; second, inside the declaration of the type `Device` we place an object of type

`Device_Monitor` but you may have noticed that the discriminant passes the address of a type, not an object. In this case the use of the type name means 'replace with the object, when declared' which means that you only need to declare an object in your code and the linking of the two records is automatic.

Subprogram access types

Ada83 did not allow the passing of procedures as subprogram parameters at execution time, or storing procedures in records and so on. The rationale for this was that it broke the ability to prove the code statically. Ada95 has introduced the ability to define types which are in effect similar to C's ability to define pointers to functions.

In C and C++ there is the most formidable syntax for defining pointers to functions:

```
typedef int (*callback_func) (int param1, int param2);

void register_device(device_instance device,
                     device_unit      unit,
                     callback_func    callback)
{
   ..
   if (device == 0)
   {
      // error
   } else
   {
      if (callback(device, input_string))
      {
         // error
      }
   }
}
```

The Ada syntax should now come as a nice surprise (a more complete version of this example is provided in source form as `Access_Test5.adb`):

```
declare
   type Callback_Func is
      access function(Device : in Device.Instance;
                      Data : in String) return Boolean;

   procedure Register_Device
      (Device           : in out Device.Instance;
       Unit_ID          : in      Device.Unit;
       Input_Callback : in      Device.Input_Callback) is

      Input_String   : String;
```

```
begin
   ..
   if Device = null or else
      Input_Callback(Device, Input_String) then
      raise Input_Error;
   end if;
end Register_Device;
```

Like C++ there is no special syntax required to call a subprogram passed in an access type. However, if you want to use the full form then:

```
*(callback) (device, input_string);       // in C

Input_Callback.all(Device, Input_String); -- in Ada
```

Ada_Store   Subprogram access types are used in our example to implement the application logic itself as a state machine. Point of Sale applications have a very distinctive state, signed-on, trading, selling, signed-off, and so forth, and so most are developed to represent these states. Another reason for using a state machine is that its use of stack resources is less: a function call-based application might have so many call levels as to exhaust system resources.

Initially we declare the types used to implement the state machine, like this:

```
declare
   type State;
   type State_Func is access procedure(Control : access State);
   type State is
      record
         Func          : State_Func;
         Current_User  : Ada_Store.User.Instance;
      end record;
```

We can now write a state. The following is a real state from the application and its job is to wait for a user to sign on. Large areas of the code have been removed to show the main points; a state must conform to the profile of the type `State_Func` which means that a control record of type `State` is passed in. When the user has been signed on then this state passes control to the state called `Main_Trading_Loop` by assigning `Main_Trading_Loop'Access` into the control record. If the user fails to sign on or hits the cancel key then the state passes control to itself.

```
procedure Wait_For_User
   (Control : access State) is

   Inp_Msg : Message_Ptr;
   Input_1 : Input_Allowed := (1 => Sign_On);
   ..
```

```
begin
   ..
   Display.Clear(Displays(Customer));
   Display.Write(Displays(Customer), 1, "SORRY LANE", true);
   Display.Write(Displays(Customer), 2, "CLOSED", true);

   Display.Clear(Displays(Cashier));
   Display.Write(Displays(Cashier), 1, "SIGN ON");

   loop
      Inp_Msg := Get_Input(Input_1, True, "USER ID");
      ..
      if Inp_Msg.Action = Cancel then

         Control.Func := Wait_For_User'Access;
         exit;
      end if;

      if Inp_Msg.Action = Enter then
         -- sign user on.
         Control.Func := Main_Trading_Loop'Access;
         exit;
      end if;
   end loop;
end Wait_For_User;
```

The code that manages this state machine is shown below. It has a state record to be passed to each state and continues until a state assigns **null** to the next state component.

```
procedure Start is
   Next_State : aliased State;
begin
   Next_State.Func := Start_Up_Application'Access;
   while Next_State.Func /= null loop

      Next_State.Func(Next_State'Access);
   end loop;
end Start;
```

Storage pool management

It is quite common in C++ to override the operators new and delete, either for a class, for a hierarchy of classes, or for the system as a whole for a number of reasons:

- To use a better or more efficient allocation mechanism.
- To implement garbage collection.

- To track memory allocation/deallocation for debugging purposes.
- To implement some other feature, for example persistence, so objects are read from disk when allocated and written back when deallocated.

In Ada95 we can accomplish a similar goal with the use of storage pool attributes and the facilities provided by the library package `System.Storage_Pools` (see Section 8.1.4).

3.6   Exceptions

Exceptions (section 11 of the reference manual) are a feature which C++ programmers, on the whole, are only just becoming familiar with. Ada, however, was designed with exceptions included from the beginning. This does mean that Ada code will use exceptions more often than not, and certainly the standard library packages and the run-time will raise a number of possible exceptions.

Unlike C++ where an exception is identified by its type, in Ada exceptions are uniquely identified by name. To define an exception for use, simply

```
parameter_out_of_range : exception;
```

These look and feel like constants: you cannot assign to them and so forth; you can only raise an exception and handle an exception.

Exceptions can be argued to be a vital part of the safety of Ada code: they cannot easily be ignored, and can halt a system quickly if something goes wrong. This is far more reliable than a returned error code which in most cases is completely ignored.

3.6.1   Ada exceptions and C++ exceptions

As we have already discussed, the biggest difference between Ada exceptions and C++ exceptions is that there is no predefined exception 'type' in C++. There is a lot of discussion on which approach is more flexible; however, it is my belief that neither is more flexible than the other, they are simply different.

In many C++ projects it is common to define class hierarchies for exceptions, and the C++ draft standard [13] even defines a set of such classes, rooted at a library class `exception` (in header `stdexcept`) which looks like:

```
namespace std {
   class exception {
   public:
      exception() throw();
      exception& exception(const exception&) throw();
      exception& operator=(const exception&) throw();
      virtual ~exception() throw();
      virtual const char* what() const throw();
   };
}
```

This class is then used by the library to signify error conditions, and subclasses exist to categorize the errors. The following library-defined subclasses exist:

```
exception
    logic_error
        domain_error
        invalid_argument
        length_error
        out_of_range
    runtime_error
        range_error
        overflow_error
```

You could then subclass these to create your own application exception classes. For instance:

```
exception
    ..
    runtime_error
        ..
        my_file_handler_error
```

This hierarchy allows us to handle exceptions in a generic way: you can query the type of the exception (assuming in the case above you have run-time type information (RTTI), a feature from the draft standard already implemented in a number of compilers) and in the case of the file-handler exception it may identify more details on the precise nature of the file error.

However, with this scheme, if you have to interface your library with a third-party library that uses a differing principle, such as the following, you now have a problem:

```
typedef const char* Cpp_Exception;

Cpp_Exception Unknown_Exception = "Unknown";
Cpp_Exception File_Exception    = "File";
Cpp_Exception Date_Exception    = "Date";

void raise_exception(Cpp_Exception the_exception);
```

Now, of course, all your carefully crafted exception-handling code using RTTI to check exception types will have to be extended to cope with the new mechanism.

```
package Project is
    ..
    Unknown : exception;
end Project;
```

```
package Project.File is
   ..
   File_Not_Found : exception;
   Access_Error   : exception;
end Project.File;
```

```
package Project.Date is
   ..
   Invalid_Day   : exception;
   Invalid_Month : exception;
end Project.Date;
```

This is the Ada approach. Although we have not covered packages yet it is clear that within these syntactic units we have declared exceptions which can be handled by name distinctively within generic code such as:

```
declare
   ..
exception
   when Project.File.File_Not_Found => ..
   when Project.Date.Invalid_Day => ..
   when Project.Scheduler.Invalid_Day => ..
   when Project.Unknown => ..
end;
```

We have lost the hierarchical structure of the C++ exception classes above, and, of course, the ability for the C++ exception class to carry information with it. However, the use of the full name including package names does provide the designer the ability to reuse standard understood names, such as the use of the exception name `Invalid_Day` within the scheduler and date packages.

Section 8.1.5 describes some standard library packages that allow us to be more flexible with our exception handling, to pass messages with an exception and to save and re-raise an exception.

3.6.2   Predefined exceptions

A number of exceptions can be raised by the standard library and/or the run-time environment. You may expect to come across at least one while you are learning Ada (and more once you know it):

- `Constraint_Error`   This exception is raised when a constraint is violated; such constraints include

  - numeric overflow,
  - range bounds exceeded,
  - reference to invalid record component,
  - de-reference of **null** access type.

- `Program_Error` This is raised by the run-time to mark an erroneous program event, such as calling a procedure before package initialization or bad instantiation of a generic package or access type level violation.
- `Storage_Error` This exception is raised when a call to **new** could not be satisfied owing to lack of memory, or a subprogram call could not be made owing to invalid stack space.
- `Tasking_Error` This is raised when problems occur during inter-task communication (see Section 7.3).

3.6.3 Suppress **pragma**

This pragma can be used to suppress certain run-time checks from taking place, usually for performance reasons. It is included in this section because if any of these run-time checks fail, they raise one of the language-defined exceptions listed above.

The pragma works from its declaration to the end of the innermost enclosing scope, or the end of the scope of the named object (see Table 3.1).

Table 3.1 Predefined language pragmas.

Pragma argument	Suppresses exception	Exception normally raised on
Access_Check	Constraint_Error	De-reference of a **null** access value
Accessibility_Check	Program_Error	Access to inaccessible object or subprogram
Discriminant_Check	Constraint_Error	Access to incorrect component in a discriminant record
Division_Check	Constraint_Error	Attempt to divide by zero
Elaboration_Check	Program_Error	Incorrect elaboration of package or subprogram body
Index_Check	Constraint_Error	Out of range array index
Length_Check	Constraint_Error	On array length violation
Overflow_Check	Constraint_Error	Overflow from numeric operation
Range_Check	Constraint_Error	Out of range scalar value
Storage_Check	Storage_Error	Not enough storage to satisfy a new call
Tag_Check	Constraint_Error	Object has an invalid tag for operation

The first use of the `Suppress` pragma below turns off checking for **null** access values throughout its enclosing scope (for the lifetime of the suppress), whereas the second only suppresses the check for the named data item.

```
pragma Suppress(Access_Check);
pragma Suppress(Access_Check, On => My_Type_Ptr);
```

The point of this section is that by default of all these checks are enabled, and so any such errors will be trapped.

Figure 3.1   Status word bit-layout.

3.7   System representation of types

In C a number of features are provided to allow the programmer a great deal of flexibility in specifying the structure of data, so for example a status word might be defined as follows:

```
#pragma pack(1)

typedef struct {
    unsigned status : 4;
    unsigned unused : 3;
    unsigned parity : 1;
} device_status_word;
```

The initial pragma (common across most C compilers, though preprocessor pragmas are not subject to standardization) packs all data structures on single byte boundaries, important for this application. The structure then uses the C bit-field syntax to define a structure which takes up a single byte as in Figure 3.1. Unfortunately this is not guaranteed. The actual implementation of bit-fields in C is compiler-dependent and can take any form the compiler decides. For example bits may be placed in a different order. Instead of from left to right as in Figure 3.1, the compiler may place them right to left. Imagine writing a value of this type to a file using one compiler and reading it with another compiler which has used a different order for the bit-fields.

   Also in C you could only use the types `int`, `signed`, or `unsigned` to specify bit-fields. C++ expands this to allow `char`, `short`, `long`, or `enum`; however, it does not attempt to specify the implementation, in fact it states (section 9.6 of [11]): 'People often try to use bit-fields to save space. Such efforts are often naïve and can lead to waste of space instead.'

   As you might expect with Ada's background in embedded and systems programming there are ways in which you can force a type into specific system representations (section 13 of the reference manual) such as the C example above. We will start with some of the more basic representation clauses, and finish with an example matching the above. All of the examples in this section are combined into the source example `System_Representation.adb`.

3.7.1   Specifying size

This first example shows the most common form of system representation clause, the size attribute. We will ask the compiler to give us modular type representing the range 0 to 255 and then forcing it to be eight bits in size.

```
declare
    type BYTE is mod 256;
    for BYTE'Size use 8;

    BYTE_Size : Integer := BYTE'Size;

    Storage   : Integer := System.Storage_Unit;
    WORD_Size : Integer := System.Word_Size;
```

We can also, as you can see, use this attribute to query the size of an object. We can also use the two values in package System to query the size of a storage unit and the size of the machine word. In most cases the Storage_Unit is a byte and so its value is 8.

3.7.2 Enumeration values

Again this is useful for system programming. It gives us the safety of enumeration range checking, so we can only put the correct value into a variable, but does allow us to define what the values are if they are being used in a call that expects specific values.

```
type Activity is  (Reading, Writing, Idle);
for Activity  use (Reading => 1, Writing => 2, Idle => 4);
```

3.7.3 Specifying location

We might find out that the activity data, represented by Activity above, is always to be found in a certain memory location, so we may write:

```
Status_Address : constant System.Address :=
    System.Storage_Elements.To_Address(16#0340#);

Device_Status : Activity;
for Device_Status'Address use Status_Address;
```

The value used to specify the address in this case must be a constant value of type System.Address. The most common way to specify an address is to convert from an Integer literal as we have in this case.

The address literal uses Ada's version of the C++ 0x340 notation, with the general form of base#value# where the base is a value between 2 and 16 and the value may include underscores for clarity, so bit masks are very easy to define, for example:

```
Is_Available  : constant BYTE := 2#1000_0000#;
Not_Available : constant BYTE := 2#0000_0000#;
```

System representation of types **101**

3.7.4 Record layout

This last example is the most complex: it declares an Ada record which will match the intention of the C structure `device_status_word` above. First we will see a normal record declaration, where we declare the components `Status`, `Unused`, and `Parity` (with more appropriate types than those allowed by C). We then move on to the representation clauses. The alignment clause is a direct equivalent to the `#pragma pack 1` used by C. The second clause specifies the bit order to assume (specified by the enumeration `Bit_Order` in the package `System`). Finally we specify the exact layout of the components; the value between the **at** and the **range** is the offset in storage units of the element and the range is the bits taken within the storage unit.

```
type Bit_Flag is mod 2**1;

type Device_Status_Word is
   record
      Status : Activity;
      Unused : Integer range 0 .. 7;
      Parity : Bit_Flag;
   end record;

for Device_Status_Word'Alignment use 1;
for Device_Status_Word'Bit_Order use Low_Order_First;
for Device_Status_Word use
   record
      Status at 0 range 0 .. 3;
      Unused at 0 range 4 .. 6;
      Parity at 0 range 7 .. 7;
   end record;
```

The example above, although a little long winded, is easy to read, easy to understand, and because of careful statement in the language reference manual we know as programmers that we will get a single byte structure with all components where we want them. This representation is absolute and holds for any compiler on any machine. We can then write the structure to a file, pass it over the network and we know that whoever receives it will be able to make sense of it.

As well as the record representation clauses a set of three attributes can be applied specifically to record components, `Position`, `First_Bit`, and `Last_Bit`. These can be used to accomplish the same as the above clause.

```
for Device_Status_Word'Alignment use 1;
for Device_Status_Word'Bit_Order use Low_Order_First;

for Device_Status_Word.Status'Position use 0;
for Device_Status_Word.Status'First_Bit use 0;
for Device_Status_Word.Status'Last_Bit use 3;
for Device_Status_Word.Unused'Position use 0;
```

```
for Device_Status_Word.Unused'First_Bit use 4;
for Device_Status_Word.Unused'Last_Bit use 6;
for Device_Status_Word.Parity'Position use 0;
for Device_Status_Word.Parity'First_Bit use 7;
for Device_Status_Word.Parity'Last_Bit use 7;
```

3.7.5 Bit sets

In C it is very easy to work with values that are considered to represent a set of discrete bits, for example:

```
#define ISBITSET(value, bit) value && (1 << (bit))
{
    int bit_set;

    get_register(&bit_set);

    if (ISBITSET(bit_set, 0))
    {
        do_something();
    }
    if (ISBITSET(bit_set, 1))
    {
        do_something_else();
    }
    ..
}
```

The macro tests if the bit specified is set (non-zero) in the value passed. The example then calls some function to set the value of `bit_set` and then proceeds to perform actions based on the values of different bits.

In Ada this is usually accomplished with a packed array of `Booleans`. The pragma `Pack` is used to represent the object in the smallest possible storage and for an array of Boolean values this is one single bit each.

```
declare
    type Bit_Set is array (Integer range 0 .. Integer'Size - 1)
        of Boolean;
    pragma Pack(Bit_Set);

    Register : Bit_set := (others => False);
begin

    Get_Register(Register);

    if Register(0) then
        Do_Something;
    end if;
```

```
   if Register(1) then
      Do_Something_Else;
   end if;
   ..
end;
```

The advantages of this approach are that we can have actual types for our bit sets rather than having to rely on integer values. I consider that the readability of the code is much greater in the Ada example and can be enhanced even further by using an enumeration type to specify the array bounds.

```
declare
   type Register_Bits is (Read_Enabled,  Write_Enabled,
                          Flush_Enabled, Restart_Enabled,
                          Async_Write_Enabled,
                          Error_Packet_Enabled,
                          Unused_Bit_0,
                          Unused_Bit_1);

   type Register is array (Register_Bits) of Boolean;
   pragma Pack(Register);

   A_Register : Register := (others => False);
begin

   Get_Register(A_Register);

   if A_Register(Read_Enabled) then
      Do_Something;
   end if;
   ..
end;
```

One further not so obvious feature of the Ada approach is that bit masks can still be used. For example, consider this C code:

```
{
   int required_capability = 15; /* 0,1,2,3 = set */
   int bit_set;

   get_register(&bit_set);

   if ((bit_set && required_capability) == required_capability)
   {
      do_something();
   }
   ..
}
```

We have declared a mask which has set all the bits which specify capabilities required to be set; the use of the logical **and** tests if the bits are set in the register. To accomplish this in Ada we declare an array with the values we require set to `True`, we then **and** the two arrays together (such logical operations are defined for array types).

```
declare
   ..
   Required_Capability : Register := (Read_Enabled    => True,
                                      Write_Enabled   => True,
                                      Flush_Enabled   => True,
                                      Restart_Enabled => True,
                                      others => False);
   A_Register : Register := (others => False);
begin

   Get_Register(A_Register);

   if (A_Register and Required_Capability)
      = Required_Capability then

      Do_Something;
   end if;
   ..
end;
```

3.8   Representing C unions in Ada

Ada has more than one way in which it can represent a union as defined in a C program; the method you choose depends on the meaning and usage of the C union.

Firstly we must look at the two ways unions are generally used. Unions are used to represent the data in memory in more than one way (like a variant): the programmer must know which way is relevant at any point in time. This variant identifier can be inside the union or outside, for example:

```
struct _device_input {
   int device_id;
   union {
      type_1_data from_type_1;
      type_2_data from_type_2;
   } device_data;
};
void get_data_func(_device_input* from_device);
union device_data {
```

```
    type_1_data from_type_1;
    type_2_data from_type_2;
};
void get_data_func(int *device_id, device_data* from_device);
```

In the first example all the data required is in the structure: we call the function and get back a structure that holds the union and the identifier that denotes which element of the union is active. In the second example only the union is returned and the identifier is separate; the union itself does not contain all the required information.

The next step is to decide whether, when converting such code to Ada, you wish to maintain simply the concept of the union, or whether you are required to maintain the memory layout also.

Note: the second choice is usually only if your Ada code is to pass such a structure to a C program or get one from it.

3.8.1   As a variant record

If you are simply retaining the concept of the union then you would *not* use a union without a variant:

```
type Device_ID is new Integer;

type Device_Input(From_Device : Device_ID) is
    record
        case From_Device is
            when 1 =>
                From_Type_1 : Type_1_Data;
            when 2 =>
                From_Type_2 : Type_2_Data;
            when others =>
                null; -- unknown.
        end case;
    end record;
```

The above code is conceptually the same as the first piece of C code; however, it will probably look very different. You could use the following representation clause to make it look like the C code. Remember that in C the layout of a **struct** is implementation-dependent so you would have to check this for each C compiler you want to pass the record to. Also note that any Ada **case** statement must cover all possibilities and therefore a **when others** clause must be included.

```
for Device_Input use
    record
        From_Device at 0 range 0 .. 15;
        From_Type_1 at 2 range 0 .. 15;
        From_Type_2 at 2 range 0 .. 31;
    end record;
```

You should be able to pass this to and from C code now. You could use a representation clause for the second C case above, but unless you really must pass it to some C code, re-code it as a variant record.

3.8.2 Using Unchecked_Conversion

We can also use the abilities of `Unchecked_Conversion` (Section 5.5.1) to convert between different types. This allows us to write the following:

```
type Type_1_Data is
   record
      Data_1 : Integer;
   end record;

type Type_2_Data is
   record
      Data_1 : Integer;
   end record;

function Type_1_to_2 is new Unchecked_Conversion
   (Source => Type_1_data, Target => Type_2_Data);
```

This means that we can read/write items of type `Type_1_Data` and when we need to represent the data as `Type_2_Data` we can simply write

```
Type_1_Object : Type_1_Data := ReadData;

Type_2_Object : Type_2_Data := Type_1_to_2(Type_1_Object);
```

3.9 Summary

Consider now our Point of Sale example. We now know how to declare new types, use control structures and write subprograms. This is enough to start considering some of the code we might want to write.

Initially we will need to declare some global types, required by our whole project, such as:

```
type Quantity          is new Positive;
type Currency          is delta 0.01  digits 10;
type Weight            is delta 0.001 digits 6;

type Short_Description is new String(1 .. 18);
type Full_Description  is new String(1 .. 75);
```

and some global constants:

```
System_Name              : constant String := "Ada Store";
System_Version           : constant String := "GENERIC_1.0.0";
```

Now we can try some more complicated types, structures with actual business meaning, departments, items, and tenders. The following are structures for departments and items; each item contains a reference to the department it is in (which manages its price range and tax rate for example):

```
-- department information.
declare
    type Department_Identifier is new Positive range 1 .. 50;

    type Instance is
       record
           Department_Number : Department_Identifier;
           Description       : Short_Description;
           Min_Price         : Currency    := 0.00;
           Max_Price         : Currency    := 0.00;
           Tax_Rate          : Percentage := 0.00;
       end record;
-- item information.
declare
    type Item_Identifier is new Positive;

    type Instance is
       record
           Item_Number       : Item_Identifier;
           In_Department     : Department_Identifier;
           Display_Descr     : Short_Description;
           Price             : Currency;
           Weight_Required   : Boolean;
       end record;
```

The next type, a representation of a tender type (type of payment, for example cash, card) is more complete and even presents its set of operations. Such business objects are usually held in a database, hence the Lookup and Remove subprograms deal with identifiers rather than objects, and the Create_New subprogram is required to insert the object in the database.

```
-- tender information.
declare
    type Tender_Identifier is new Positive range 1 .. 20;

    type Tender_Type_Instance is
       record
            Tender_ID : Tender_Identifier;
```

```
         Description       : Short_Description;
         Min_Amount        : Currency   := 0.00;
         Max_Amount        : Currency   := 0.00;
      end record;

   function Lookup
      (Tender_ID : in Tender_Identifier)
       return Tender_Type_Instance;

   procedure Create_New
      (Tender_ID    : in Tender_Identifier;
       Description : in Short_Description;
       Min_Amount   : in Currency;
       Max_Amount   : in Currency);

   procedure Remove
      (Tender_ID : in Tender_Identifier);

   function Authorize
      (Tender : in Tender_Type_Instance;
       Amount : in Currency)
       return Boolean;

   function Description
      (Tender : in Tender_Type_Instance)
       return Short_Description;

Invalid_Identifier : exception;
```

Items, departments, and other database-held objects would follow a similar pattern with `Create_New`, `Lookup`, and `Remove` subprograms.

What we cannot do so far is package this code in a form that the compiler can truly accept. The next chapter will add a little more to our understanding by introducing Ada packages and describing the Ada compilation model.

Packages for structured programming

4.1	C++ vs Ada compilation models
4.2	Package structure
4.3	Accessing packages
4.4	Package data hiding
4.5	Nested packages
4.6	Some fine detail
4.7	Summary

One of Ada's prime goals was to support the development of very large software projects. One feature of large software systems is their division into units; whatever they are called – layers, subsystems, modules, or services – what matters is that in between layers there is an interface and it is the communication over these interfaces that causes so many problems in a large team.

In C and C++ there is currently no support for the management or packaging of the interfaces between software systems. A number of languages have attempted to solve this problem, notable the Modula family with the concept of modules, a unit of code with a given interface that provides the public view of a software component.

It is necessary to understand the differences between C/C++ and Ada at a more fundamental level before we discuss Ada packages (section 7 of the reference manual). We need to discuss the backgrounds of the languages and the models used in their design.

4.1 C++ vs Ada compilation models

4.1.1 C and C++ stream model

C was initially developed as a portable assembly/system programming language for the development of the UNIX operating system, a single-project, single-vendor development. As such, issues such as maintenance, productivity, readability, safety,

109

security, and large-scale systems were not considered. This led to a compilation model that looks very much like most assembly languages, a single file that defines sets of external symbols for the linker to resolve. With the increase in complexity of the work expected of the early C compilers a pre-processor was developed which allowed extensions to the language, the most notable being the `#include` statement which introduced the text of one file into the current.

C++ was developed [11] as an attempt to marry the performance and system level characteristics of C with the powerful abstraction techniques, based around the concept of classes, found in Simula. One of the design goals of C++ was to maintain as much backwards compatibility with C as possible and this has included the compilation model.

The resulting stream of text produced by the pre-processor (by stripping out the comments and merging all `include` files) means that the compiler has very little context information to work with and certainly no partitioning of declarations.

As an example, consider the following three header files; firstly `part_a.h`:

```
// --- part_a.h

#include "part_b.h"

#define A_STRING B_STRING

void part_a_func(char*, int);
```

now `part_b.h`:

```
// --- part_b.h

#define B_STRING    "hello world"
```

now `part_c.h`:

```
// --- part_c.h

#define C_LENGTH 10
```

and the main program:

```
#include "part_a.h"
#include "part_c.h"

void main(void)
{
    part_a_func(A_STRING, C_LENGTH);
}
```

The compiler will simply see the following after the preprocessor has removed **#defines** and flattened the headers:

```
void part_a_func(char*, int);
void main(void)
{
    part_a_func("hello world", 10);
}
```

This leads to two classic problems, name clashes and order dependency.

Name clashes

The first problem, that of name clashes, is fairly easy to see. Imagine that a file `main.c` includes two header files, `my_file.h` and `3rd_party.h` like so:

```
#include <3rd_party.h>
#include "my_file.h"

void main(void)
{
    ;
}
```

where both header files declare an object called `VERSION_INFO`, so the compiler will flag an error to tell you that the object has been multiply declared. The standard answer is to prefix a tag to each so you might get `MY_VERSION_INFO` and `3RD_PARTY_VERSION_INFO`. This is not a nice approach, and is required far too often.

Multiple includes   Another problem is including the same file many times: you may not include it twice (that would be silly) but you may include *a* then *b* where *b* also includes *a*, and so on. To get around this each header becomes *protected* by a rather haphazard manner such as:

```
#if !defined( part_b_h )
#define  part_b_h
// --- part_b.h

#define B_STRING    "hello world"

#endif
```

Namespaces

The new draft C++ standard [13] has included **namespaces**, an idea to add contexts or partitions into the compilation stream. Each header can then be wrapped in a name-space to identify its contents, so we would have:

```
// my_file.h
namespace my_name_space {
```

```
    const int VERSION_INFO = 10;
    ..
};
```

This means that `main.c` can reference an object called `my_name_space:`
`:VERSION_INFO`. The inclusion of namespaces in C++ will help with the mixing of
third party software and the management of software modules, though it will take
some time to reach mainstream usage and for its implications to be fully understood
by programmers.

Order dependency

Now consider `part_a.h` and `part_b.h` again:

```
// ——— part_a.h

#include "part_b.h"

#define A_STRING B_STRING


// ——— part_b.h
#if defined(FEATURE_OK)
    #define B_STRING    "hello world"
#else
    #define B_STRING
#endif
```

Now the client of `part_a.h` has to know to define `FEATURE_OK`, because it is
required to get a legal definition of `B_STRING` in `part_b.h`. This sort of coding
occurs frequently, often when a single large header is included and macros are used to
declare which bits of the header to use.

```
#define INCLUDE_FEATURE_aaaa
#define INCLUDE_FEATURE_bbbb
#define INCLUDE_FEATURE_cccc
#include <large_and_complex_header.h>
```

The `#include` directive knows nothing about what it is including and can lead to all
sorts of problems, such as people who `#include "thing.c"`. This sharing of code
by the pre-processor leads to the `#ifdef` construct as there would be different interfaces for different people. The other problem is that C++ compilations can sometimes
be very slow because `file_a` included `file_b` included `file_c`. Or the near fatal
`file_a` included `file_a` included `file_a` and so on.

Stroustrup [11] has tried (in vain, as far as I can see) to convince C++ programmers to remove dependence on the pre-processor but all the drawbacks are still
there. In effect the C and C++ compilation model is file-based: you compile a source

file and it includes header files (which means that you can even put a fully qualified path name in the `include` statement, that is `#include "/home/skj/include/myfile.h"`).

4.1.2 Ada library model

The Ada model of compilation is built around the idea of a central library. All successful compilations result not in an object file, but in a new entry in the library. This library is capable of being shared within a project, a company, or private to the individual – the choice is between you and the facilities provided by the compiler vendor.

Library units

This model results in the unit of compilation being not a stream of text, but a **library unit**. The *Language Reference Manual* defines a library unit as '. . . a separately compiled program unit, and is always a package, subprogram or generic unit. Library units may have other (logically nested) library units as children, and may have other program units physically nested within them.' Any library unit consists of a specification and a body (described in Section 2.4 on subprograms); these two halves are tightly bound together and no discrepancy between the two will be accepted by the compiler. This means that the mapping of source to files is not important in the compilation model; you compile *this function*, or *that package*, and so it is much easier for the compiler to provide cross-module static checks. A standard called ASIS (Ada Semantic Interface Specification) defines a number of Ada packages which can be used to query the library programmatically and can form the basis of library-independent browsers.

The specification contains an explicit list of the visible components of a library unit and so there can be no internal knowledge exploited as is often the case in C code. Consider the following example of a C module called `server`:

```
// server.h

void start(void);
void stop(void);

int send_message(int message_id, char* message_text);

// server.c

void start(void)
{
    ..
}

void stop(void)
{
    ..
}
```

```
int actual_code(int message_id, char* message_text)
{
    ..
}

int send_message(int message_id, char* message_text)
{
    ..
    actual_code(message_id, message_text);
    ..
}
```

You will notice in the code file the `send_message` function calls a function `actual_code`, which does the main processing. If you have even read-only access to the source code of the server module you might decide to do the following in your client module:

```
// client file

extern int actual_code(int message_id, char* message_text);

void some_other_func(void)
{
    ..
    //(void)send_message(message_1, "A test message");
    // removed above call, it was too slow, the following
    // is much better !

    actual_code(message_1, "A test message");
    ..
}
```

The `extern` statement tells the compiler that at link time a function called `actual_code` will exist; however, the programmer of the module server is at liberty to remove the function – it is his or her private code after all – or he or she could do what they should have done in the first place: mark it as `static`.

Packages

An Ada package, however, is a little like a namespace, but more powerful. The package specification is a completely encapsulated entity which can be compiled on its own and so must include specifications from other packages to do so (unlike C++ where the order of inclusion in the source file using a header is used to make sure all declarations are visible). An Ada package body at compile-time will refer to its package specification to ensure legal declarations, but in some Ada environments it would look up a compiled version of the specification.

Note: Ada has *no* pre-processor!

4.2   Package structure

Below is the skeleton of a simple package. First, its specification file:

```ada
package Ada_Store_Trading is

    type State is (Trading, Not_Trading, Consolidating);

    procedure Start;
    procedure Stop;

    function Current_State return State;

    Invalid_Trading_Time : exception;
end Ada_Store_Trading;
```

Now its body, or implementation, file. The most important note is the keyword **body**: forget this and you will find the compiler will become rather upset at finding subprogram bodies in a package specification!

```ada
package body Ada_Store_Trading is

    Trading_State : State;

    procedure Start is
    begin
        if Some_Time_Test then
            Trading_State := Trading;
        else
            raise Invalid_Trading_Time;
        end if;
    end Start;

    procedure Stop is
    begin
        if not Some_Time_Test then
            Trading_State := Not_Trading;
        else
            raise Invalid_Trading_Time;
        end if;
    end Stop;

    function Current_State return State is
    begin
        return Trading_State;
    end Current_State;
begin
    Trading_State := Not_Trading;
end Ada_Store_Trading;
```

The package specification contains nothing you have not seen, a type declaration, an exception, and three simple subprograms. However, in the package body you will notice an object called `Trading_State` which holds the current state. This is not accessible to any client of the package `Ada_Store_Trading`. This is equivalent to an object in C which is marked static within a code module.

You should also have noticed that the package itself has a statement part, in which it sets the initial state of the object `Trading_State`. This code part may be used to open files and to perform initialization. In some cases nearly all the work is done here, with functions and procedures used by the package simply to access data set up during this initialization (see Section 4.6.1 for discussion on initialization).

This package initialization should solve the sort of problem which causes code like the following to be found frequently in a C source module:

```
/* source module */

struct something important_data;
int               important_data_initialized = 0;

void function_1(void)
{
   if (!important_data_initialized)
   {
       /* initialize important_data */
   }
}
```

A number of strategies exist in C++, usually using a class to represent the important data and using its constructor to initialize it correctly. The Ada approach is more flexible and is certainly easier to read and understand as most of the C and C++ solutions are cobbled together.

4.3   Accessing packages

Working with the example package above, let us assume that we need to include our `Ada_Store_Trading` package so that we can start trading (you must start trading before you can issue any other command to the system).

4.3.1   `with`

Firstly how and where do we include it? Like C, package specifications can be added to either a specification or body, depending on who is the client. In C it is usual to use `#include` only in a C module, so clients must manage header dependencies; in C++ it is more usual to make each header stand alone and include all the headers it requires.

A package specification is included for use with the keyword **with** (see below),

and its contents are then made available to the client. All **with** clauses must appear
before the library unit which is to use them; this is so that you can quickly and easily
see the dependencies on any particular unit.

    Note: the body of a library unit automatically **with**s its specification and so
any declarations there are visible. The body also has access to any library unit **with**-
ed by its specification.

```
with Ada_Store_Trading;

package Ada_Store_PoST_Application is

    type State_1 is (Signed_On, Signed_Off, Secured);

    type State is
        record
            User_State  : State_1;
            Store_State : Ada_Store_Trading.State;
        end record;

    function Current_State return State;
    ..
end Ada_Store_PoST_Application;

with Ada.Text_IO;
package body Ada_Store_PoST_Application is

    Application_State : State;

    function Current_State return State is
    begin
        return Application_State;
    end Current_State;

    Temp : Ada_Store_Trading.State;
begin
    Temp := Ada_Store_Trading.Current_State;

    Application_State := (User_State => Signed_Off,
                          Store_State => Temp);

    if Temp = Ada_Store_Trading.Not_Trading then

        Ada.Text_IO.Put_Line("Store not trading");
    end if;
end Ada_Store_PoST_Application;
```

You can see here the basic visibility rules: the specification has to **with** the package
`Ada_Store_Trading` so that it can declare its own type `State`. As we said above,
the body automatically has access to the units included in its specification. You can see
that although the body does not **with** `Ada_Store_Trading` the package is used in
the body to get the trading status into the object `Temp`. The body also **with**s another
package `Ada.Text_IO` to make a call to `Put_Line`; the specification is unaware of
this **with** and so cannot use `Ada.Text_IO` unless it has its own **with** statement. Any

other client of this package cannot make use of the **with** statement in its specification, therefore

```
with Ada_Store_PoST_Application;

procedure Test is
   Application_State : Ada_Store_PoST_Application.State; -- legal
begin
   Ada_Store_Trading.Start; -- illegal
end Test;
```

The second line is illegal because the **with** statement in the `Ada_Store_PoST_Application` specification is not visible to `Test` as a client; `Test` will have to put its own **with** in.

Note: it is illegal to generate a circular dependency between packages, that is, it is obvious if package A depends on package B which in turn depends on package A – where do you start? However, because the Ada compiler understands each package as a logical and separate entity it can detect circular dependencies with many layers between A and B.

As you can see, to use a declaration from the package `Ada_Store_Trading` you must qualify it with the package name. So in the specification above to declare the record component `Store_State` we had to use the type `Ada_Store_Trading.State`. In C or C++ when you #include a file you do not have to qualify entries, and it is possible to achieve this in Ada. Consider the following helper function:

```
with Ada.Text_IO;
use  Ada.Text_IO;

with Ada_Store_Trading;
use  Ada_Store_Trading;

procedure Start_Trading is
begin

   Start;
exception
   when Invalid_Trading_Time =>
      Put_Line("Could not start trading, invalid trading time");
      raise;
end Start_Trading;
```

4.3.2 use

The **use** clause makes all components of the specified package directly visible; the **with** statement in effect only brings the package name into scope. We said before that the **with** statement must appear before the library unit; the **use** statement may appear before, or inside the unit.

Note: if we had also put a **use** for the package Ada_Store_Trading into the specification for Ada_Store_PoST_Application above we would have had a serious problem; consider:

```
with Ada_Store_Trading;
use  Ada_Store_Trading;

package Ada_Store_PoST_Application is

    type State_1 is (Signed_On, Signed_Off, Secured);

    type State is
       record
          User_State  : State_1;
          Store_State : State; -- which state !!!
       end record;

    function Current_State return State;
    ..
end Ada_Store_PoST_Application;
```

Now we know that Store_State is of type State defined in Ada_Store_Trading, but the compiler does not. It believes you are trying to create a structure with a component of the enclosing type – illegal, so even if you have provided a **use** statement Ada still allows you to qualify names to avoid this sort of ambiguity.

4.3.3   use type

There is a special form of the **use** clause which can simply include the primitive operations of a type from a package; consider:

```
package Ada_Store_Transactions is

    type Identifier is new Positive;

    Invalid_Operator : exception;

    function "+"(L,R : Identifier) return Identifier;
    function "-"(L,R : Identifier) return Identifier;
    function "&"(L,R : Identifier) return Identifier;
    function "*"(L,R : Identifier) return Identifier;
    function "/"(L,R : Identifier) return Identifier;
    function "**"(L,R : Identifier) return Identifier;
    function "mod"(L,R : Identifier) return Identifier;
    function "rem"(L,R : Identifier) return Identifier;
    function "abs"(L,R : Identifier) return Identifier;

    function Next_Identifier return Identifier;

    ..
end Ada_Store_Transactions;
```

If we now wanted to write some client code, which could not **use** this package, perhaps because of a name clash with something in another package, we would have to qualify all use of types and subprograms in `Ada_Store_Transactions`, thus:

```
with Ada_Store_Transactions;

procedure Test is
   Transaction_ID : Ada_Store_Transactions.Identifier;
begin
   Transaction_ID := Ada_Store_Transactions.Next_Identifier;

   Transaction_ID := Ada_Store_Transactions."+"(Transaction_ID, 1);
end Test;
```

We have had to qualify the addition operator, which does not look good. Ada95 recognized this and added a **use type** clause which makes all primitive operations for the type directly visible, so we could, however, have done the following:

```
with Ada_Store_Transactions;
use type Ada_Store_Transactions.Identifier;

procedure Test is
   Transaction_ID : Ada_Store_Transactions.Identifier;
begin
   Transaction_ID := Ada_Store_Transactions.Next_Identifier;

   Transaction_ID := Transaction_ID + 1;
end Test;
```

As you can see we still have to qualify the type name itself with its package name in the declaration of `Transaction_ID` and the use of the function `Next_Identifier`; we do not, however, have to qualify the use of the addition operator.

4.3.4   Brief summary

We have seen so far how to use packages to provide a level of code structure and how to manage relationships between packages. So far we have not introduced anything radically new; in C++ using namespaces and a good development standard you could achieve something similar although the C++ compiler would not be performing the same level of checks on your code. What follows are additional topics that cannot be achieved in C++.

4.4   Package data hiding

We saw before how we can declare objects within the package body, thus hiding it from prying eyes; however, it is difficult to work with this as our only method of data hiding. Encapsulation requires, for any level of safe reuse, a level of hiding. That is to say we need to defer the declaration of some data to a future point so that no client can depend on the structure of the data and allow the provider the ability to change that structure if the need arises.

In C this is most usually done by presenting the 'private type' as a `void*` which means that you cannot know anything about it, but implies that no one can do any form of type checking on it. So the `dev_create` function actually creates a real device and passes back a `void*` pointer to it. Conversely other functions would have to convert the `void*` to a `real_device*`; if the passed pointer was not created by `dev_create` then there is the possibility that the use of the passed `device` will crash the application.

```
/* C code header file */
typedef void* device;

device dev_create(int unit_id);

void dev_open(device a_device);
void dev_close(device a_device);
..

/* C code source module */
typedef struct {
    int unit_id;
    int mode;
    int status;
    int buffering;
} real_device;

device dev_create(int unit_id)
{
    real_device* new_device;

    new_device = (real_device*)malloc(sizeof(real_device));
    ..
    return (device)new_device;
}

void dev_open(device a_device)
{
    real_device* actual = (real_device*)a_device;
    ..
}
```

In C++ we would put the device data in the private part of the class declaration. The `private` part of the class is available to see, but cannot be used by clients. This gives us a much better implementation which might look like the following. Note the use of inline member functions to return private data.

```
// C++ header file
class Device {
public:
   Device(int unit_id);   // constructor instead of explicit
                          // create command.
   void open(void);
   void close(void);
   ..
   int current_mode(void)    { return mode; }
   int current_status(void) { return status; }
   ..
private:
   int unit_id;
   int mode;
   int status;
   int buffering;
};
```

4.4.1 'Smileys'

The next C++ example goes even further: it actually delegates the details of how the class is represented into its implementation. By simply forward declaring a new class, and a pointer to one, we get the effect called a **smiley**, named after the Cheshire cat in *Alice in Wonderland* who vanished, leaving simply its smile behind.

This construct is frequently used where you want a client of a class to know absolutely nothing about the representation of a class, possibly in case you need to change it. Although this technique requires more careful implementation to handle the embedded `Device_Impl` pointer, it is very safe.

```
// C++ header file
class Device {
public:
   Device(int unit_id);   // constructor instead of explicit
                          // create command.
   ~Device(void);

   void open(void);
   void close(void);
   ..
   int current_mode(void);
   int current_status(void);
   ..
private:
   class Device_Impl;
   Device_Impl* Implementation;
};
```

```
// C++ source module
class Device::Device_Impl {
public:
    int device_id;
    int mode;
    int status;
    int buffering;
};

Device::Device(int)
{
    Implementation = new Device_Impl;

    ..

}

Device::~Device(void)
{
    delete Implementation;
}
```

4.4.2 `private`

Each Ada package has an optional `private` part (section 7.3 of the reference manual), analogous to the private section of a C++ class. Below is an Ada (Ada83) version of the first C++ example above.

```
package Ada_Store_PoST_Device is

    type Instance is private;

    type Unit is range 1 .. 9;
    type Device_Mode is ( Input, Output, Both );
    type Device_Status is ( Closed, Idle, Busy, Locked,
                            Off_Line, Error );

    procedure Open
       (Device : in out Instance;
        Unit_ID : in     Unit);

    procedure Close
       (Device : in out Instance);

    procedure Lock
       (Device : in out Instance);

    procedure UnLock
       (Device : in out Instance);
```

```
procedure ReStart
    (Device : in out Instance);

--
-- Query functions
--
function Current_Mode
    (Device : in Instance)
    return Device_Mode;

function Current_Status
    (Device : in Instance)
    return Device_Status;

function Unit_ID
    (Device : in Instance)
    return Unit;
..
private
    type Buffer_State is ( Disabled, Empty, Buffering );

    type Instance is
       record
           Unit_ID          : Unit           := 1;
           Current_Mode     : Device_Mode    := Output;
           Current_Status   : Device_Status  := Closed;
           Buffer_Status    : Buffer_State   := Disabled;
       end record;

    procedure Flush_Buffer
        (Device : in out Instance);

end Ada_Store_PoST_Device;
```

Above we noted that this is the Ada83 equivalent to the C++ class above. It is an object-based aproach, or you can view `Instance` as an abstract data type; it is not a class or object in C++ or object oriented terms. When we get to Chapter 6 we will rewrite this example in Ada95 in an object oriented way, much closer to the C++ example.

4.4.3 private types

The structure of the above example should be fairly easy to follow. Firstly we declare our new type `Instance` and tell clients that it is a **private** type; in effect we are forward declaring it (this is termed in Ada the partial view, or partial declaration). We can then quite happily use it (as in the function `Open`) until we come to the keyword **private** where we must finally complete the declaration (full view or full declaration).

When declaring a type simply for use in the private part of an Ada package specification, such as the `Buffer_State`, you do not need to forward declare it in the public part. You can include other declarations in the private part, like a C++ class, such as subprograms, objects, or even further packages (see later on).

Note: unlike C++ the private part in an Ada package specification can only appear once and at the end of the package specification.

4.4.4 private implications

A type declared as **private** can only be passed by a client of the package as a parameter to a function, used as a return type, assigned to (:=) or checked for equality (=) or inequality (/=); no other operations are supported (unless explicitly declared). This is because the client cannot see the structure of the full declaration and so cannot act upon the type fully.

Such a type can be used by a client to declare other types, so it could for example be used as part of a record declaration:

```
with Ada_Store_PoST_Device;

declare
   type My_Type is
      record
         Some_Data : Integer;
         A_Device  : Ada_Store_PoST_Device.Instance;
      end record;
```

4.4.5 limited private

We can even restrict use of the assignment and equality operators by declaring the type as **limited private** which means that all you can do is create objects of the type and pass them as parameters to functions. As the type we are dealing with is a peripheral device, there seems little sense in giving the client the ability to assign one to another, therefore we will make `Instance` a limited private type.

You may not in the public part of a package specification declare objects of the private type as the representation is not yet known. You can declare constants of the type, but you must declare them in both places, forward declare them in the public part with no value, and then again in the private part to provide a value once the type is known.

```
package Ada_Store_PoST_Device is

   type Instance is limited private;

   Null_Device : constant Instance;

   ..
```

```
private
   type Buffer_State is ( Disabled, Empty, Buffering );

   type Instance is
      record
         Unit_ID            : Unit           := 1;
         Current_Mode    : Device_Mode    := Output;
         Current_Status  : Device_Status  := Closed;
         Buffer_Status   : Buffer_State   := Disabled;
      end record;

   Null_Device : constant Instance := (Unit_ID       => 1,
                                       Current_Mode   => Output,
                                       Current_Status => Closed,
                                       Buffering => Disabled);

end Ada_Store_PoST_Device;
```

Ada will allow us to implement smileys (see above) for data hiding, although this is not usual practice in Ada programs.

```
package Ada_Store_PoST_Device is

   type Instance is limited private;

   Null_Device : constant Instance;

   ..

private
   type Device_Impl;
   type Device_Impl_Ptr is access Device_Impl;

   type Instance is
      record
         Implementation : Device_Impl_Ptr := null;
      end record;

   Null_Device : constant Instance := (Implementation => null);

end Ada_Store_PoST_Device;
```

4.4.6   Deferred type

We have now covered the term **private** type, a type whose complete declaration is not yet known. The complete declaration of `Device_Impl` has been deferred until the package body, so surprisingly enough it is termed a **deferred type**.

4.4.7 Abstract data types

The `Device` example above provides the basis for an **abstract data type**. This method for object-based programming has been well known and understood for years: the creation of an encapsulated type with a set of operations – the forerunner to today's object oriented programming systems. Let us consider an example:

```
with Ada_Store_PoST_Device;
with System_Printer;

procedure Device_Test is

    The_Device  : Ada_Store_PoST_Device.Instance;
    The_Printer : System_Printer.Instance;
begin

    Ada_Store_PoST_Device.Open(The_Device, 1);
    System_Printer.Open(The_Printer, "A4.Drilled");

    Ada_Store_PoST_Device.Write(The_Device, ..);
    System_Printer.Write(..);

    Ada_Store_PoST_Device.Read(The_Device, ..);

    Ada_Store_PoST_Device.Close(The_Device);
end Device_Test;
```

This may not seem very clever to C++ programmers, but it is as big a leap forward from C as C++ classes, it solves namespace problems, and provides a level of encapsulation previously not possible with C. Note how the package name becomes a type name, so you get in effect:

```
Type_Name.Operation(Instance, Args ..);
```

Also we have used a convention of naming the primary type of a package `Instance`. Again, this becomes very readable: when you look at the declarations for `The_Device`, you request an instance of `Ada_Store_PoST_Device`. This readable abstract data type concept is very powerful and is used to great effect to package objects, though as yet we have not touched on *true* object oriented programming in any way.

4.5 Nested packages

Like C++ namespaces Ada packages can be nested, one inside another. Ada83 supported nested packages, but Ada95 has extended this concept to introduce the term **child library units**.

For this chapter we will use the term physical nesting to cover the features available in Ada83 and logical nesting to cover the additional features added by Ada95.

4.5.1 Physically nested

What follows is a simple example of a nested package:

```
package Ada_Store_PoST_Device is

    type Instance is private

    Null_Device : constant Instance;

    ..

    package Message is

        type Instance is
            record
                Data   : String(1 .. 40);
                Length : Positive;
            end record;
        end Message;

    private
    ..
    end Ada_Store_PoST_Device;
```

This introduces a new package into the device package that handle messages sent to and from devices. A client of this code cannot **with** the nested package separately, it can **with** the outer package and simply **use** the inner.

```
with Ada_Store_PoST_Device;

procedure Device_Test is
    use Ada_Store_PoST_Device.Message;

    A_Device   : Ada_Store_PoST_Device.Instance;
    A_Message  : Ada_Store_PoST_Device.Message.Instance;
    Whats_This : Instance;
begin
    null;
end Device_Test;
```

The answer to the question `Whats_This` is that the object is of type `Instance` declared in the nested package `Message` because that is the only package which has been **use**-d.

4.5.2   Logically nested

The logical nesting of packages or subprograms to create *child library units* is done by using a dotted notation in the package name, like we did to declare A_Message above. You may have noticed this use of a dotted notation in previous examples when we **with**-ed the library package Ada.Text_IO.

This is a difficult topic to explain so it might be better to show an example. We will now rearrange our current packages into some logical order, thus:

```
package Ada_Store is
   -- overall project package
end Ada_Store;

package Ada_Store.PoST is
   -- to do with the PoS terminal
end Ada_Store.PoST;

package Ada_Store.PoST.Device is
   -- holds the ADT for a PoST peripheral device
end Ada_Store.PoST.Device;

package Ada_Store.Transaction is
   -- holds the ADT for a sale transaction
end Ada_Store.Transaction;
```

Each of these packages is a separate library unit, and the dotted notation logically groups them, so the compiler when compiling Ada_Store.Transaction has to ensure that a legal package called Ada_Store exists first and can act as the parent.

As a client of a logically nested package accessing it is slightly different from accessing a physically nested package; you do not need to **with** its parent. So to access the type Instance in Ada_Store.PoST.Device you only have to write:

```
with Ada_Store.PoST.Device;
```

and not necessarily (although perfectly legal):

```
with Ada_Store;
with Ada_Store.PoST;
with Ada_Store.PoST.Device;
```

4.5.3   Visibility of private declarations in child units

Before we continue it is important that you understand the visibility rules at work within the parent–child package relationship. Let us consider the package Ada_Store as the top of our hierarchy of packages:

```
package Ada_Store is

    type Currency is delta 0.01 digits 10;

private
    type Internal_Currency is delta 0.001 digits 15;

end Ada_Store;
```

We can then look at the following package and say simply that the declaration of Item_1 is legal and that Item_2 is illegal; this all follows from what we have learned so far.

```
with Ada_Store;

package Test is

    Item_1 : Ada_Store.Currency;            -- legal
    Item_2 : Ada_Store.Internal_Currency;  -- illegal
end Test;
```

A package cannot use anything declared in the private part of a package specification; however, consider the following two child packages:

```
package Ada_Store.Test_1 is

    Item_1 : Currency;           -- legal
    Item_2 : Internal_Currency; -- illegal
end Ada_Store.Test_1;

package Ada_Store.Test_2 is

    Item_1 : Currency;           -- legal

private
    Item_2 : Internal_Currency; -- legal !
end Ada_Store.Test_2;
```

The first example package also demonstrates that the child of a package does not need to either **with** its parent or qualify declarations from its parent (unless they clash), therefore Item_1 in Test_1 is of type Currency, not necessarily Ada_Store. Currency. The second example is also a child, and does not look that different, except that we have now made Item_2 private, and it becomes legal.

The reason for this is quite simple; all declarations in the public part of the parent specification become visible, without qualification, in the public part of the child package. All declarations in the private part of the parent specification also become visible, without qualification, in the private part of the child package. This simple rule allows us to treat the private part of a package like the protected area of a C++ class definition. Clients using the class may not access protected members; classes deriving from it, however, may have access to the protected area. This will become more important as we get to the Ada95 constructs for object oriented programming, tagged types, in Chapter 6.

Note: it is legal to nest a package physically within a child package, but you may not physically nest child packages within anything; they must be library units.

4.5.4   Use of with in child units

We said above that there was no need for a child package to **with** its parents explicitly, much like a package body does not need to **with** its specification. However, there are some other rules that apply to the use of **with** with child packages:

- You do not need to **with** your parent explicitly.
- A specification may not **with** one of its own child packages (it becomes a cyclic dependency) although a body may **with** one of its own child packages.
- You do need to **with** a sibling.
- You may **with** a child of a sibling.

These simple rules again help ensure a static dependency between packages which allows the compiler to detect illegal dependencies.

Another useful feature is that declarations in your parent are directly visible in your package specification and body. This includes both physically and logically nested packages.

```
with Ada_Store.User;
with Ada_Store.Transaction;

package Test is

    A_User          : Ada_Store.User.Instance;
    A_Transaction : Ada_Store.Transaction.Instance;
end Test;
```

Each declaration must fully qualify the types used. We could, of course, **use** the two packages and make them fully visible, but it might introduce name problems we want to avoid. However, this is the situation if package **Test** becomes a child of package Ada_Store:

```
with Ada_Store.User;
with Ada_Store.Transaction;

package Ada_Store.Test is

    A_User          : User.Instance;
    A_Transaction : Transaction.Instance;
end Ada_Store.Test;
```

We still have to qualify the use of type `Instance` in both cases, except that we do not need to include `Ada_Store` as in effect we have access to that scope.

4.5.5 Child subprograms

So far we have discussed child packages, but we can logically nest subprograms, in the same way we can nest subprograms in normal packages. Therefore we could exercise the package above with the procedure:

```
-- specification file.
procedure Ada_Store.Test.Main;

-- body of procedure.
procedure Ada_Store.Test.Main is
begin
   ..
end Ada_Store.Test.Main;
```

The reason for creating child subprograms is the same as that for creating child packages; the new rules on visibility make test programs easier and can mean that the procedure above can exploit features in the test package not publicly available.

4.5.6 Private child units

It is possible to create **private child units** which heavily restrict the number and type of clients allowed to access them. Let us consider a package hierarchy for a moment:

```
Ada_Store
    Log
    PoST
        Application
        Device
            CashDrawer
            Display
            Keyboard
            OS_Interface (private)
            Printer
            Scanner
            Input_Queue

    Station
    Support
            List
            Trace
```

```
Trading
   Department
   Item
   Tender
   Transaction
User
```

We have introduced a private package, OS_Interface, which is specific to the handling of the terminal's peripherals. OS_Interface wraps access to the physical hardware.

The visibility rules for private child packages are as follows:

- All normal unit **with** rules apply.
- Only the bodies of units rooted at the parent of the private unit (in this case Device) may **with** the private unit.
- Only private units within this sub-hierarchy may **with** the private unit in their specifications.

The effect of this is that in our example the package Application cannot **with** one of the private packages at all because it is not in the hierarchy rooted at Device. The packages Display, Keyboard, Printer, and Input_Simulator may **with** the private package OS_Interface in their bodies, but only Input_Simulator (another private unit) may **with** it in its specification.

A private unit is denoted by the keyword **private** before either **package**, **procedure**, or **function**, as we see below:

```
private package Ada_Store.PoST.Device.OS_Interface is

   type Device_Handle is new Positive;

   type Byte is mod 2**8;
   type Byte_Array is array (Positive range <>) of Byte;

   function   Open
      (Device_Name : in String)
       return Device_Handle;

   procedure Close
      (Device : in out Device_Handle);

   procedure Write
      (Device : in Device_Handle;
       Data   : in Byte_Array);

   procedure Read
      (Device : in Device_Handle;
       Data   : out Byte_Array);
```

```
    procedure Flush
        (Device : in Device_Handle);

end Ada_Store.PoST.Device.OS_Interface;
```

We do not want anyone but the device objects themselves to be able to access this package, but if we make it internal to `Device` then the `Keyboard` package cannot access it.

4.5.7 Brief summary

The addition of child units, and private child units, enables us to design Ada systems into hierarchies with better cohesion between related packages and a flexibility previously unavailable. The Ada library (see Part 2) is hierarchical in structure and has three root packages, `Ada`, `Interfaces`, and `System`, of which all other library units are children.

4.6 Some fine detail

The following sections deal with some of the messy details which can confuse programmers new to Ada when dealing with packages. It may be that you want to skip this section if you are just trying to get to grips with the language itself; however, you should read it before you attempt any Ada development as the issues here relate to both implementation and, to a certain extent, design of software in Ada.

4.6.1 Elaboration

We spoke before (Section 4.2) about the ability to have an initialization section in a package: how do we know in what order these are run, and who runs them?

In Ada the term *elaboration* is used to denote the process by which library units are initialized before execution commences. Two main processes are required, initialize objects declared at the library level and execution of package initialization code.

So for the following relatively complicated example the objects `Trace_File` and `Trace_File_Name` must be created and initialized, `Trace_File_Name` with the given string. Once this has been done then the initialization code is executed; this ensures that the trace file we are writing to is open. This requires calls to the library package `Ada.Text_IO`, and if that package is not already elaborated then the exception `Program_Error` is raised. Therefore it would be nice if someone worked out the correct order of elaboration.

```ada
with Ada;
use  Ada;
with Ada.Text_IO;
with Ada.Calendar;
with Ada.Task_Identification;

package body Ada_Store.Support.Trace is

    package Tasks renames Task_Identification;
    Trace_File        : Text_IO.File_Type;
    Trace_File_Name : constant String := "ada_store.trc";

    procedure Put
        (Trace_This : in String) is

          Seconds : Calendar.Day_Duration;
    begin
          Seconds := Calendar.Seconds(Calendar.Clock);

          Text_IO.Put_Line(Trace_File,
                              "**** Task " &
                              Tasks.Image(Tasks.Current_Task) &
                              " At " &
                              Calendar.Day_Duration'Image(Seconds) &
                              " Wrote:");

          Text_IO.Put_Line(Trace_File,
                    Trace_This);
          Text_IO.Flush(Trace_File);
    end Put;

begin
    Text_IO.Open(Trace_File,
                    Text_IO.Out_File,
                    Trace_File_Name);
exception
    when Ada.IO_Exceptions.Name_Error =>
        Text_IO.Create(Trace_File,
                          Text_IO.Out_File,
                          Trace_File_Name);
end Ada_Store.Support.Trace;
```

Binding

In C and C++ for each source module the compiler pre-processes it and compiles it to object code; you then link the object code. In Ada each library unit is compiled, and then before linking an additional step called binding usually takes place. It is the binder's job to produce the elaboration code and attempt to produce it in the correct order.

Note: elaboration is also the process by which declarations become objects, or rather when at run-time we reach a declaration part the objects are created, for example:

```
procedure example is
begin

   ..

   declare
      I : Integer; -- this is a declaration
   begin
      .. -- in here we have an object called I of type
         -- Integer, because the compiler elaborated the
         -- declaration above when we entered this block.
   end;

   ..

end example;
```

Elaboration pragmas

To assist the binder you may include certain pragmas which control the order of elaboration (section 10.2.1 of the reference manual). These are as follows:

- **pragma** Elaborate (*Library_Unit_Names*);   This specifies that the given library units must be elaborated before the current unit. This could have been used in the tracer example above to ensure that the Ada.Text_IO package is elaborated by adding:

```
package body Ada_Store.Support.Trace is
   pragma Elaborate(Ada.Text_IO);
```

- **pragma** Elaborate_All(*Library_Unit_Names*);   This pragma ensures that each library unit *required* by the given library units is elaborated before the current unit.

- **pragma** Elaborate_Body(*Library_Unit_Name*);   This pragma is used to ensure that the body of the given library unit is elaborated immediately after its declaration. Many library packages specify this to put themselves as high up the list of elaboration as possible.

- **pragma** Preelaborate(*Library_Unit_Name*);   This pragma informs the binder that the named library unit can be pre-elaborated, which means that its initialization code is restricted to a safe set of operations.

- **pragma** Pure(*Library_Unit_Name*);   Like the above, this pragma informs the binder that the library unit initialization is safe; in the case of a package declared as pure it means that no initialization code exists and no objects are declared at the library level.

Elaboration is a complex process, both to understand initially and for the compiler and run-time to implement. However, seeing as many C++ compiler vendors have similar problems with the constructors of globally declared C++ objects then the Ada approach can be seen as more satisfactory.

4.6.2 Implementation separation

In some cases it may be that a nested unit becomes quite large and actually makes maintenance of the containing unit difficult. It is then possible to extract it from the containing unit and tell the compiler that it exists separately. For example in the Point of Sale application there is a single control loop, which slowly grows until it is larger than the rest of the code in the module; at this point it is decided to separate it. The module then looks like this:

```
package body Ada_Store.PoST.Application is

    -- object declarations.

    -- support subprograms.

    procedure Main_Loop is separate;
begin
    -- initialization.
end Ada_Store.PoST.Application;
```

The keyword **separate** is used to inform the compiler that it has been removed. You must then create a new file to contain it, which looks like this:

```
separate(Ada_Store.PoST.Application)
procedure Main_Loop is
begin
    ...
end Main_Loop;
```

In this case **separate** is used again, this time to signify where the code was separated from.

There are other good reasons for using **separate**, for instance if one subunit is developed by one programmer, when the rest of the unit is developed by someone else it might make sense to separate it to aid in source control.

Another reason commonly used will be of interest to C and C++ programmers: system-dependent code; for example:

```
/* C (or C++) source module */

void an_important_function(void)
{
```

```
#ifdef SYS_WIN32
    /* an implementation */
#elsif SYS_OS2
    /* an implementation */
#elsif SYS_UNIX
    /* an implementation */
#endif
}
```

The pre-processor is used to insert the operating system-specific code into a function that can then be called by clients on any system. In Ada we cannot accomplish this; however, we can do the following:

```
package Important is

    procedure An_Important_Procedure;
end Important;

package body Important is

    procedure An_Important_Procedure is separate;
end Important;
```

It is now possible to produce one implementation of the subprogram for each environment, using source control mechanism, or compiler search paths to pick the right one for the current system.

4.6.3   Renaming

This is not a package-specific topic, but is introduced here as it crops up more using packages than anywhere else. Consider:

```
with Ada_Store.PoST.Device.Display;

procedure Display_Test is
begin
    package Displays renames Ada_Store.PoST.Device.Display;
    package Instance renames
                  Ada_Store.PoST.Device.Display.Instance;

    A_Display : Instance;
begin
    Displays.Open(A_Display);
    ..
    Displays.Close(A_Display);
end Display_Test;
```

The use of `Displays` not only saves us a lot of typing, but if you wanted to deal in this case with a new type of display then you simply change the **renames** clause, and the rest of the procedure stays exactly the same (if all operations on `Display.Instance` are identical for both `Displays` packages).

Similarly if you want to include two functions from two different packages with the same name, then, rather than relying on overloading, or to clarify your code text, you could:

```
with Package1;
with Package2;
function Function1 return Integer renames Package1.Function;
function Function2 return Integer renames Package2.Function;
```

Another example of a renaming declaration is where you are using some complex structure and you want in effect to use a synonym for it during some processing. In the example below we have a device handler structure which contains some procedure types that we need to execute in turn. The first example contains a lot of text which we do not really care about, so the second removes most of it, thus leaving bare the real work we are attempting to do:

```
for device in Device_Map loop
   Device_Map(device).Device_Handler.Request_Device;
   Device_Map(device).Device_Handler.Process_Function(
      Process_This_Request);
   Device_Map(device).Device_Handler.Relinquish_Device;
end loop;

for device in Device_Map loop
   declare
      Device_Handler : Device_Type renames
         Device_Map(device).Device_Handler;
   begin
      Device_Handler.Request_Device;
      Device_Handler.Process_Function(Process_This_Request);
      Device_Handler.Relinquish_Device;
   end;
end loop;
```

4.7   Summary

We have covered probably more new ground in this chapter than in everything else so far. To recap, we now know how to write packages, how to use packages, that you can nest packages, how to implement hierarchical package libraries, what the visibility rules on packages are, how to use packages to develop abstract data types, and some tips and tricks for successful package development.

4.7.1 Package hierarchy

Where does all this get us? We have said already that we can now restructure our example into a sensible package hierarchy, which will look something like this (so far):

```
Ada_Store
    Log
    PoST
        Application
        Device
            CashDrawer
            Display
            Keyboard
            OS_Interface (private)
            Printer
            Scanner
        Input_Queue

    Station
    Support
            List
            Trace

    Trading
        Department
        Item
        Tender
        Transaction
    User
```

This hierarchy has one single root, which contains three complete packages (`Log`, `Station`, and `User`) and three subsystems, `PoST`, `Support`, and `Trading`. The specification for the root package follows. It declares the standard types used throughout the system; note also that it is declared as a `Pure` package and that it does not require a body or any substantial elaboration.

```ada
package Ada_Store is

    pragma Pure(Ada_Store);

    ----------------------------------------------------------------
    -- Basic types used throughout application
    --
    type Quantity           is new Positive;
```

```
type Currency          is delta 0.01 digits 8;    -- 999,999.99
type Weight            is delta 0.001 digits 6;   -- 999.999
type Percentage_Base is delta 0.01  digits 5;     -- 999.99
subtype Percentage     is Percentage_Base range 0.00 .. 100.00;

type Short_Description is new String(1 .. 18);

------------------------------------------------------------

-- Some constants used throughout application
--

System_Name            : constant String := "Ada Store";
System_Version         : constant String := "GENERIC_1.0.0";
end Ada_Store;
```

To review we will include the specification for Ada_Store.Support.Trace (seen above) and another important package Ada_Store.PoST.Input_Queue which is used to manage an ordered queue of input from the peripheral devices.

```
package Ada_Store.Support.Trace is

   procedure Put(Trace_This : in String);
end Ada_Store.Support.Trace;

package Ada_Store.PoST.Input_Queue is

   type Input_Action is ( Unknown,
                           Enter, Cancel,
                           Sign_On, Sign_Off, Close_Down,
                           Item, Department, Subtract, Enquiry,
                           Sub_Total, Payment );

   Max_Input_Text : constant Positive := 40;

   type Message is
      record
         Action : Input_Action := Unknown;
         Input  : String(1 .. Max_Input_Text);
         Length : Natural := 0;
      end record;

   type Message_Ptr is access all Message;

   procedure Append
      (Message : in Message_Ptr);

   function   Get
      (Wait : in Boolean := False)
       return Message_Ptr;
```

```
function   Peek
   (Wait : in Boolean := False)
   return Message_Ptr;
end Ada_Store.PoST.Input_Queue;
```

This chapter has brought to you one of the most important language features of Ada: the package. It is essential to understand packages before you can develop and code beyond single procedure applications such as *hello world*.

The following two chapters build upon packages extensively so I suggest a break at this point: review the examples (in the text and on the CD) and even try writing some of your own (using the Aonix compiler from the CD).

Generics for reusable programming

The draft C++ standard [13] includes a new library, the Standard Template Library (or STL) developed by Alexander Stepanov. This is the first widely available use of templates so far in the C++ community. Templates can be considered as the major tool in developing non-object oriented generic code; however, when coupled with object oriented design and implementation they provide a flexibility previously not found in C++ implementations. It is apparent that at this time few C++ programmers have access to a stable STL implementation, fewer in a position to use the STL, and even fewer who understand the implications of using the STL. With this in mind I felt it was unwise to base work in this chapter on comparisons with the STL although some examples are used. A good paper [26] exists that describes efforts underway to implement the STL in Ada95. It should be of interest to C++ programmers familiar with STL or Ada programmers interested in the new standard C++ library.

Historically C++ templates owe a lot to Ada generics [11], and the STL has grown from work originally done by Stepanov in Ada83.

This chapter will lead you through the reasons we require generics, the cases where we might use them, and a discussion of Ada generics and C++ templates.

5.1   Generic programming in C and C++

What do we mean by generic programming? We want to find a simple means of expressing an algorithm or concept in a way in which it can be applied to the largest

143

possible range of objects. This section will demonstrate techniques for generic programming starting with C, discussing C++, and finally using the new Standard Template Library.

The example we will use is the development of a generic sorting algorithm, using the inefficient, yet easy to understand, bubble sort, and starting with a nice simple case.

Example 5.1   Sorting an array of integers in C ————————————

```
/* file: sort.h */
void sort(int *array, int num_elements);

/* file: sort.c */
#include <sort.h>

void sort(int *array, int num_elements)
{
    int top, item, temp;

    for (top = num_elements; top >= 0; top --)
    {
        for (item = 0; item < top - 1; item ++)
        {
            if (array[item] > array[item + 1])
            {
                temp = array[item];

                array[item] = array[item + 1];
                array[item + 1] = temp;
            }
        }
    }
}

/* file: test.c */
#include <sort.h>

void main(void)
{
    int test_array[10];

    sort(test_array, 10);
}
```

The example shows the three files used, `sort.c` containing the sort algorithm itself, `sort.h` which contains its declaration, and `test.c` which sorts an array of ten integers.

———————————————————————————————————————

The above *is* simple, easy to write, and easy to use, and the code is easy to read; however, when you come to sort an array of floats or an array of structures you either have to rewrite the function, write a set of **sort_***thing* functions, or you may end up with a **generic** sort function which in C can look pretty horrendous.

Example 5.2   Sort anything in C ————————————————————————————

```
/* file: sort2.h */
void sort(void *array, int element_size, int element_count);

/* file: sort2.c */
#include <sort.h>
#include <string.h>

void sort(void *array, int element_size, int element_count)
{
    int    top, item;
    char*  temp;

    temp = (char*)malloc(element_size);

    for (top = num_elements; top >= 0; top --)
    {
        for (item = 0; item < top - 1; item ++)
        {
            if (memcmp(array[item], array[item + 1], element_size)
                == 0)
            {
                memcpy(temp, array[item], element_size);

                memcpy(array[item], array[item + 1], element_size);
                memcpy(array[item + 1], temp, element_size);
            }
        }
    }
    free(temp);
}

/* file: test2.c */
#include <sort2.h>

 void main(void)
{
    int test_array[10];

    sort((void*)test_array, sizeof(int), 10);
}
```

This example takes an unsafe address for the start of the array, user-supplied parameters for the size of each element, and the number of elements and a function that compares two elements. C does not have strong typing, but you have just stripped away any help the compiler might be able to give you by using **void***.

If you get the size of an element, or number of elements in the array, wrong you can cause all sorts of damage. You also have to use the standard library routines `memcpy` to copy items as you do not know their size and have to make do with `memcmp` to compare two values.

In C++ the usual manner for constructing generic type-independent facilities is to use templates. Templates are a relatively new addition to the C++ language (introduced in version 2.1 of the language, see [11]) and they do use some rather complex syntax which can make heavily templated code rather more difficult to read. Having said this it is important that C++ programmers who have not yet got to grips with templates should do so as they complement more traditional object oriented programming techniques to produce the most effective reuse.

Example 5.3   Possible templated sort ────────────────────────────

```
// file: cppsort.h
template<class elem_type> void sort(elem_type* array,
                                     int length,
                                     bool (*test)(elem_type one,
                                                  elem_type two));

// file: cppsort.cc
#include <cppsort.h>

template<class elem_type> void sort(elem_type* array,
                                    int length,
                                    bool (*test) (elem_type one,
                                                  elem_type two))
{
    for (int top = num_elements; top >= 0; top --)
    {
        for (int item = 0; item < top - 1; item ++)
        {
            if (test(array[item], array[item + 1]) == 0)
            {
                elem_type temp = array[item];

                array[item] = array[item + 1];
                array[item + 1] = temp;
            }
        }
    }
}

// file: cpptest.cc
#include <cppsort.h>

bool compare_ints(int first, int second)
```

```
{
    if (first < second)
    {
        return -1;
    } else if (first > second)
    {
        return 1;
    } else
    {
        return 0;
    }

}

void main(void)
{
    int test_array[10];

    sort(test_array, 10, compare_ints);
}
```

This is considerably safer; we now know the type of each element in the array, though will still have to be passed the length, and this time we pass a compare function as we cannot use memcmp if the objects in the array are class types.

We now have a sort function which will sort ints, floats, structs, or class objects.

In many C++ libraries you will find sort functions such as the following:

```
template<class elem_type> void sort(array<elem_type>);
```

This is the simplest we can go, fully type safe and nice to read. The problem with this solution is that you cannot now use "int test_array[10]"; you must use the library class array to store data as it is the array class which provides our length safety. You also do not need to pass a comparison function as the library *assumes* that all objects you might want to sort will have overloaded the <or> operators. This is not generic programming, it is type safe, simple but library-specific programming!

The Standard Template Library gets around this problem by using the concept of **iterators**, objects that are used to manipulate containers of other objects and act as the plumbing between generic containers and generic algorithms. STL iterators use a syntax akin to pointer manipulation and so actual array pointers can also be used where STL expects iterators. This flexibility is what most programmers feel is the greatest benefit of the STL, safety within a flexible and extensible framework.

Example 5.4   Sorting an array of integers using the C++ STL _____

```
// file: teststl.cpp
#include <algo.h>

void main(void)
{
   int array[10];

   sort(&array[0], &array[10]);
}
```

The above uses the STL header `algo.h` which provides the definitions of the standard templated algorithms, including `sort`. This function is then used on the array, simply passing the first element and the element beyond the end. This example is important as the STL has provided a safe sort which uses iterators to move around the array and so can be used on any container supporting the iterator syntax.

   The following shows the same sort algorithm being used to sort items in a `vector` – an STL safe array.

```
// file: teststl2.cpp
#include <vector.h>
#include <algo.h>

void main(void)
{
   vector<int> array[10];

   // add data to vector ..

   sort(array.begin(), array.end());
}
```

It is this use of templates which interests us most, as it is the use of template-like constructs in Ada called *generics* which we will focus on next.

5.2   Generic programming in Ada

We will begin our tour of Ada's generic programming facilities with an Ada generic subprogram which encapsulates the sort example.

Example 5.5   Ada generic sort specification _____

```
-- file: Bubble_Sort.ads
generic
   type Index_Type is (<>);
   type Element_Type is private;
   type Element_Array is array (Index_Type range <>)
      of Element_type;
```

```
with function ">" (el1, el2 : Element_Type) return Boolean;
procedure Bubble_Sort(The_Array : in out Element_Array);
```

This specification shows us many of the features of Ada generics. For example note that we have said quite a few things about what we are going to sort: it is an array, for which we do not know the bounds (so it is specified as **range** <>); we also cannot expect that the range of the array is an integer range and so we must also make the range type a parameter, `Index_Type`. Then we come on to the element type: this is simply specified as private, so all we know is that we can test equality and assign one to another. This provides us complete type safety; we know the type, bounds, and size of the array and its components, better than C++ can give us.

Ada must also have a function to compare two elements, similar to the C++ Example 5.3 above. However, in this case we will *ask* for the function (notice the use of the keyword **with**) which, although it looks like an operator, can be any function that matches the signature.

You should already be able to see the difference between the Ada code and C code as far as readability (and therefore maintainability) and safety are concerned and why, therefore, Ada promotes the reuse philosophy.

The Ada `Bubble_Sort` specification may look a little daunting, somewhat large and possibly complex. However type-independent programming is difficult in a type-safe language and so generics have to be rigorous in their specification of what types are allowed and how they are to be used.

We can now look at how we might implement the sort algorithm itself.

Example 5.6   Ada generic sort body _____

```
-- file: Bubble_Sort.adb
procedure Bubble_Sort(The_Array : in out Element_Array) is
begin
    for Loop_Top in reverse The_Array'Range loop
        for Item in The_Array'First .. Index_Type'Pred(Loop_Top)

        loop
            if The_Array(Item) > The_Array(Index_Type'Succ(Item))
            then
                declare
                    Element : Element_Type := The_Array(Item);

                begin
                    The_Array(Item) :=The_Array(Index_Type'Succ(Item));
                    The_Array(Index_Type'Succ(Item)) := Element;
                end;
            end if;
        end loop;
    end loop;
end Bubble_Sort;
```

Note the use of the scalar and discrete attributes to calculate the bounds of the array in a type safe and truly generic manner (for instance the use of `Index_Type'Succ(Item)` instead of the more usual C code `[Item + 1]`). Also we compare two array elements in the central **if** statement using the passed `">"` function, just as we might in C++ if we have provided the type `Element_Type` with an overloaded operator; in the Ada code it is not treated as an operator call, simply a call to the provided function.

We can now use our generic to sort a simple array of integers, using the supplied comparison operator.

```
-- file: Sort_Test1.adb
with Bubble_Sort;

procedure Sort_Test1 is

    subtype Index    is Positive     range 1 .. 10;
    type     An_Array is array (Index range <>) of Integer;

    procedure Test_Sort is new Bubble_Sort(Index,
                                           Integer,
                                           An_Array,
                                           ">");

    Sort_This : An_Array := (5, 6, 7, 1, 3, 2, 4, 10, 9, 8);
begin
    Test_Sort(Sort_This);

    for Item in Sort_This'Range loop
        Ada.Text_IO.Put(Integer'Image(Sort_This(Item)));
    end loop;
end Sort_Test1;
```

The first two types simply declare the type of the array index, in this case a subtype of `Positive`, and an array we are going to sort.

We then instantiate the generic with the parameters required, the array index type, the type of the array component, the type of the array and finally the comparison function (in this case the primitive operator for type `Integer`). Of course we then declare an array and sort it and print the array, just in case.

In comparison with C++ we must explicitly instantiate each and every use of a generic subprogram before use. In C++ templated functions are automatically instantiated where they are used, taking their type parameters from the parameters used at the call site. The explicit instantiation is important in Ada as it follows the static typing principles and therefore provides very explicit compile-time type checking.

5.2.1   Slicing

Some C programmers may be looking at the first example and saying to themselves that because you must specify the bounds of the array by hand, it is actually more flexible;

therefore you can specify a bound smaller than the overall array to sort only part of it like this:

```
int test_array[10];

sort(test_array, 8);      /* sort only first 8 */
sort(&test_array[1], 8); /* sort 1 .. 9 */
```

Where the second example is quite interesting, we have sorted a slice of the array, which is exactly what we would consider doing in the Ada examples above.

```
declare
   ..
   Sort_This : An_Array(0 .. 9);
begin
   Test_Sort(Sort_This(0 .. 7));

   Test_Sort(Sort_This(1 .. 8));
```

However, what is the result of the following code in the respective languages?

```
int test_array[10];

sort(test_array, 11); /* possible crash! */

declare
   ..
   Sort_This : An_Array(0 .. 9);
begin
   Test_Sort(Sort_This(0 .. 11)); -- compiler error
```

Example 5.7   General sorting in Ada ————————————————————

```
-- file: Sort_Test2.adb
with Bubble_Sort;
use  Bubble_Sort;

procedure Sort_Test2 is

   type Area_Details is
      record
         Area_Code       : Positive
         Representative : Person_ID;
         Area_Size       : Natural;
         Sales_To_Date   : Decimal;
      end record;

   type Sales_Figures is array(Positive range <>) of Area_Details;

   function Compare_Size(L, R : Area_Details) return Boolean;
```

```
      procedure Sort_By_Size is new Bubble_Sort(Positive,
                                                Area_Details,
                                                Sales_Figures,
                                                Compare_Size);

      function Compare_Sales(L, R : Area_Details) return Boolean;
      procedure Sort_By_Sales is new Bubble_Sort(Positive,
                                                 Area_Details,
                                                 Sales_Figures,
                                                 Compare_Sales);

      .. -- declare Print_Sales_Data and Sales_Array
   begin
      Print_Sales_Data(Sales_Array);

      Sort_By_Size(Sales_Array);
      Print_Sales_Data(Sales_Array);

      Sort_By_Sales(Sales_Array);
      Print_Sales_Data(Sales_Array);
   end Sort_Test2;
```

We have now used the same sort function on a more realistic example. The important thing to note in this example is that in each instance of the generic the formal parameter '<' has been replaced with a function that compares a single component of the structure; therefore two different sorting methods can be achieved with the same sort algorithm.

It is even possible to reverse sort the array by passing an operator '>' where the operator '<' is expected: when the generic is instantiated only the signature of the passed subprogram is checked and both < and > have the same signature, just different results.

5.3   Generic packages

Ada packages and generics (section 12.7 of the reference manual) were designed to go together and you will find generic packages used extensively in the Ada standard library. For example, the generic package Ada.Direct_IO looks like this:

```
generic
   type Element_Type is private;

package Ada.Direct_IO is

   ..
end Ada.Direct_IO;
```

This package is the standard method for writing out files of identical components (like an array in a disk file), and may be used like this:

```
type My_Struct is
   record
      ..
   end record;

package My_Struct_IO is new Ada.Direct_IO(My_Struct);
use My_Struct_IO;

Item : My_Struct;
File : My_Struct_IO;

My_Struct_IO.Write(File, Item);
```

The instantiation of the package `My_Struct_IO` provides us with a package that can act on random access files whose record type is `My_Struct`. See Section 8.2.2 for a more detailed study of these packages and how they are used.

Example 5.8   Generic list package ─────────────────────────────

```
generic
   type Element_Type is private;
package Ada_Store.Support.List is

   type Instance is limited private;

   type Element_Ptr is access all Element_Type;

   procedure Append
       (List    : access Instance;
        Element : across Element_Type);

   function  Get
       (List    : access Instance) return Element_Ptr;

   function  Peek
       (List    : access Instance) return Element_Ptr;

   List_Empty : exception;
private
   type Element_Holder;
   type List_Ptr        is access Element_Holder;

   type Element_Holder is
      record
         Actual : Element_Ptr;
         Next   : List_Ptr := null;
      end record;
```

```
type Instance is limited
   record
        Head    : List_Ptr := null;
        Tail    : List_Ptr := null;
   end record;
```

end Ada_Store.Support.List;

This example demonstrates a generic package that manages a linked list of items. The generic parameter is again marked simply as private so we can only compare and assign objects of type Element_Type within the body of the package. Our list object, type Instance, is marked as **limited private** because you may not assign one list to another, or compare two lists.

Three functions are provided to access the list, Append, Get, and Peek; the list is strictly first in, first out (FIFO) and so no insert, delete, or iterator functions are provided. The list will raise the exception List_Empty if you call either Get or Peek when there are no items in the list.

All the really interesting things about this specification are in the private part: a type Element_Holder which acts as the link in the list, holding an element in the list, and providing the list pointer. Finally we complete the type Instance, which simply contains a pointer to the top and a pointer to the end of the list.

We will now briefly look at how we might implement the same list in C and then C++.

Example 5.9   Generic list handling in C ———————————————

```
struct element_holder {
   void* actual;
   struct element_holder* next;
};

struct _list_instance {
   struct element_holder* head;
   struct element_holder* tail;
};
typedef struct _list_instance* list_instance;

void append(list_instance list, void* actual);

void* get(list_instance list);

void* peek(list_instance list);
```

In C we have had to use a void pointer to represent the data itself and reveal the full structure of the list.

In C++ we would expect to use a class to represent the list, and we then have the option of either using a void pointer to represent the data, or using a templated class,

in which case we could of course save ourselves a lot of trouble by simply including the
STL header file `list.h` and use the templated list container provided by the library.
   For completeness a templated version of our simple list is shown.

Example 5.10   Generic list handling in C++ ───────────────────────────

```
class basic_list {
public:

    basic_list(void);

    void append(void* actual);

    void* get(void);
    void* peek(void);

private:
    struct element_holder {
        void* actual;
        struct element_holder* next;
    };

    struct element_holder* head;
    struct element_holder* tail;
};

template<class Element_Type> class template_list {
public:
    basic_list(void);

    void append(Element_Type* actual);

    Element_Type* get(void);
    Element_Type* peek(void);

private:
    struct element_holder {
        Element_Type* actual;
        struct element_holder* next;
    };

    struct element_holder* head;
    struct element_holder* tail;
};
```

You will notice the similarities between the C++ template example and the Ada specification above: even though the two encapsulation constructs (class vs package) are
different, the concepts are so close that the result becomes very similar.

───

   The body of the `Ada_Store.Support.List` package should provide
no great surprises, except perhaps that we have introduced the use of

Unchecked_Deallocation (see Section 5.5.2) to make sure that when we get an item from the list we free the memory associated with the Element_Holder record.

```ada
with Unchecked_Deallocation;

package body Ada_Store.Support.List is

    procedure Free is
        new Unchecked_Deallocation(Element_Holder, List_Ptr);

    procedure Append
        (List    : access Instance;
         Element : access Element_Type) is
    begin
        if List.Tail = null then

            List.Tail := new Element_Holder'(Actual => Element,
                                             Next   => null);

            List.Head := List.Tail;
        else

            List.Tail.Next := new Element_Holder'(Actual => Element,
                                                  Next   => null);

            List.Tail := List.Tail.Next;
        end if;
    end Append;

    function Get
        (List    : access Instance) return Element_Type is

        Element : Element_Type;
    begin
        if List.Head = null then

            raise List_Empty;
        end if;

        Element := List.Head.Actual;

        List.Head := List.Head.Next;

        if List.Head = null then

            List.Tail := null;
        end if;

        Free(List.Head);

        return Element;
    end Get;

    function Peek
```

```
   (List    : access Instance) return Element_Type is
begin
   if List.Head = null then

       raise List_Empty;
   end if;

   return List.Head.Actual;
end Peek;

end Ada_Store.Support.List;
```

5.3.1 Ada_Store

This list package may now be used anywhere in our code, and is used in our
Ada_Store example application in the package Ada_Store.PoST.Input_Queue
which uses an instance of the list internally, like this:

```
package Unsafe_List is new Support.List(Message_Ptr);

type List_Ptr is access Unsafe_List.Instance;

Real_List : List_Ptr := new Unsafe_List.Instance;
```

Firstly Input_Queue instantiates the package Unsafe_List which is a generic list
of pointers to Message records. It then creates a new instance of the
List.Instance to use internally. The reason the list we have instantiated is called
Unsafe_List will become clear in Chapter 7 when we have to deal with task-safe
data.

5.3.2 Nested generics

It is possible to treat generic library units just as any other library unit. They may thus
be physically and logically nested within other library units and may have units nested
within them. The most important reason for nesting a generic within another package
is the declaration of exceptions.

   In our list example we have an exception List_Empty which may be raised by
Get or Peek. It is this exception that will give us problems, for example:

```
with Ada.Text_IO;

with Ada_Store.Support.List;
use Ada_Store.Support.List;

procedure Test_List_Exceptions is

   type A is ..
   type B is ..
```

```
      package List_Of_A is new Instance(A);
      package List_Of_B is new Instance(B);

      A_Object : A;
      B_Object : B;
   begin
      ..
      A_Object := List_Of_A.Get;
      B_Object := List_Of_B.Get;
      ..
   exception
      when List_Of_A.List_Empty =>
         Ada.Text_IO.Put_Line("List of A's empty");

      when List_Of_B.List_Empty =>
         Ada.Text_IO.Put_Line("List of B's empty");
   end Test_List_Exceptions;
```

It should be fairly clear that each instantiation of the list package introduces a new package, and therefore we have two exceptions to check; it is very useful in this case to identify which list has actually become empty. However, there are cases where you need to have one overall exception for failures in any instance of a generic package, and this is where nested packages come in.

It is possible to create an outer package that contains the exceptions and other instance-independent declarations and then nest the generic within it. In Ada83 it was only possible to nest the generic physically within the outer package or create a separate package to hold the exceptions. In Ada95 you can also use child units.

One solution might therefore be to have an outer package that deals with general list exceptions, like this:

```
   package Ada_Store.Support.Lists is

      List_Instance_Error,
      List_Empty,
      List_Full : exception;
   end Ada_Store.Support.Lists;
```

We can then create a number of generic child packages for differing types of lists, and our example might become:

```
   generic
      type Element_Type is private;

   package Ada_Store.Support.Lists.Single_Linked is

      ..
   end Ada_Store.Support.Lists.Single_Linked;
```

Another possibility is to have a completely separate package which simply contains the exceptions. This approach is used by the Ada95 standard library; the IO packages in the library (`Ada.Text_IO`, `Ada.Sequential_IO`, and `Ada.Direct_IO`, for example) all have to raise the same exceptions, so a separate package `Ada.IO_Exceptions` is used:

```
package Ada.IO_Exceptions is
    pragma Pure (IO_Exceptions);

    Status_Error : exception;
    Mode_Error   : exception;
    Name_Error   : exception;
    Use_Error    : exception;
    Device_Error : exception;
    End_Error    : exception;
    Data_Error   : exception;
    Layout_Error : exception;

end Ada.IO_Exceptions;
```

5.4 Specifying parameters for generics

We have seen a number of possible argument types used already in the examples above, and will now go through the list of argument types. The set of parameters that can be passed to an Ada generic cover just about any eventuality and, as you can see with the sort example above, are much more expressive than C++ templates. A complete discussion of parameter types is found in section 12.4 of the language reference manual.

Note: I use italics in the following definitions to denote optional keywords.

5.4.1 Type parameters

- **type** X **is** (<>); -- Discrete: Integer, Character, Enumeration ..
  type X **is range** <>; -- Signed integer: Integer, Positive ..
  type X **is mod** <>; -- Unsigned integer. (Ada95).
  type X **is digits** <>; -- Floating point.
  type X **is delta** <>; -- Fixed point.
  type X **is delta** <> **digits** <>; -- Decimal. (Ada95).

  The above set covers all the scalar types (Chapter 3), the first matches any discrete type, the second and third match integer types either signed or unsigned, and the last three match the different real types.

- **type** X **is array(..) of** Y; This, as we have already seen, specifies an array type. I have omitted the specification of the array range as it may take any legal form, including the use of other parameters.

- **type** X(*Arg : type*) **is** *limited* **private;** This denotes a so-called definite type. If not limited then the body of the generic can only assume that assignment and equality tests are available for the type; if it is limited then even these operations are unavailable.

- **type** X(<>) **is** *limited* **private;** This type parameter was added with Ada95 and denotes a type that is indefinite (usually meaning unconstrained). Because of this you may not declare any uninitialized objects of the type as they may not be constrained, and of course you cannot pass objects of this type to subprograms expecting constrained types.

```
generic
   type Indefinite(<>) is private;
procedure Something;
procedure Something is
   An_Object : Indefinite; -- illegal
begin
   ..
end Something;

procedure Some_String is new Something(String);
```

The example above declares a generic procedure and instantiates it with the unconstrained type String. Because the type is unconstrained then the declaration of An_Object is illegal. It is possible in the code to see if the parameter is definite with an attribute of the same name:

```
procedure Something  is
begin
   if Unconstrained'Definite then
      ..
   else
      ..
   end if;
end Something;
```

- **type** X **is access** *all*|*constant* Y;
  type X **is access** *procedure*|*function* Y ..;

  These type parameters are used to denote access types. You can also pass in access to subprogram types using the second notation.

- **type** X(*Arg : type*) **is new** Y; This is a very useful parameter which actually constrains the passed type by specifying that it must be derived from the specified type. There are two reasons for this: first to ensure some minimum physical requirement, or second to ensure some other requirement, for example:

```
generic
   type X is range <>;
procedure ..

generic
   type X is new Integer;
procedure ..
```

It would appear that the above are identical in effect, since they both require a signed integer type to be specified at instantiation; however, for the second we know that the specified type has at least the physical properties of the type `Integer`, even if further constrained by the specified subtype. Another example might be that we require some primitive operation to be available to us, so for example:

```
type X_Base is
   record
      ..
   end record;

function "+"(L, R : X_Base) return X_Base;
function "−"(L, R : X_Base) return X_Base;

generic
   type X is new X_Base;
procedure ..
```

This example is far more interesting: we require that the type specified at instantiation is derived from the type `X_Base`, which has certain properties, including two primitive operations.

- ```
  type X(Arg : type) is abstract new Y with private;
  type X(Arg : type) is abstract tagged limited private;
  ```

The **type X** is an Ada95 tagged type. We will return to generics and tagged types in the next chapter.

5.4.2 with parameters

We saw above how to pass a function to a generic, using the keyword **with**. There is one other parameter that may be passed to a generic package by using **with**, another generic package added for Ada95.

```
with Ada_Store.Support.List;

generic
   with package A_List is new Ada_Store.Support.List(<>);
package Ada_Store.Support.List_Iterator is

   ..

end Ada_Store.Support.List_Iterator;
```
```

This says that we have some package called `List` (seen above) which is a generic package implementing a linked list of items. We want to be able to iterate through any such list and so we have a new generic package which takes a parameter which must be an instantiated package. The `(<>)` in this case denotes that the generic package has a set of parameters; note that it does not indicate a single parameter but any set of parameters. This could be used as:

```
package A_List is new Ada_Store.Support.List(Message_Record);
package Message_View is
   new Ada_Store.Support.List_Iterator(A_List);
```

We could actually specify parameters to be passed to the **with**-ed package, like this:

```
with Ada_Store.Support.List;

generic
   type Element_Type is private;
   with package A_List is new Ada_Store.Support.List (Element_Type);
package Ada_Store.Support.List_Iterator is
   ..
end Ada_Store.Support.List_Iterator;
```

5.4.3   Parameter defaults

When passing parameters to a subprogram it is possible to supply default values, for example:

```
procedure Something(Value : Integer := 1);
```

The same is true for generic parameters. The only point worth noting is that when specifying the default for a **with**-subprogram parameter you can use an interesting value for the default; consider our sort procedure again:

```
generic
   type Index_Type is (<>);
   type Element_Type is private;
   type Element_Array is array (Index_Type range <>)
     of Element_Type;
   with function "<" (el1, el2 : Element_Type) return Boolean is
     <>;
   procedure Bubble_Sort(The_Array : in out Element_Array);
```

Note the addition of the '**is** <>' to the declaration of the parameter: this means that if it is not specified at instantiation time a matching primitive operation should be used if it can be found. Thus, for the example where we sorted integers we could have omitted the last parameter because '<' is a specified primitive operation of the type `Integer`.

5.5   Unchecked programming

We have talked a lot about the safety issues dealt with by Ada. Type safety implies very strict rules on converting objects of one type into another type, access type rules prevent memory leaks and dangling references, and so on.

Sometimes it is important to be able to subvert this safety. For example in Section 3.8 we discussed passing unions to and from a C program and we introduced the generic function `Unchecked_Conversion`. In Section 3.5 when discussing access types we also introduced the generic `Unchecked_Deallocation` as the only available method for returning memory allocated from a storage pool to that pool.

The following two sections cover these generic library subprograms in more detail.

5.5.1   `Unchecked_Conversion`

This generic function is defined as:

```
generic
   type Source (<>) is limited private;
   type Target (<>) is limited private;
function Ada.Unchecked_Conversion (Source_Object : Source)
   return Target;
```

and should be instantiated as in the example below (taken from one of the Ada95 standard library packages `Ada.Interfaces.C`).

```
function Character_To_char is new
   Unchecked_Conversion (Character, Interfaces.C.char);
```

It can then be used to convert an Ada character to a C char, thus

```
A_Char : Interfaces.C.char := Character_To_char('a');
```

5.5.2   `Unchecked_Deallocation`

This generic function is defined as:

```
generic
   type Object (<>) is limited private;
   type Name is access Object;
procedure Ada.Unchecked_Deallocation (X : in out Name);
```

This function deallocates pool-specific access values created with the **new** operator. We have already seen it used in the list example above to deallocate link nodes. To recap on its use:

```
with Unchecked_Deallocation;

package body Ada_Store.Support.List is

    procedure Free is
        new Unchecked_Deallocation(Element_Holder, List_Ptr);

    ..

    function Get is

        ..
        if List.Head = null then

            List.Tail := null;
        end if;

        Free(List.Head);

        return Element;
    end Get;
```

We instantiate it with the type of the object to deallocate, and its access type, and then we simply call the new function `Free` with an access object to deallocate the node.

5.6 Summary

Here is a brief summary of the generic parameters; the actual syntax for generic sub-programs and packages should be fairly simple to grasp.

```
type X is (<>);                      -- Discrete type
type X is range <>;                  -- Signed integer type
type X is mod <>;                    -- Modular integer type
type X is digits <>;                 -- Floating point type
type X is delta <>;                  -- Fixed point type
type X is delta <> digits <>;        -- Decimal fixed point type
type X is array (..) of Y;           -- Array of Ys
type X is private;                   -- Any definite type
type X(<>) is private;               -- Any indefinite type
type X is access all Y;              -- Access to object type
type X is access procedure ..        -- Access to procedure
type X is access function ..         -- Access to function
type X is tagged private;            -- Any tagged type
type X is new Y with private;        -- A tagged extension of Y
```

```
X : in X_Type := X_Value;        -- Formal object

with procedure X(..);            -- Formal procedure
with function X(..);             -- Formal function
with package X is new Y(..);     -- Formal package
```

We have introduced two new elements to our application example, the generic sub-program `Ada_Store.Support.Sort` and the generic package `Ada_Store.Support.List`.

Tagged types for object oriented programming

In [11] Stroustrup describes the history of C++ and its forerunner *C with classes* as an amalgam of C and Simula. Ada95 is not *Ada with classes*, as you will come to realize.

Ada95 terminology may seem a little alien to many C++ programmers, or even programmers of other object oriented languages. For example we have already seen how even Ada83 supports type derivation and inheritance of primitive operations well before the introduction of so-called object oriented programming features. Beware that many of the rules governing object oriented programming in Ada95 with the new tagged type are exactly the same as those we have already met and used for elementary types described above.

This chapter has been organized in a similar way to *The Annotated C++ Reference Manual* (C++ ARM)[12] chapters 9–11; each section header consists of the Ada term with the C++ term bracketed (where possible).

6.1 Classes in C++

Example 6.1   The standard introductory example ⎯⎯⎯⎯⎯⎯⎯⎯⎯

```
class animal {
    animal(char* animal_name) : name(animal_name) ;
```

```
public:
   virtual void  make_a_sound(void) = 0;

            char* name(void) { return name; };

   static  char* class_name(void) { return_class_name; };
protected:
   char* name;
private:
   static const char* _class_name;
};
```

This classic object oriented example provides a useful example as it provides a small, but rich, set of features including:

- a private constructor,
- a pure virtual function,
- an inline static function,
- a data member,
- a static data member.

We will be using this example quite a lot through this chapter, diverting from our `Ada_Store` example which we will return to in due course.

As we know, the main language feature for supporting object oriented programming in C++ is the class; the C++ ARM defines a class as (commentary, chapter 9):

> '"Class" is the key concept of C++. A class is a user-defined type. The class is the unit of data hiding and encapsulation. The class is the mechanism supporting data abstraction by allowing representation details to be hidden and accessed exclusively through a set of operations defined as part of the class. Polymorphism is supported through classes with virtual functions. The class provides a unit of modularity. In particular, a class with only static members provides a facility akin to a "module" in many languages: a named collection of objects and functions in their own names space.'

If we analyze the role of the class in C++ we will find that we have already introduced many of the features in Ada. Firstly 'A class is a user-defined type': in Ada we can create user-defined types with primitive operations already including type derivation. 'The class is the mechanism supporting data abstraction': in Ada the package provides data abstraction and supports data hiding and access through subprograms. 'The class provides a unit of modularity': again in Ada we use the package for a much more flexible and safe mechanism.

It is the statement 'Polymorphism is supported through classes with virtual functions' and the statement not made above that 'Class derivation can include the extension of the parent type' that were not provided with the features of Ada83.

6.2   Tagged types

In a number of places in the text so far we have made mention of tagged types, a feature added in Ada95 to provide for object oriented programming. Tagged types are an extension to the existing concept of a record, and provide the run-time information required to make dispatching calls to primitive operations (virtual functions), therefore providing polymorphism. They also provide a method for extending a type when deriving it and so complete our C++ class feature list above.

Example 6.2   The `Animal` class in Ada ─────────────────────────────

```
-- file: Animal.ads
package Animal is
   type Instance is abstract tagged private;

   procedure Make_A_Sound
      (Animal : in Instance'Class)
       is abstract;

   function  Name
      (Animal : in Instance)
       return String;

   function  Class_Name return String;

private
   type Instance is abstract tagged
      record
          Name : String(1 .. 30);
      end record;

   Private_Class_Name : constant String := "Animal";
end Animal;
```

You have now seen a tagged type declaration. Please note the following additional features:

- The use of the keyword **tagged** when declaring the type `Instance`.
- The use of the keyword **abstract** when declaring both the procedure `Make_A_Sound` and the type `Instance`.
- The use of the attribute `'Class` on the formal parameter to the procedure `Make_A_Sound`.
- The absence of an enclosing construct such as the class in C++ which delimits its members. The tagged type does not act in this way.

```
package body Animal is

   function Name
```

```
    (Animal : in Instance) return String is
begin
    return Animal.Name;
end Name;

function Class_Name return String is
begin
    return Private_Class_Name;
end Class_Name;

end Animal;
```

The above is a simple form of the package body for the package `Animal`.

Note: in the above package the main type is called `Instance`. This is a common convention which does have some advantages. Mainly it uses the package/type relationship and the namespace management of Ada to provide meaningful names. Other conventions are to use plurals for package names and to use the singular for the type, for instance:

```
package Animals is
    type Animal is tagged ..

    ..

    An_Animal : Animal;
    A_Dog     : Animals.Dogs.Dog;
```

6.2.1   Use of tagged types and packages

We now need to discuss the statement 'The class provides a unit of modularity' and its relation to tagged types. Where is the class? Where is the unit that wraps up the components and operations and presents them as a single programmatic entity?

We have already seen packages used to provide abstract data types by using the package scope to present a type and its operations as a single unit. We have seen that C++ classes can be used to accomplish the same effect in 'In particular, a class with only static members provides a facility akin to a "module" in many languages: a named collection of objects and functions in their own names space.' Can we then reserve this situation and use the package to present the scoping and namespace management provided by C++ classes?

The answer is yes; the combination of a tagged type and its operations declared within a package provides the closest approximation to a C++ class that Ada can provide.

Example 6.3   Real tagged type declaration _____

```
with Ada_Store.Trading.Department;

package Ada_Store.Trading.Item is
```

```ada
type Instance  is tagged private;

type Identifier is new Natural;

function  Lookup
   (Item_Number : in Identifier)
     return Instance;

procedure Create_New
   (Item_Number       : in Identifier;
    In_Department      : in Department.Identifier;
    Display_Descr      : in Short_Description;
    Price              : in Currency;
    Weight_Required : in Boolean := False);

procedure Remove
   (Item_Number : in Identifier);

function  In_Department
   (Item : in Instance)
     return Department.Identifier;

function  Display_Description
   (Item : in Instance)
     return Short_Description;

function  Price
   (Item : in Instance)
     return Currency;

function  Weight_Required
   (Item : in Instance)
     return Boolean;

Invalid_Identifier : exception;
Invalid_Price      : exception;
private
   Null_Identifier : constant Identifier := 0;

   type Instance is tagged
      record
          Item_Number      : Identifier;
          In_Department     : Department.Identifier;
          Display_Descr     : Short_Description;
          Price             : Currency;
          Weight_Required : Boolean;
      end record;
end Ada_Store.Trading.Item;
```

This is a tagged type from our **Ada_Store** example. It is used to hold details about
a sale item such as its price, description, department, and so on.

6.2.2   Tagged type components (Class members)

Because the tagged type is built around a normal Ada record, class data members are simply represented as components of the tagged record, in fact any legal record declaration is allowed, including discriminants. In the example above the string Name is a member of the equivalent of the C++ class member name.

Unfortunately because the tagged type is built around a normal Ada record you can only declare components in one place; you need to make the decision to put your complete record declaration in either the public part or the private part (as above).

6.2.3   Tagged type primitive operations (Class member functions)

Primitive operations for tagged types are similar to primitive operations for other types: they are subprograms declared before the freezing point for the type (see Section 6.2.5) with an argument or return value of the tagged type.

Our Animal example has two primitive operations, Make_A_Sound and Name, which have a parameter of the tagged type Instance.

Note: if you have two tagged types declared together you cannot declare a primitive operation which has arguments of both types: primitive operations can only be primitive to a single type. The following is therefore illegal:

```
package Animal is
    type Pet_Instance is abstract tagged private;
    type Owner_Instance is abstract tagged private;

    procedure Purchase
        (Me      : in Owner_Instance;
         Animal : in Pet_Instance);

    ..
```

In some object oriented languages this is known as a *multi-method*; in Ada it is known as a *compiler error*.

One feature of C++ which has come into common use especially when engineering large projects is the use of const member functions, a member function that has the keyword const following its signature. In the example below we have rewritten the member function name on the animal class to be const. This means that a call to this member function does not affect the state of the class in any way.

```
class animal {
    animal(char* animal_name) : name(animal_name) ;
public:
    virtual void  make_a_sound(void) = 0;
            char* name(void) const;
    static  char* class_name(void);
    ..
};
```

This can be achieved in Ada using, again, existing simple rules. Consider the following two primitive operations on the `Animal` tagged type. The first we know already: it returns the name of the animal. The second subprogram is a procedure to set the name of the animal: it obviously will change the state of the type, and will assign to the `Name` component.

```
function Name
   (Animal : in Instance)
      return String;

procedure Name
   (Animal    : in out Instance;
    New_Name : in      String);
```

The access specifier for the parameter `Animal` in the first subprogram states that it is an input-only parameter and so the object inside the body of the function is read-only. The corresponding parameter in the following procedure makes the object read–write. This simple rule provides the same functionality as the C++ `const` keyword except that it cannot be bypassed as it frequently is in C++ code.

6.2.4   Static members

Static member functions and static data members have no distinct syntax in Ada; however, by using the package to provide class scope any non-primitive operation of the tagged type declared in the scope behaves in the same way as a C++ static member.

In our example above the function `Type_Name` is a non-primitive operation and acts like a static member.

6.2.5   Freezing points

The *freezing point* is the term used to specify the point at which you may not specify any further primitive operations for a type. The section in the language reference manual that deals with freezing, 13.14, starts with the following helpful statement:

> 'This clause defines a place in the program text where each declared entity becomes "frozen". A use of an entity, such as a reference to it by name, or (for type) an expression of the type, causes freezing of the entity in some contexts, as described below. The Legality Rules forbid certain kinds of uses of an entity in the region of text where it is frozen.'

The simplest way to view this lawyer-speak is that the complete structure of an entity must be known before it can be used. The freezing point itself is always at the end of the enclosing declarative part unless use of the type (an object declared of the type, an expression resulting in the type or a new type derived from it) causes its freezing before this point.

With tagged types the freezing point is important as no further primitive operations can be declared for a tagged type after it has been frozen; the act of freezing the type constructs the internal details required for dispatching (analogous to a C++ v-table).

6.3   Derived tagged types (derived classes)

In C++ we use the term inheritance to mean a very specific case where one C++ class is derived from another. In Ada the term inheritance is used in all cases of type derivation, for example:

declare
    type Transaction_ID **is new** Integer;

The derived type `Transaction_ID` inherits the primitive operations of the type `Integer`. From this we can see how to derive a new type from a tagged type.

Example 6.4   Inheritance in C++ and Type extension in Ada95 ————————

```
class dog : public animal {
public:
    dog(void);

    void make_a_sound(void);

    static char* class_name(void);
private:
    static const char* _class_name;
};
-- file: Animal.Dog.ads
package Animal.Dog is
    type Instance is new Animal.Instance with null record;

    procedure Make_A_Sound(Dog : in Animal.Instance'Class);

    function  Class_Name return String;

private

    Private_Class_Name : constant String := "Dog";
end Animal.Dog;
```

The new type `Dog.Instance` is derived from `Animal.Instance`. Note that when deriving from the parent we add the keyword **with** to provide for the derived type to add further components. In the case above no further components were needed, so we added a null record. If we had required any further components we might have had:

```ada
package Animal.Dog is
   type Instance is new Animal.Instance with private;

   procedure Make_A_Sound(Dog : in Animal.Instance'Class);

   function  Class_Name return String;
private
   type Instance is new Animal.Instance with
      record
         Has_Fleas : Boolean := False;
      end record;

   Private_Class_Name : constant String := "Dog";
end Animal.Dog;
```

The second of these specifications can be found in `Animal.Dog.ads`.

As with many declarations seen so far we have split the declaration of both `Animal` and `Dog` into the public and private parts of the package specification and specified its parent type in both. In Ada it is legal to omit the specification of a tagged types parent type in the partial declaration, so we could have written:

```ada
package Animal.Cat is
   type Instance is tagged private;
   ..
private
   type Instance is new Animal.Instance with
      record
         Likes_Water : Boolean := False;
      end record;
   ..
end Animal.Cat;
```

This feature is useful because a client of this package has to use the first, partial, declaration whereas the package body uses the full declaration in the private part and therefore has the knowledge that the type `Cat.Instance` is derived from `Animal.Instance`. The following procedure becomes quite interesting:

```ada
-- file: Test1.adb
with Animal;
with Animal.Cat;
with Animal.Dog;

procedure Test1 is
   type Animal_Ptr is access all Animal.Instance;

   Ptr        : Animal_Ptr;
   An_Animal : Animal.Instance;
```

```
   A_Cat      : Animal.Cat.Instance;
   A_Dog      : Animal.Dog.Instance;
begin
   Ptr := An_Animal'Access;               -- perfectly legal.
   Ptr := Animal.Instance(A_Cat)'Access; -- illegal.
   Ptr := Animal.Instance(A_Dog)'Access; -- legal.
end Test1;
```

Base class pointers

We have declared an access type which accesses any animal, so we should also be able to use it to hold access values for any derived type. We then declare an animal object, a cat object and a dog. Placing the access value of an animal into an animal access type works, as we would expect, and placing the access value of the dog into the animal access works (once it has been cast to an animal). However, the attempt to place the cat's access value into the animal access fails. This is because the public view of the type `Cat.Instance` does not relate the cat to an animal in any way; that information is private.

This rule can be simplified to state that

'the public view may identify the parent type for a new tagged type; if, however, it does specify a parent type then the private full declaration may derive the type from any type in the class of the public parent. A client's knowledge of the parent of the new type is limited to the specification in the public part'.

This means that if the partial declaration of `Dog.Instance` says the parent is `Animal.Instance` then the private full declaration may specify the parent to be any type derived from `Animal.Instance`; `Mammal.Instance` for example.

6.3.1   Abstract tagged types (abstract classes)

We saw in our original `Animal` example the use of the keyword **abstract** to denote both a pure virtual function and an abstract tagged type. In Ada if a tagged type has any abstract primitive operations (marked with **is abstract**) then it too must be marked as abstract. Also if a tagged type is abstract then any functions that return objects of the type *must* also be marked abstract (you cannot create an instance of an abstract object even in the package body, so such a function cannot be implemented).

The rules for using abstract tagged types are similar to those for abstract class in C++. Any tagged type with abstract primitive operations must be marked as abstract, though a type marked abstract does not necessarily have to have abstract operations.

You may not declare an object of an abstract type:

```
declare
   An_Animal : Animal; -- illegal.
```

You may, however, declare objects of an access to abstract tagged type:

```
declare
   type Animal_Ptr is access Animal;

   An_Animal : Animal_Ptr := Animal_Ptr(new Dog);
```

Any type derived from an abstract tagged type that does not overload all abstract operations is also deemed to be abstract; it must be marked with **is abstract**.

In the previous section we described how the partial and full declarations of a tagged type can, legitimately, have different views on the parent of the type. It is also legal for the two declarations to have a different view on whether the type is abstract.

Example 6.5   Partial and full declarations ───────────────────────────

```
with Ada.Calendar;
with Ada_Store.Station;

package Ada_Store.Log is

   type Element is abstract tagged private;

   function To_String
     (Log_Element : in Element)
       return String;

   procedure Put
     (Element_In : in out Element'Class);

private
   type Sequence_Number is
     new Long_Integer range 1 .. Long_Integer'Last;

   type Element is tagged
     record
            Sequence_Number : Ada_Store.Log.Sequence_Number;
            Calendar_Time   : Ada.Calendar.Time;
            Station_ID      : Ada_Store.Station.Identifier;
         end record;

end Ada_Store.Log;
```

The type `Element` is meant to be the parent of specific log elements, therefore we do not want clients creating instances of `Element`. Marking the type as abstract accomplishes this; however, note that there are no abstract operations, so the type does not *need* to be abstract and in fact the full declaration is not abstract. This has another implication: the package body uses the full declaration of the type, and so does not know that the client believes the type is abstract; thus code within the body of the package can declare objects of type `Element`.

We will discuss this again in Section 6.5.

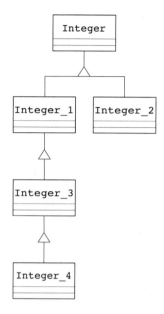

Figure 6.1   Inheritance hierarchy for Integer types.

6.3.2   'Class and 'Tag (run–time type identification)

We have not so far discussed the attribute 'Class used in the declaration of the sub-program Make_A_Sound:

  procedure Make_A_Sound(Animal : **in** Instance'Class);

This attribute is used to denote a class of types; again this is a term previously in use in Ada83 and denotes a set of derived types rooted at a given type. So for example in Ada83 we might have

  declare
      type Integer_1 **is new** Integer;
      type Integer_2 **is new** Integer;
      type Integer_3 **is new** Integer_2;
      type Integer_4 **is new** Integer_3;

This can be viewed as an inheritance hierarchy represented by the OMT class diagram shown in Figure 6.1. Each new type has a class of types derived from it, so the class of types rooted at type Integer includes all our new types; the class of types rooted at type Integer_3 is simply Integer_4. The class of types rooted at Integer_4, however, is *currently* an empty set.

   In Ada95 this terminology becomes important when discussing tagged types where type derivation is enhanced with type extension. Consider if we now derived a set

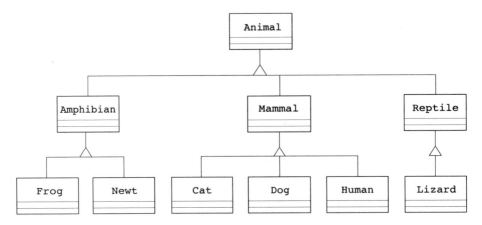

Figure 6.2 Inheritance hierarchy for `Animal` types.

of types from our abstract base type `Animal`, as shown in Figure 6.2. It can be seen that the type `Cat` is derived from `Mammal` and so is part of the Mammals class. The `'Class` attribute is used to denote this class and is used in two ways, firstly to declare objects which may take any object in the class, and secondly to check whether an object is in the class.

For example (following from Example 6.4):

```
-- file: Test2.adb
with Animal;
with Animal.Mammal;
with Animal.Mammal.Cat;
with Animal.Mammal.Dog;

procedure Test2 is
    type Animal_Ptr is access all Animal.Instance'Class;
    Ptr        : Animal_Ptr;
    An_Animal : Animal.Instance;
    A_Cat      : Animal.Cat.Instance;
    A_Dog      : Animal.Dog.Instance;
begin

    Ptr := An_Animal'Access;
    Ptr := A_Cat'Access;
    Ptr := A_Dog'Access;
end Test 2;
```

Class-wide types

We do not need to cast the objects `A_Cat` and `A_Dog` to be of type `Animal.Instance` any longer because the access type can explicitly hold access values for any type in the class of types rooted at `Animal.Instance`.

Derived tagged types (derived classes) **179**

A type declared as `Animal.Instance'Class` is called a class-wide type, and therefore the type `Animal_Ptr` above is called an access to class-wide type, or a class-wide access type. Although the Ada terminology is different, a class-wide type is directly analogous to a pointer to a base class in C++.

As we have said, we can check whether a given object is in a class of types, so that:

```ada
-- file: Test3.adb
with Ada.Text_IO;

with Animal;
with Animal.Mammal;
with Animal.Mammal.Cat;
with Animal.Mammal.Dog;

procedure Test3 is
   type Animal_Ptr is access all Animal.Instance'Class;

   procedure What_Is(Animal : Animal_Ptr) is
   begin
      if Animal.all in  Animal.Mammal.Cat.Instance'Class then

         Ada.Text_IO.Put_Line("Animal is a cat");
      elsif Animal.all in Animal.Mammal.Dog.Instance'Class then

         Ada.Text_IO.Put_Line("Animal is a dog");
      else

         Ada.Text_IO.Put_Line("Animal is an unknown animal");
      end if;
   end What_Is;

   An_Other : Animal.Instance;
   A_Cat    : Animal.Cat.Instance;
   A_Dog    : Animal.Dog.Instance;
begin

   What_Is(A_Cat);
   What_Is(A_Dog);
   What_Is(An_Other);
end Test3;
```

The procedure `What_Is` takes a class-wide access type and then checks to see what type the access value is and prints a message to that effect, so that when we run this we will get the message that the first object is a cat, the second is a dog, and the third is an unknown object. Note that to use the 'in class' test we have to de-reference the access type `Animal` as the test compares the tag attached to an object.

Consider what would have happened if we had written `What_Is` to test the order of type derivation:

```
procedure What_Is(Animal : Animal_Ptr) is
begin
   if Animal.all in Animal.Instance'Class then

      Ada.Text_IO.Put_Line("Animal is an unknown animal");
   elsif Animal.all in Animal.Mammal.Instance'Class then

      Ada.Text_IO.Put_Line("Animal is a mammal");
   elsif Animal.all in Animal.Mammal.Cat.Instance'Class then

      Ada.Text_IO.Put_Line("Animal is a cat");
   elsif Animal.all in Animal.Mammal.Dog.Instance'Class then

      Ada.Text_IO.Put_Line("Animal is a dog");
   end if;
end What_Is;
```

All the objects we pass to `What_Is` would have produced the message 'Animal is an unknown animal' because `'Class` checks whether the object is in the specified class, not if it is of a specific type.

'Tag *Attribute*

There is another important attribute associated with tagged types, `'Tag`, which returns the tag associated with each tagged type that is used internally to identify it. The attribute can be applied to a type, or to any object of a class-wide type. We can then use this tag to check for explicit type equality, and could rewrite the above as:

```
procedure What_Is(Animal : Animal_Ptr) is
begin
   if Animal. all'Tag = Animal.Instance'Tag then

      Ada.Text_IO.Put_Line("Animal is an unknown animal");
   elsif Animal.all'Tag = Animal.Mammal.Instance'Tag then

      Ada.Text_IO.Put_Line("Animal is a mammal");
   elsif Animal.all'Tag = Animal.Mammal.Cat.Instance'Tag then

      Ada.Text_IO.Put_Line("Animal is a cat");
   elsif Animal.all'Tag = Animal.Mammal.Dog.Instance'Tag then

      Ada.Text_IO.Put_Line("Animal is a dog");
   end if;
end What_Is;
```

Or we could use the library package `Ada.Tags` (Section 8.1.6) to simplify this further and write:

```
procedure What_Is(Animal : Animal_Ptr) is
begin
   Ada.Text_IO.Put_Line("Animal is of type " &
      Ada.Tags.Expanded_Name(Animal.all'Tag));
end What_Is;
```

The package `Ada.Tags` supplies the function `Expanded_Name` which will return a string containing the fully qualified name of the type, and so we might see something like:

```
Animal is of type ANIMAL.MAMMAL.CAT.INSTANCE
```

6.3.3   Polymorphism and `'Class` (virtual functions)

We have seen how the Ada run-time can identify types using the attribute `'Tag` and identify class types with the attribute `'Class`. The Ada95 run-time also uses these attributes to provide so-called dispatching calls, the Ada term for what we call virtual functions in C++.

Virtual functions

In C++ there is a general problem with the use of the keyword `virtual`: when designing a class you must be fairly sure of how a client may use it, or derive from it so that some functions are correctly assigned virtual. For each virtual function there is a slight overhead so you should not make all functions virtual, and in many cases you specifically do not want a function to exhibit virtual behavior. It is still, as the class designer, your problem to assign this behavior to your class and it is very difficult to change a function once the class has been completed and is in use by clients.

In Ada95 the responsibility for this behavior is more distributed because it is actually the type of the actual parameter of an operation which designates its behavior. If a parameter is of a class-wide type when the subprogram is called then the actual type must be determined before the call and so dispatching occurs. Firstly the designer of a tagged type can declare that some primitive operations are always dispatching operations by making the formal parameter class-wide; secondly a client may pass a class-wide type to a subprogram, forcing a dispatched call.

```
with Animal;
use  Animal;
with Animal.Mammal;
use  Animal.Mammal;
with Animal.Mammal.Cat;
use  Animal.Mammal.Cat;
with Animal.Mammal.Dog;
use  Animal.Mammal.Dog;
```

```
procedure Test is
   type Animal_Ptr is access all Animal.Instance'Class;
   Any_Animal : Animal_Ptr;
   ..
begin
   ..
   Make_A_Sound(Any_Animal.all);
end Test;
```

In the case of `Make_A_Sound` above it is obvious that the call will dispatch as the formal parameter is declared as `Instance'Class` and we have passed an actual parameter of class-wide type. Because we have used a number of packages each of which has a procedure `Make_A_Sound` we could have created objects of a number of types, and with one call to this subprogram we can dispatch to the correct object. But what if we add a call to `Name`, whose parameter is not a class-wide type?

```
begin
   ..
   Ada.Text_IO.Put_Line(Name(Any_Animal.all));
   Make_A_Sound(Any_Animal.all);
end Test;
```

Both the calls to `Name` and `Make_A_Sound` will dispatch because the actual parameter is class-wide, so why did we specify the formal parameter for `Make_A_Sound` as class-wide? Ada95 enables you to specify that some operations must always dispatch, but lets you decide whether you want dispatching at call-time.

6.3.4   Class-wide objects

A class-wide object is considered to be unconstrained, and its exact type is unknown and so an object declared as a class-wide type must be explicitly initialized with an object within the class, so:

```
-- file: Test4.adb
with Ada.Text_IO;

with Animal;
with Animal.Mammal;
with Animal.Mammal.Cat;
with Animal.Mammal.Dog;

procedure Test4 is
   subtype Animal_Class is Animal.Instance'Class;
   type    Animal_Ptr is access all Animal.Instance'Class;
```

```
      Some_Animal : Animal_Class;                          --illegal.
      A_Cat        : aliased Animal.Mammal.Cat.Instance; --legal.
      An_Animal    : Animal_Class := A_Cat;               --now legal.
      Animal       : Animal_Ptr;
   begin
      Ada.Text_IO.Put_Line(Name(A_Cat));        -- normal call.
      Ada.Text_IO.Put_Line(Name(An_Animal));    -- normal call.

      Animal := A_Cat'Access;
      Ada.Text_IO.Put_Line(Name(Animal));       -- dispatched.
   end Test4;
```

There are three calls to Name, the second we would expect to dispatch as a class-wide
type is used; however, most compilers will optimize out the dispatch as the actual type
is known through the static initialization. The last call still has to be dispatched because
the access type can hold objects of any type within the class.

This may seem like a problem; however, consider the following code:

```
-- file: List_Test.adb
with Ada_Store.Support.List;

procedure List_Test is

   type     Object is tagged null record;
   subtype O_Class is Object'Class;

   package Object_List is new Ada_Store.Support.List(O_Class);
   type List_Ptr is access Object_List.Instance;

   List : List_Ptr := new Object_List.Instance;

begin
   -- put items into list.

   loop
      declare
         An_Object : O_Class := Get(List);
      begin
         -- Process An_Object.
      end;
   end loop;
end Test;
```

We have used our linked list from before and instantiated the generic with a class-wide
type, which means it can hold any object derived from the base type Object. The loop
extracting items from the list is the most important: as each element is extracted from
the list it sets the actual type of the object An_Object. This ability to have class-wide

objects can be a saving from the traditional C++ method of storing heterogeneous lists by using pointers.

6.4 Unsupported C++ features

Ada95 is not C++ and the language designers did not set out to make it so. This is not a criticism of C++: many Ada programmers have wanted true object oriented programming for some time now, but they did not want features rushed into the language for the sake of fashion. The language designers were also having to work other features into the language, not just object oriented programming constructs, while not breaking existing features.

The object oriented programming features added to the language exist within already well-understood rules and frameworks and as such some features could not (at least not sensibly) be added.

The following sections outline major areas where Ada95 does not provide a construct or feature which C++ does; in most cases it will then proceed to show you how to synthesize that feature.

6.4.1 Nested classes

It may have become clear that Ada cannot provide the nesting of classes in the same way that C++ does, for example:

```
class outer {
public:

    outer();

    void function_1(void);
    void function_2(void);
protected:

    class inner {
    public:

      ..
    };
};
```

In Ada we can model something similar with nested packages, so that:

```
package Outer is

    type Instance is tagged private;

    procedure procedure_1;
    procedure procedure_2;
```

```
private

    package Inner is

        type Instance is tagged private;
        ..
    end Inner;
end Outer;
```

This example is similar in result to the example above, but cannot always be used to synthesize some of the cases where nested classes are used. If you have to convert a body of C++ code into Ada95 then you must consider each use of nested classes and decide whether you can synthesize or whether you should make it non-nested.

6.4.2   Base class access specifiers

```
class base_class { .. };

class public_derived : public base_class { .. };

class private_derived : private base_class { .. };
```

The above simple example shows you what we mean by base class access specifiers. When defining a base-derived class relationship in C++ you specify how the base class is visible to the derived (one of `public` or `private` and possibly `virtual` as well). The C++ ARM [12] in section 11.2 defines access specifiers for base classes as:

'If a class is declared to be a base class for another class using the `public` access specifier, the `public` members of the base class are `public` members of the derived class and `protected` members of the base class are `protected` members of the derived class. If a class is declared to be a base class for another class using the `private` access specifier, the `public` and `protected` members of the base class are `private` members of the derived class. Private members of a base class remain inaccessible even to derived class unless `friend` declarations within the base class declaration are used to grant access explicitly.'

In Ada there are no access specifiers; the nearest that can be achieved is the use, or not, of parent–child packages. For example:

```
package Parent is

    type Instance is tagged
        record
            ..
        end record;
end Parent;
```

Child packages

Any package that wants to derive from and possibly extend `Parent.Instance` can do so and has full access to the components of the type. Any other client also has full access to the type, like a C++ class where every member is defined public.

We should, however (as we have so far), declare a partial view in the public part of the specification and hide the implementation, like this:

```
package Parent is

    type Instance is tagged private;

private

    type Instance is tagged
        record

            ..

        end record;
end Parent;
```

We then have two forms of client, those who simply **with** the package and use the type `Instance` and those who are child packages, thus:

```
with Parent;
package Child_1 is

    type Instance is new Parent.Instance with private;

private

    type Instance is new Parent.Instance with tagged
        record

            ..

        end record;
end Child_1;

package Parent.Child_2 is

    type Instance is new Parent.Instance with private;

private

    type Instance is new Parent.Instance with tagged
        record

            ..

        end record;
end Parent.Child_2;
```

The package specifications do not look too different, but the bodies will be. The body of `Child_1` has no access to the private part of the package **Parent** and so no operation of its tagged type can act on components of the parent.

The body of `Parent.Child_2` is different, though; it will be able to see the private part of `Parent` and so its operations can act on its parent types' components and call private operations of the parent.

Private types

It is also possible to use the feature introduced in Section 6.3 where we do not need to declare the parent for a derived tagged type in the partial view of a type to synthesize C++'s private inheritance:

```
with Parent;
package Child_3 is

    type Instance is tagged private;

private

    type Instance is new Parent.Instance with tagged
        record
          ..
        end record;
end Child_3;
```

Private inheritance is generally used in C++ where internally a class wants to use the implementation of one class to provide the facilities for a new class without inheriting the operations of that class. For example, to implement a stack using an array to store elements you might find in C++:

```
class stack : private array {
public:
    stack(void);

    ..
};
```

In many cases it is better to internalize this implementation, like this:

```
class stack {
public:
    stack(void);

    ..
private:
    array the_internal_array;
};
```

This alternative is completely possible in Ada and both examples are provided below:

```
with Safe_Array;
package Stack is

    type Instance is tagged private;

private

    type Instance is new Array.Instance with tagged
        record
            ..
        end record;
end Stack;

with Safe_Array;
package Stack is

    type Instance is tagged private;

private

    type Instance is tagged
        record
            The_Internal_Array : Safe_Array.Instance;
            ..
        end record;
end Stack;
```

6.4.3 Friends

Friends are a ridiculous feature in C++. They allow a class to specify either another class or a function that acts as a friend. This friend then has complete access to all public, protected, and private members of the main class. Consider the following example:

```
class nice_and_safe {
public:

    nice_and_safe(void);

    int access_my_data(void);

private:
    int private_data;

    friend void not_so_safe(nice_and_safe an_instance);
};

void not_so_safe(nice_and_safe an_instance)
{
    an_instance.private_data = 0;
}
```

The function `a_function` is not a member of the class `nice_and_safe` but has complete access to it.

Ada does not have friend functions or friend classes. There is no way to synthesize the same semantics as the C++ friend directly; we have seen previously, however, that child library units can be used to access private information.

```
-- file: Nice_And_Safe.ads
package Nice_And_Safe is

   type Instance is tagged private;

   function Access_My_Data
     (Object : in Instance)
       return Integer;

private
   type Instance is tagged
      record
         Private_Data : Integer;
      end record;

end Nice_And_Safe;

-- file: Nice_And_Safe-Not_So_Safe.ads
procedure Nice_And_Safe.Not_So_Safe
  (Object : in out Nice_And_Safe.Instance'Class);
-- file: Nice_And_Safe-Not_So_Safe.adb
procedure Nice_And_Safe.Not_So_Safe
  (Object : in out Nice_And_Safe.Instance'Class) is
begin
   Object.Private_Data := 0;
end Nice_And_Safe.Not_So_Safe;
```

The resulting Ada package `Nice_And_Safe` contains a tagged type and so is a good representation of the C++ class above. The procedure `Not_So_Safe` in the Ada case above becomes its own library unit which is a child of `Nice_And_Safe`; this gives it access to the private part of its parent so that it can assign into the record element. Note that we have had to declare the parameter as a class-wide object, because the type `Instance` has already been frozen.

6.4.4 Multiple inheritance

Ada95 does not support multiple inheritance for tagged types. The designers of Ada95 viewed it as a feature that made both the language design and implementation more difficult, and because it was a feature that was not fully understood and little exploited it was not really required.

Mix-in inheritance is a term used to cover the technique where you have a hierarchy of objects, like our `Animal` hierarchy, and instead of having additional subclasses to add additional properties, or declaring all possible properties, you can have an additional class which you can add at any point. The technique of mix-in inheritance can be completely synthesized by using tagged types and generics.

In our `Animal` hierarchy we may wish to take note of animals that have been domesticated. We have a number of options:

- Add details to be stored about domesticated animals to the base class, though if an animal is not domesticated this is a waste of space.
- For each animal have a `Domesticated_Animal` and a `Wild_Animal` type.
- Mix-in the properties from a `Domesticated_Animal` class when you identify a possibly domesticated animal.

In C++ or other languages supporting multiple inheritance it is easy. For example, if we want to distinguish between domesticated dogs and wild dogs we can have:

```
class Domesticated {
public:

    ..
};

class Dog : public Mammal {
public:

    ..
};

class Domesticated_Dog : public Dog, public Domesticated {
public:

    ..
};

{
    Dog              Wolf;
    Domesticated_Dog Collie;

    ..
}
```

We have already said that Ada does not support any form of multiple inheritance, so how can we distinguish between our `Collie` and `Wolf`? The following generic might enable us to accomplish this:

```
-- file: Domesticated.ads
with Animal;

generic

    type Wild_Animal is new Animal.Instance with private;
```

```
package Domesticated is

    type Instance is new Wild_Animal with private;

    procedure Set_Purpose
       (Domesticated_Animal : in out Instance;
        Purpose              : in      String);

    function Get_Purpose
       (Domesticated_Animal : in Instance)
        return String;
private
    type Instance is new Wild_Animal with
       record
            Purpose : String(1 .. 30);
       end record;
end Domesticated;
```

This means that we can add an instantiation of Domesticated, passing in our Dog.
Instance type and resulting in a new type available to us, a Domesticated_
Dog.Instance. We can now even inform others why man should domesticate a collie.

```
-- file: Test5.adb
with Animal.Mammal;
use  Animal.Mammal;
with Animal.Mammal.Dog;
with Domesticated;

procedure Test5 is

    package Domesticated_Dog is new Domesticated(Dog.Instance);

    A_Wild_Wolf    : Dog.Instance;
    My_Pet_Collie : Domesticated_Dog.Instance;
begin

    Domesticated_Dog.Set_Purpose(My-Pet-Collie
                                       "Herd sheep and tear slippers");
end Test5;
```

As most dogs will be domesticated it is not unreasonable to add the package instantiation to the dogs package:

```
package Animal.Dog is
    type Instance is new Animal.Instance with private;

    package Domesticated_Dog is new Domesticated(Instance);
    subtype Domestic_Instance is Domesticated_Dog.Instance;

    ..
end Animal.Dog;
```

If we return quickly to the specification for `Domesticated`, we will see that the generic formal parameter is a tagged type derived (directly or indirectly) from `Animal.Instance`. This means that we have introduced a constraint so that we cannot pass in a tagged type representing a building or a car; the attributes of domestication are specifically for this problem.

```
with Animal;

generic

    type Wild_Animal is new Animal.Instance with private;

package Domesticated is
    ..
```

What if we want to mix-in something more general like color? We might want to specify the color of a building or a car, so we do not want to constrain the type that might be passed. The formal parameter can be relaxed to accept any tagged type, so:

```
generic

    type A_Thing is tagged private;

package Colored is
    ..
```

This means we can now apply color to any tagged type. We can even specify the color for our collie:

```
-- file: Test6.adb
with Animal.Mammal;
use  Animal.Mammal;
with Animal.Mammal.Dog;
with Domesticated;
with Colored;

procedure Test6 is

    package Domesticated_Dog is new Domesticated(Dog.Instance);
    package Pet_Dog is new Colored(Domesticated_Dog.Instance);

    A_Wild_Wolf   : Dog.Instance;
    My_Pet_Collie : Pet_Dog.Instance;
begin

    Domesticated_Dog.Set_Purpose(My-Pet-Collie
                                 "Herd sheep and tear slippers");
    Pet_Dog.Set_Color(My-Pet-Collie
                      Pet_Dog.Black & Pet_Dog.White);
end Test6;
```

This technique is very powerful and requires no additional support from the language. It exists as just another clause in the Ada83 type derivation rules. Mix-in inheritance is the most frequent use of multiple inheritance in C++ projects and so this synthesized version was considered enough for most Ada projects.

6.4.5   Constructors and destructors for Ada

Ada does not provide a specific constructor or destructor function for tagged types. However, there are four basic methods for synthesizing constructors (only one way for destructors):

- component defaults,
- use of discriminants,
- explicit create functions and abstract types,
- use of `Ada.Finalization`.

Component defaults

Each component in a record may have a default value as we have seen, and in many cases this is all a constructor does, initialize members to known safe values. We could therefore implement this simply by:

```
package Animal is
    type Color    is (Red, Blue, Green, Yellow, Brown, Black);

    type Instance is abstract tagged private;

    ..
private
    type Instance is abstract tagged
        record
            Name      : String(1 .. 30) := (others => ' ');
            My_Color  : Color            := Brown;
        end record;

    ..
end Animal;
```

We therefore know the initial value of each component and in many cases this is all C++ constructors are written for; thus we have solved the simplest constructor problem.

Discriminants

The complete record declaration for a tagged type may contain any legal components, as well as discriminants, so consider the following:

```
package Animal is
    type Color     is (Red, Blue, Green, Yellow, Brown, Black);

    type Instance(Its_Color : Color) is abstract tagged private;

    ..
private
    type Instance(Its_Color : Color) is abstract tagged
        record
            Name     : String(1 .. 30);
            My_Color : Color := Its_Color;
        end record;

    ..
end Animal;
```

The discriminant works to initialize the record, so to declare an object of type
`Instance` we are forced to provide the animals's color, like this:

```
with Animal;
with Animal.Dog;

procedure Test;
    Rover : Animal.Dog.Instance(Animal.Brown);
begin
    Animal.Make_A_Sound(Animal.Instance'Class(Rover));
end Test;
```

The use of component initialization and discriminants is certainly moving us in the
right direction, though again we have not addressed the lack of a destructor.

Create *function*

It is possible to include a function which creates an object, initializes it and returns it
to the client. In fact in abstract data types it is common and so many programmers will
be used to developing `Create` functions.

For example the package `Ada_Store.Trading.Item` we saw above
manages sale items, which reside in some database somewhere; a client should not
explicitly declare objects of the item type, but should either look them up from the
database, or call a `Create` function which ensures they are put into the database.

A possible form of this package may look like this:

```
with Ada_Store.Trading.Department;

package Ada_Store.Trading.Item is

    type Instance         is abstract tagged private;
    type Instance_Ptr     is access all Instance;
```

```
   type Identifier        is new Natural;

   function Lookup
     (Item_Number : in Identifier)
      return Instance_Ptr;

   procedure Create_New
     (Item_Number     : in Identifier;
      In_Department   : in Department.Identifier;
      Display_Descr   : in Short_Description;
      Price           : in Currency;
      Weight_Require  : in Boolean := False);

     ..
private
   Null_Identifier : constant Identifier := 0;

   type Instance is tagged
      record
         Item_Number     : Identifier;
         In_Department   : Department.Identifier;
         Display_Descr   : Short_Description;
         Price           : Currency;
         Weight_Require  : Boolean;
      end record;

end Ada_Store.Trading.Item;
```

Abstract partial view

We have declared the partial view of `Instance` as an abstract tagged type, so clients cannot create their own objects. We have then presented the function `Lookup` which returns access to `Instance` objects (remember a primitive operation of an abstract tagged type may not return an object of the type). The body may look something like this:

```
package body Ada_Store.Trading.Item is

function Lookup
  (Item_Number : in Identifier)
   return Instance is

   Returned_Item : Instance_Ptr;
begin
   -- lookup in database
   if Record_Found then

      Returned_Item := new Instance;
```

```
            -- populate Returned_Item;
            return Returned_Item;
            end if;
        end Lookup;

    procedure Create_New
        (Item_Number    : in Identifier;
         In_Department  : in Department.Identifier;
         Display_Descr  : in Short_Description;
         Price          : in Currency;
         Weight_Require : in Boolean := False) is
         Database_Item  : Instance;
    begin
        -- populate Database_Item;
        -- add to database
        if not Record_Written then

            -- raise an exception
        end if;
    end Create_New;

  end Ada_Store.Trading.Item;
```

Because the package body knows that the full declaration of the type Instance is not abstract it can allocate objects of the type and return them.

This technique does not solve the destructor problem, although it is possible to add another subprogram, Free for example, which is used to clear up the object and in this case deallocate the storage from the allocator.

Discriminants

Another way to accomplish this is to declare the partial view of the type with unknown discriminants:

```
  with Ada_Store.Trading.Department;
  package Ada_Store.Trading.Item is
      type Instance(<>) is tagged private;

      ..
  private
      type Instance is tagged
         record
             Item_Number    : Identifier;
             In_Department   : Department.Identifier;
             Display_Descr   : Short_Description;
             Price           : Currency;
         end record;
  end Ada_Store.Trading.Item;
```

The unknown discriminant means that the client cannot create an object of the type `Instance` because he or she cannot correctly initialize the discriminants. The full view is again devoid of the discriminant and so the body can create objects and return them to the client.

The advantage of this approach is that the type `Instance` does not need to be tagged; an unknown discriminant can be added to a normal record.

```
with Ada_Store.Trading.Department;

package Ada_Store.Trading.Item is

    type Instance(<>) is private;

    ..

private
    type Instance is
        record
            Item_Number        : Identifier;
            In_Department       : Department.Identifier;
            Display_Descr       : Short_Description;
            Price               : Currency;
        end record;

end Ada_Store.Trading.Item;
```

Controlled types

Ada does provide a standard library package `Ada.Finalization` which can provide constructor- and destructor-like facilities for tagged types. This package will be discussed further in Section 8.1.6. Basically it provides an abstract tagged type from which you derive new types. The types `Controlled` and `Limited_Controlled` have three abstract functions, which are called by the Ada run-time at certain points, including allocation and deallocation.

6.5 Summary

We have now covered nearly all of the Ada95 core language; in particular we have now covered the Ada95 object oriented programming constructs and facilities. In most cases it is relatively easy to rewrite C++ classes as Ada95 tagged types. If multiple inheritance, base class access, or friends are extensively used, then some class libraries may require some redesign. In general, though, the object oriented features of Ada95 are well integrated into a safer, more complete language than C++ and the effort required to rework some of the more archaic C++ in use today is worth the investment.

Ada95 was not re-engineered to be a *pure* object oriented language such as Smalltalk. It was meant to provide a set of additional programming features to programmers who were used to a safe, productive language and did not want to have to fix code broken by a new language version. This is a similar goal to that of the original designers of C++ when moving from C.

How many times has a new C++ compiler arrived which has introduced new type rules, new types, new headers, and a lot of backwards compatibility problems? The designers of Ada95 have tried to minimize the impact of the language changes, though of course if you have a variable called `aliased` or `tagged` then you do have a minor problem.

The following is a brief summary of tagged type features:

```
package Animal is

    -- abstract tagged type.
    type    Instance   is abstract tagged private;

    -- class wide type.
    subtype Any_Animal is Instance'Class;

    -- virtual subprogram.
    procedure Eat
       (Animal : in Any_Animal;
        Amount : in Integer);

    -- pure virtual subprogram.
    procedure Make_A_Sound
       (Animal : in Instance)
        is abstract;

private
    type Instance is abstract tagged
       record
           -- data member.
           Food_Reserves : Integer := 100;
       end record;

    -- protected subprogram.
    function Is_Hungry
       (Animal : in Instance)
        return Boolean;

end Animal;

package Animal.Dog is

    -- derived type.

    type Instance is new Animal.Instance with private;

    -- override pure virtual subprogram.
    procedure Make_A_Sound
       (Dog : in Instance);
```

```
      -- additional subprogram.
      procedure Chase_Stick
         (Dog : in Instance);

   private
      type Instance is abstract tagged
         record
            -- additional data member.
            Has_Fleas : Boolean := False;
         end record;

   end Animal.Dog;
```

6.5.1   Ada_Store

We have also introduced some new features and packages into our example. We introduced in 6.2 the `Ada_Store.Trading.Item` package, which also referenced another package, `Ada_Store.Trading.Department`. The packages below `Ada_Store.Trading` represent entities required as part of the store's trading operations and as well as items and departments, tenders (payment types) and customer sales have packages. All the types represented by these packages are marked tagged in case we need to derive from them at later stages. We can also introduce one of our most important tagged types, the device type, an abstract type from which we will derive individual peripheral handling types.

```
   with Ada_Store.PoST.Input_Queue;

   package Ada_Store.PoST.Device is

      type Instance        is abstract tagged private;
      type Instance_Ptr    is access all Instance'Class;

      type Unit            is range 1 .. 9;
      type Device_Mode     is ( Input, Output, Both );

      type Device_Status   is ( Closed, Idle, Busy, Locked,
                                Off_Line, Error );
   procedure Open
     (Device   : in out Instance'Class;
      Unit_ID : in      Unit);

   procedure Open
     (Device : in out Instance)
      is abstract;

   procedure Close
     (Device : in out Instance);

   procedure Lock
     (Device : in out Instance);
```

```
procedure UnLock
  (Device : in out Instance);

procedure ReStart
  (Device : in out Instance);

--
-- Query functions
--
function Current_Mode
  (Device : in Instance)
  return Device_Mode;

function Current_Status
  (Device : in Instance)
  return Device_Status;

function Unit_ID
  (Device : in Instance)
  return Unit;


--
-- Flushes any internal data
--
procedure Flush
  (Device      : in Instance;
   Flush_Mode  : in Device_Mode)
  is abstract;


--
-- Accept an Input Message.
--
procedure Accept_Input
  (Device : in out Instance;
   Input  : in       Input_Queue.Message_Ptr)
  is abstract;


--
-- exceptions raised, possibly not by this base, but by
-- members of the class
--
Device_Not_Found   : exception;
Incorrect_Status   : exception;
Incorrect_Mode     : exception;
Transport_Error    : exception;
Invalid_Input      : exception;
```

```
private
   type Instance is abstract tagged
      record
         Unit_ID          : Unit           := 1;
         Current_Mode   : Device_Mode     := Output;
         Current_Status: Device_Status   := Closed;
      end record;

end Ada_Store.PoST.Device;
```

The type itself is an abstract tagged type, and so when derived to provide a concrete type (as in the scanner case below) the abstract subprograms Open, Flush, and Accept_Input must be implemented.

The example below also shows how we can overload a function specified in a parent type, in this case Current_Status, with an additional meaning.

```
package Ada_Store.PoST.Device.Scanner is

   type Instance is new Ada_Store.PoST.Device.Instance
      with private;

   type Laser_Status is ( On, Off, Unknown );

   function Current_Status
      (Scanner : in Instance)
       return Laser_Status;

   procedure Open
      (Scanner : in out Instance);

   procedure Flush
      (Scanner      : in Instance;
       Flush_Mode   : in Device_Mode);

   procedure Accept_Input
      (Scanner : in out Instance;
       Input    : in Input_Queue.Message_Ptr);
private
   type Instance is new Ada_Store.PoST.Device.Instance
      with null record;

end Ada_Store.PoST.Device.Scanner;
```

Here is the body to our base device package:

```
package body Ada_Store.PoST.Device is

   procedure Open
      (Device   : in out Instance'Class;
       Unit_ID : in       Unit) is
```

```
begin
   if Device.Current_Status = Closed then

      Device.Current_Status := Idle;
      Device.Unit_ID         := Unit_ID;

      Open(Device);
   else

      raise Incorrect_Status;
   end if;
end Open;

procedure Close
   (Device : in out Instance) is
begin
   if Device.Current_Status /= Closed or
      Device.Current_Status /= Locked then

      Device.Current_Status := Closed;
   else

      raise Incorrect_Status;
   end if;
end Close;

procedure Lock
   (Device : in out Instance) is
begin
   if Device.Current_Status /= Locked then

      Device.Current_Status := Locked;
   else

      raise Incorrect_Status;
   end if;
end Lock;

procedure UnLock
   (Device : in out Instance) is
begin
   if Device.Current_Status = Locked then
      Device.Current_Status := Idle;
   else

      raise Incorrect_Status;
   end if;
end UnLock;

procedure ReStart
   (Device : in out Instance) is
```

```
begin
    if Device.Current_Status = Off_Line or
       Device.Current_Status = Error then

       Device.Current_Status := Idle;
    else

       raise Incorrect_Status;
    end if;
end ReStart;

function  Current_Mode
   (Device : in Instance)
    return Device_Mode is
begin
    return Device.Current_Mode;
end Current_Mode;

function  Current_Status
   (Device : in Instance)
    return Device_Status is
begin
    return Device.Current_Status;
end Current_Status;

function  Unit_ID
   (Device : in Instance)
    return Unit_ID is
begin
    return Device.Unit_ID;
end Unit_ID;

end Ada_Store.PoST.Device;
```

7 Tasking for concurrent programming

Many more programmers are having to work in multi-threaded environments today: most modern operating systems support threads (or light-weight processes) to some extent. The problem with threads is that they are not standard and so are not portable. Every operating system has a differing set of application programmers' interfaces (APIs) and frequently differing scheduling and priority rules. Thread programming is also notoriously difficult to manage in C and difficult to encapsulate in C++. Neither C nor C++ provides any support for important issues in multi-threaded programming: features such as re-entrant functions and interprocess communication (IPC).

Unlike C++ Ada defines a model for concurrent programming as part of the language itself. Few other languages (Occam and Java[19] are examples) provide language level concurrency; other languages (Modula-3) provide a concurrency model through the use of standard library abstractions. In Ada there are two base components: the task which encapsulate a concurrent process, and the protected type, which is a data structure that provides guarded access to its data. This chapter will deal with how to use these features to develop responsive, high-performance applications utilizing one of the few truly cross-platform models for concurrent processing.

7.1   Tasks and threads

The task is an active component, it is the Ada construct encapsulating a light-weight process, and it provides a simple model for executing multiple code blocks concurrently.

204

If you have not worked in a multi-threaded environment you might like to consider the advantages. In a non-multi-threaded UNIX (for example) the granularity of concurrency is the process. This process is an atomic entity; to communicate with other processes you must use sockets, IPC, etc. The only way to start a cooperating process is to initialize some global data and use the fork function to start a process which is a copy of the current process and so inherits these global variables. The problem with this model is that the global variables are now replicated in both processes: a change to one is not reflected in the other. In a multi-threaded environment multiple concurrent processes are allowed within the same address space, that is, they can share global data.

As an example, consider the word processor I used to write this book. It is version 7.0 of Microsoft Word and it has some great features. One that has been very useful is that it spell checks words as I write them, underlining them in red if they are incorrect (some reviewers of the typescript pointed out that it did not do a very good job!). It also paginates the text as I write, which with the amount of formatting involved must be a relatively complex task. Traditionally, one of two approaches had to be taken to such intensive tasks: first it had to be an off-line process initiated from a menu, or periodically the word processor would stop, refuse further input, and repaginate.

The reason for the use of such user-unfriendly mechanisms is that such applications had a single thread of execution which has to handle the user input and the graphical output and could not spare time for more complex tasks. When I run the Microsoft process viewer application I notice that Word now has three threads running, and although I do not know what each thread is doing, it is plain to see that it is the introduction of these threads that allows the word processor to offer me so many new features.

The breaking of these application performance bottlenecks is the most common application for threads, although they are often used within server software to manage connections from clients in a more secure and controlled manner than was previously possible with multiple process environments.

Bearing this application example in mind we will start by looking at how to program threads in the Windows NT environment.

7.1.1   A Windows NT thread

The following example is code which will work on a Microsoft Win32 operating system (Windows NT or Windows 95). It has the initial function of starting a new thread which will run in parallel to main.

Example 7.1   A simple Windows NT multi-threaded program ⎯⎯⎯⎯⎯⎯⎯⎯⎯

```
#include <windows.h>

DWORD Thread_X(LPVOID lpParam)
{
    while (1)
    {
```

```
        printf("Thread_X here\n");
    }
}

int main(void)
{
    DWORD       dwThreadId;
    HANDLE      hThread;

    hThread = CreateThread(NULL,
                           0,
                           (LPTHREAD_START_ROUTINE)Thread_X,
                           NULL,
                           0,
                           &dwThreadId);
    while (1)
    {
        printf("main here\n");
    }
}
```

The parameters to the function `CreateThread` provide a security descriptor (`NULL`), the size of the stack for the new thread (0 indicates a default value is to be used), the function to run, any parameters to be passed to the new thread (`NULL` again), creation flags (0 indicates no additional flags), and finally the identifier for the thread is passed back and a handle to the thread is returned from the function.

The exact order of the output from the two threads above depends on the operating system's scheduling rules, priorities, load on the system, and time-slice durations. We should, however, see enough intermixed messages to prove that the two threads are running.

Just to show the problems associated with threads, here is some code developed for IBM OS/2. It simply does what we achieved with Win32 above. The problem is that, although there are similarities, it is the differences in the code that we notice most. In particular in the OS/2 example the client has to allocate the stack for the thread, in the Windows NT example `CreateThread` allocates it, and in the OS/2 example we do not pass parameters to the new thread; we can in Windows NT.

```
#define INCL_DOSPROCESS
#include <os2def.h>
#include <bsedos.h>

#include <stdio.h>

VOID Thread_X(VOID)
{
    while (1)
```

```
    {
        printf("Thread_X here\n");
        DosSleep(500);
    }
}
int main(void)
{
    USHORT  usReturnCode;
    USHORT  usThreadId;
    SEL     selector;
    PBYTE   pbStackTop;

    usReturnCode = DosAllocSeg(4192,
                                   &selector,
                                   SEG_NONSHARED);

    if (usReturnCode = 0)
    {
        pbStackTop = (PBYTE)(MAKEP(selector, 0) + 4192);

        usReturnCode = DosCreateThread(Thread_X,
                                         &usThreadId,
                                         pbStackTop);
    }
    while (1)
    {
        printf("main here\n");
    }
}
```

7.1.2   An Ada task

In the example below an Ada task is presented which will act in the same way as the
threads seen above:

```
-- file: First_Task.adb
with Ada.Text_IO;

procedure First_Task is

    task X;

    task body X is
    begin
        loop
            Ada.Text_IO.Put_Line("task X here");
        end loop;
    end X;
```

```
begin
   loop
      Ada.Text_IO.Put_Line("First_Task got here");
   end loop;
end First_Task;
```

As with packages and subprograms a *task unit* comes in two parts, the specification and the body. Both of these are shown above; the task specification simply declares the name of the task and nothing more. The body of the task is equally uninteresting, the task starts and enters the loop.

The major advantage to a concurrency model within the language is that this example will work in exactly the same way with any Ada compiler supporting tasking on any operating system, even those that do not support threads, for example Unix or even MS-DOS.

7.1.3   Task types

Tasks can be defined as types, which means that objects can then be created in the usual way.

```
-- file: Three_Tasks.adb
with Ada.Text_IO;

procedure Three_Tasks is

   task type X(id : Integer);

   task body X is
   begin
      loop
         Ada.Text_IO.Put_Line("task" &
                               Integer'Image(id) &
                               " here");
      end loop;
   end X;

   Task_1 : X(1);
   Task_2 : X(2);
   Task_3 : X(3);
begin
   loop
      Ada.Text_IO.Put_Line("Three_Tasks got here");
   end loop;
end Three_Tasks;
```

We have also declared a discriminant part for the task, so we can pass parameters on declaration to a task easily.

Task types are inherently **limited** and so no equality test or assignment is valid for them.

7.2   Traditional interprocess communication (IPC)

In a traditional multi-processing environment it was discovered that in many cases processes are required to communicate with each other by means other than shared files or network connections. Facilities such as semaphores and shared memory were developed to cater for these needs. In multi-threaded environment (such as OS/2 or Windows NT) these facilities are heavily used to synchronize the threads within a process allowing them to cooperate; once a thread is started it will run until the end of the given function, unless stopped by an outside event.

7.2.1   Semaphores

Semaphores are a well-understood mechanism for communication between cooperating processes or threads; a semaphore has a discrete counter (which is initially zero) and two operations, `signal` and `wait`. The `signal` operation simply increments the counter by one. The `wait` operation on the other hand decrements the counter by one, except in the case that `wait` is called and the counter is already zero in which case the caller is blocked until the counter is greater than zero (someone else calls `signal`).

You can see how we might use this to tell a process that an event is occurring, for example a network service waits for a request and then signals to a worker thread to do something; for example:

```
semaphore work_pending;

void worker_thread(void)
{
   ..
   while (1)
   {
      work_pending.wait();
      ..
   }
}

void network_reader(void)
{
   ..
   start_thread(worker_thread);
   ..
   while (1)
```

```
    {
       ..
       network_read(&data);

       work_pending.signal();
       ..
    }
}
```

The main function `network_reader` starts its worker thread and then waits for a request from the network. It will obviously have to decode this message and perform some action on it, then it signals the semaphore and `worker_thread`, which was previously blocked, awakes and processes the request.

The most important aspect of all these IPC mechanisms is that each operation is atomic. The operation `work_pending.wait()` performs two operations: initially it waits until the count is greater than one and then decrements it. It is important that both these operations are considered to be one: there must never be a case where the test is performed and then some other action occurs before the counter can be decremented.

7.2.2 Mutual exclusion

These are binary semaphores; they have a single state which is either acquired or not. As such they can be used to protect a shared resource by acting as a lock. The `signal` and `wait` operations on mutual exclusion semaphores (mutexes) are frequently renamed to either `release` and `acquire` or `unlock` and `lock`. As such a call to `lock` or `acquire` is like a call to `wait` and will block until whoever has the lock currently frees it.

In our example above, how do we cope with the fact that there must be a shared buffer between the `network_reader` and `worker_thread` where details of the request are stored? We cannot have the `network_reader` updating the buffer while the `worker_thread` is still using it.

```
semaphore    work_pending;
data_buffer shared_data;
mutex        data_lock;

void worker_thread(void)
{
    ..
    while (1)
    {
        work_pending.wait();

        data_lock.acquire();
        my_data = shared_data;
```

```
            data_lock.release();
            ..

        }
    }
    void network_reader(void)
    {
        ..
        start_thread(worker_thread);
        ..
        while (1)
        {
            ..
            network_read(&net_data);
            data_lock.acquire();
            shared_data = net_data;
            data_lock.release();

            work_pending.signal();
            ..
        }
    }
```

This example now uses a shared buffer and a mutex to protect it. The two functions lock the buffer long enough to copy data into it or out of it into their own storage area.

7.2.3   Shared memory

Shared memory is not usually used in multi-threaded programming because the global scope is shared between all threads. It is frequently used, however, between different processes in a multiprocessing environment. Each section of shared memory is identified in some way by the system when you create it and it becomes mapped into your process address space. Other processes can then open this section and the memory area is shared between each process which has opened it.

In this chapter we are dealing with Ada's facility for multi-threaded programming; in Section 9.4 we will deal with the Ada95 distributed systems programming annex and we will recap on the idea of shared memory.

7.2.4   Deadlock

Consider the following example of two cooperating threads and two mutexes. If these threads are run at the same time both will block for ever!

```
    mutex        first_lock;
    mutex        second_lock;
```

```
void first_thread(void)
{
   ..
   while (1)
   {
      first_lock.acquire();
      ..
      second_lock.acquire();
      ..
      second_lock.release();
      ..
      first_lock.acquire();
   }
}
void second_thread(void)
{
   ..
   while (1)
   {
      second_lock.acquire();
      ..
      first_lock.acquire();
      ..
      first_lock.acquire();
      ..
      second_lock.release();
   }
}
```

For instance if `first_thread` is scheduled first it will acquire `first_lock` and continue on for a little while. If in the meantime `second_thread` has a chance to run then it may acquire `second_lock` before `first_thread` and continue on to a deadlock: `first_thread` cannot continue past the attempt to acquire `second_lock` because it is already locked and `second_thread` cannot acquire `first_lock`. Once the deadlock has happened there is no way to break it, since neither thread can continue to the point where it might release one of the locks.

It is very important that you manage IPC resources very carefully so that you avoid deadlock by good design.

7.3   Task synchronization (the Rendezvous)

The advantage of Ada tasking is that the Ada task model provides much more than the task as a thread; it offers us a model for IPC as well. Specifically the Ada tasking model defines methods for intertask cooperation and much more in a system-independent way using constructs known as *entries*.

A `Rendezvous` is just what it sounds like, a meeting place where two tasks arrange to meet up; if one task reaches it first then it waits for the other to arrive. The tasks rendezvous at an entry construct declared by the task; the task does not care who meets it there, it simply announces its intention to wait for someone.

In actual fact a FIFO queue is formed for each rendezvous of all tasks waiting; this can even be queried by clients to decide whether to call a rendezvous, or by rendezvous themselves.

7.3.1 entry and accept

The **entry** is a construct used in a task specification to declare a rendezvous:

```
task type X is

    entry A_Rendezvous;
end X;
```

An **entry** is a little like a procedure: it may take parameters but may not return values, and is matched in the task body by an **accept**. The only items which may appear in a task specification are entries, not subprograms or objects, and although a private part is allowed, it too must only contain entries.

```
task body X is
    ..
begin
    accept A_Rendezvous do
        ..
    end A_Rendezvous;
end X;
```

The **accept** body appears with the statement part of the task body for reasons that will become clear as we continue.

Consider the example below. A system of some sort has a cache of elements and it requests an element from the cache; if it is not in the cache then the cache itself reads an element from the master set. If this process of reading from the master fills the cache then it must be reordered. When the process finishes with the item it calls `PutBack` which updates the cache and if required updates the master.

```
task type Cached_Items is

    entry Request(Item : out Item_Type);
    entry PutBack(Item : in  Item_Type);
end Cached_Items;
```

```
task body Cached_Items is

    Log_File : Ada.Text_IO.File_Type;
begin
    -- open the log file.
    loop
        accept Request(Item : out Item_Type) do
            -- satisfy from cache or get new.
        end Request;

        -- if had to get new, then check cache
        -- for overflow and consistency.

        accept PutBack(Item : in Item_Type) do
            -- replace item in cache.
        end PutBack;

        -- if item put back has changed
        -- then possibly update original.
    end loop;
end Cached_Items;
```

Below is some typical client code using the task type above:

```
declare
    Cache : Cached_Items;
    Item  : Item_Type;
begin
    Cache.Request(Item);
    ..
    Cache.PutBack(Item);
end;
```

It is the sequence of processing which is important here. First, the client task (remember, even if the client is the main program it is still, logically, a task) creates the cache task which executes its body. The first thing the cache performs is some procedural code, its initialization, in this case to open its log file. Next we have an accept statement, a rendezvous, and in this case the two parties are the owner task, when it reaches the keyword **accept**, and the client task that calls `Cache.Request(Item)`.

If the client task calls `Request` before the owner task has reached the **accept** then the client task will wait for the owner task. However, we would not expect the owner task to take very long to open a log file, so it is more likely that it will reach the **accept** first and wait for a client task.

When both client and owner tasks are at the rendezvous then the owner task executes the **accept** code while the client task waits. When the owner task reaches the end of the rendezvous both the owner and the client are set off again on their own way.

If you look closely at the `Cached_Items` task body you can see why the

accept bodies are within the statement part of the task: we have enclosed the two **accept**s within a loop. If we had not then after the rendezvous `PutBack` the task would have completed.

7.3.2   select

If we look closely at `Cached_Items` you might notice that if the client task calls `Request` twice in a row, you have a deadly embrace; the owner task cannot get to `Request` before executing `PutBack` and the client task cannot execute `PutBack` until it has satisfied the second call to `Request`.

To get around this problem we use a **select** statement which allows the task to specify a number of entry points that are valid at any time.

```
task body Cached_Items is

   Log_File : Ada.Text_IO.File_Type;
begin
   accept Request(Item : Item_Type) do
      -- open the log file.
      -- satisfy from cache or get new.
   end Request;

   loop
      select
         accept PutBack(Item : Item_Type) do
            -- replace item in cache.
         end PutBack;

         -- if item put back has changed
         -- then possibly update original.
      or
         accept Request(Item : Item_Type) do
            -- satisfy from cache or get new.
         end Request;

         -- if had to get new, then quickly
         -- check cache for overflow.
      end select;
   end loop;
end Cached_Items;
```

We have done two major things. First we have added the **select** construct which says that during the loop a client may call either of the entry points (in effect the **select**   becomes the rendezvous waiting for either `PutBack` or `Request`). The second point is that we moved a copy of the entry `Request` into the initialization section of the task so that we must call `Request` before anything else (also by moving the open log file code into this rendezvous it is only ever done if the task is used; if we create a task but do not use it we do not have to worry about opening the log file). It is worth noting that we can have many entry points with the same name and they may be the same or may do something different but we only need one entry in the task specification. This is an important point: so far we have not changed the specification of the task at all.

7.3.3   Guarded entries

Within a **select** statement it is possible to specify the conditions under which an **accept** may be valid, so:

```
task body Cached_Items is

    Log_File          : Ada.Text_IO.File_Type;
    Number_Requested : Integer := 0;
begin
    accept Request(Item : Item_Type) do
        -- open the log file.
        -- satisfy from cache or get new.
    end Request;

    loop
        select
            when Number_Requested > 0 =>
                accept PutBack(Item : Item_Type) do
                    -- replace item in cache.
                end PutBack;

                -- if item put back has changed
                -- then possibly update original.

        or

            accept Request(Item : Item_Type) do
                -- satisfy from cache or get new.
            end Request;

            -- if had to get new, then quickly
            -- check cache for overflow.
        end select;
    end loop;
end Cached_Items;
```

This (possibly erroneous) example adds an internal counter to keep track of the number of items in the cache. If no items have been read into the cache then you cannot logically put anything back.

Be careful when using guarded entries. First, it is obvious from the example above that an unguarded entry is always treated as a guarded entry which is always true.

This is important as you must make sure that when the select is evaluated at least one rendezvous is true or the exception `Program_Error` will be raised. Second, the guard conditions are re-evaluated each time the **select** is reached.

7.3.4 **select else** (conditional entry calls)

The **else** clause on a **select** statement is executed if no other branch of the **select** is eligible for execution. For example the **else** clause allows us to implement a non-blocking **select** statement:

```
select
    accept Do_Something do
        ..
    end Do_Something;
else
    -- do something else if no-one waiting.
end select;
```

The **select** statement so far in our example checks the cache once an item has been changed, but this means that the task cannot service new calls while this housekeeping is being performed, so we could write:

```
select
    when Number_Requested > 0 =>
        accept PutBack(Item : Item_Type) do
            -- replace item in cache.
        end PutBack;
or
    accept Request(Item : Item_Type) do
        -- satisfy from cache or get new.
    end Request;
else
    -- if item put back has changed
    -- then possibly update original.

    -- if had to get new, then quickly
    -- check cache for overflow.
end select;
```

This means that the housekeeping code is only executed when no other call is outstanding.

7.3.5 Delays (timed entry calls)

It is possible to put a **delay** statement into a task. This statement has two modes, delay for a given amount of time, or delay until a given time. So:

```
delay 5.0;                    -- System.Duration
delay until A_Time;           -- Ada.Calendar.Time
```

The first use of **delay** is simple: delay the task for a given number, or fraction, of seconds. This mode takes a parameter of type `Duration` specified in the package `System`. The second use waits until a specified time is reached and takes a parameter of type `Time` from package `Ada.Calendar`.

It is more interesting to note the effect of one of these when used in a **select** statement. For example, if you want to know if someone has not called an **accept** before some given timeout then you can use a **select .. or**.

```
select
    accept An_Entry do
        ..
    end An_Entry;
or
    delay 5.0;
    Ada.Text_IO.Put_Line("An_Entry: timeout");
end select;
```

This effectively starts the delay and waits for calls on any of the specified entries. If no one calls `An_Entry` then the delay will terminate, the message is printed and the task continues execution after the end of the **select** statement. If someone does call the entry before the delay terminates then the code for that entry is executed, the message is not printed, and execution once again resumes after the **select** statement. Note the difference between the code above and the following fragment:

```
select
    accept An_Entry do
        ..
    end An_Entry;
else
    delay 5.0;
    Ada.Text_IO.Put_Line("An_Entry: timeout");
end select;
```

The above fragment does not have the same effect at all. In the first the **delay** is run while waiting for the entry to be called. In this example if no one is waiting to execute the entry `An_Entry` when the **select** statement is reached then the **delay** is called.

Let us now amend our example by adding a time-out to the entries so we can check the cache for old values.

```
task body Cached_Items is

    Log_File : Ada.Text_IO.File_Type;
    Number_Requested : Integer := 0;
```

```
begin
   accept Request(Item : Item_Type) do
      -- open the log file.
      -- satisfy from cache or get new.
   end Request;

   loop
      select
         when Number_Requested > 0 =>
            accept PutBack(Item : Item_Type) do
               -- replace item in cache.
            end PutBack;
      or
         accept Request(Item : Item_Type) do
            -- satisfy from cache or get new.
         end Request;
      or
         delay 2.0;
         -- check for old items in the cache.
      end select;
   end loop;
end Cached_Items;
```

Let us consider a different example briefly. In our example we are managing a set of peripheral devices; imagine one that requires you to send a status message to it periodically:

```
task body Peripheral_Controller is

   Status_Interval : constant System.Duration := 2.5;
   Next_Status     : Ada.Calendar.Time;
begin

   Next_Status := Ada.Calendar.Time + Status_Interval;

   loop
      select
         accept Device_Command(..) do
            ..
         end Device_Command;
      or
         delay until Next_Status;
         Send_Device_Status_Command;
         Next_Status := Ada.Calendar.Time  + Status_Interval;
      end select;
   end loop;
end Peripheral_Control;
```

It is useful to note that using a delay of 0.0 in a **select** statement is identical in effect to the **select .. else** introduced above. Thus the two following fragments achieve the same result:

```
select
    accept Do_Something do
        ..
    end Do_Something;
else
    -- do something else if no one waiting;
end select;

select
    accept Do_Something do
        ..
    end Do_Something;
or
    delay 0.0;
    -- do something else if no one waiting.
end select;
```

Client timed calls

This form of the **select** statement is not simply restricted to use within a task. The client can also use timed entry calls when calling services, for example:

```
declare
    Cache : Cached_Items;
    Item  : Item_Type;
begin
    select
        Cache.Request(Item);
    or
        delay 2.5;
        raise Request_Took_Too_Long;
    end select;
    ..
    Cache.PutBack(Item);
end;
```

Callable Attribute

A client can also decide whether to call a task entry at all depending on whether the task is still running, so for example to make sure the cache is still available:

```
begin
   if Cache'Callable then
      Cache.Request(Item);
   end if;
end;
```

Count *Attribute*

There is a similar facility for use within tasks which gives the number of tasks queued up to call a given entry:

```
accept Request(Item : Item_Type) do
   if PutBack'Count = 0 then
      -- do something?
   end if;
end Request;
```

7.3.6   Termination

The example we have been working on does not end, it simply loops forever. We can terminate a task by using the keyword **terminate** which executes an orderly clean-up of the task. (We can also kill a task in a more immediate way using the **abort** command; this is *not* recommended.)

terminate

The **terminate** alternative is used for a task to specify that the run-time environment can terminate the task if all its actions are complete and no clients are waiting. This means that if the task has any dependent tasks they must be complete, and the task that created this task must be complete:

```
loop
   select
      accept Do_Something do
         ..
      end Do_Something;
   or
      terminate;
   end select;
end loop;
```

abort *statement*

The **abort** statement is used by a client to terminate a task, possibly if it is not behaving correctly. The statement takes a task identifier as an argument, so if we were to add a new entry In_Error to our example above we might say:

```
if Cache.In_Error then
    abort Cache;
end if;
```

This aborts the task itself, and any dependent tasks and subprograms called by the task. The client can then check if a task has terminated by using an attribute which returns a Boolean value:

```
if Cache'Terminated then
    Ada.Text_IO.Put_Line("Cacheing has been turned off");
end if;
```

then abort

The **then abort** clause (asynchronous transfer of control) is used to abort some code part of a **select** statement. This is achieved by a construct which involves two distinct parts, the **triggering alternative** (a select alternative containing either an entry call or a delay statement followed by some other statements) which is run asynchronously with the **abortable part** which is also a **select** alternative. This has the following characteristics:

- If the triggering alternative completes before the abortable part is executed then the optional code is executed and the **select** completes.
- If the triggering alternative completes before the abortable part completes then the optional code is executed, the abortable part is aborted, and the **select** completes.
- If the abortable part completes before the triggering alternative then the triggering alternative is cancelled, the optional code is not run, and the **select** completes.

```
select
    delay 5.0;                    -- triggering alternative
    Put("An_Entry: timeout");     -- optional other code
then abort
    -- abortable part
    accept An_Entry do

        ..

    end An_Entry;
end select;
```

This implements a true time-out for the entry `An_Entry`. If it is not called, or fails to complete before the delay statement completes, then it is aborted and the message is displayed. If, however, it is called and the call completes before the time-out then the message is not displayed and the **select** statement is complete. We can also use an entry call instead of a delay statement, as in the following example:

```
select
   Another_Task.Their_Entry;   -- triggering alternative
   Put("An_Entry: timeout");   -- optional other code
then abort
   -- abortable part
   accept An_Entry do

      ..

   end An_Entry;
end select;
```

In this case if the call to `Their_Entry` on the task `Another_Task` completes before `An_Entry` it is aborted.

   Note: beware the conditions under which tasks may be aborted, by whatever means, and the implication of doing so. It is well worth reading the language reference manual [1] section 9.8 to review the details.

7.3.7   requeue

Because each entry blocks access to the task we cannot call one entry from another (we would block ourselves and therefore any other client as well). The **requeue** statement is used to allow one entry to call another.

   Section 7.4.1 presents an example of the use of **requeue**.

7.4   Protected types

Protected types are a new feature introduced in the Ada95 language standard. They act like the monitor constructs found in some other languages, which means that they provide mutually exclusive access to their internal data by ensuring that no two tasks can access the object at the same time.

   A basic protected type is presented below.

```
protected type Cached_Items is

   procedure Request(Item : out Item_Type);
   procedure PutBack(Item : in  Item_Type);

private
   Log_File : Ada.Text_IO.File_Type;
   Number_Requested : Integer := 0;

end Cached_Items;

protected body Cached_Items is
   procedure Request(Item : out Item_Type) is
   begin
      -- initialize, if required
```

```
            -- satisfy from cache or get new.
            -- if had to get new, then quickly
            -- check cache for overflow.
      end Request;

      procedure PutBack(Item : in Item_Type) is
      begin
            -- initialize, if required
            -- replace item in cache.
            -- if item put back has changed
            -- then possibly update original.
      end Request;
   end Cached_Items;
```

This is an implementation of our cache from the task discussion above. Note now that the names `Request` and `PutBack` are now simply subprogram calls like any other. Protected types can also declare objects in their specification (though only in their private part); in fact it is unusual to find one which does not since the task-safe management of data is their main aim.

This does show some of the other differences between tasks and protected types, for example the protected type above, because being a passive object it cannot completely initialize itself, so each procedure and/or function must check if it has been initialized. Also we must do all processing within the stated procedures.

7.4.1 IPC as protected types

It may be useful to have at our disposal some of the traditional IPC mechanisms. Rather than using the operating system primitives we can simulate most of them with Ada's tasking facilities. The example below provides a counting semaphore and a mutual exclusion semaphore for use in our example application (these are frequently used textbook examples in Ada95; ours are different in that they come from a real application). It also demonstrates the use of entries within a protected type; entries must be used over subprograms where guard conditions or the **requeue** statement is required.

It is interesting to note that such IPC mechanisms are used internally by the Ada run-time to provide facilities of the task and protected type. By using the Ada types to reproduce semaphores we are adding quite a lot of complexity, and certainly the performance of such an implementation comes into question, so why would we do it? The simple answer is that the Ada task and protected type is a standard mechanism which becomes cross platform, rather than using operating system facilities which have to be rewritten for each supported platform. As well as this, not all problems can easily be modelled as tasks or protected types: in some cases a client may wish to *lock* an object for many operations rather than the mutual exclusion guaranteed for each individual call to a protected type. For this reason it is often found that producing such a language level facility does actually aid in the maintenance of the complete system. It is also a textbook example with some merit in teaching real world uses for such facilities.

```
package Ada_Store.Support.IPC is

    protected type Mutex is

        entry     Acquire;
        procedure Release;

    private
        Locked : Boolean := False;
    end Mutex;

    protected type Semaphore(Auto_Reset : Boolean := True) is

        entry Wait;
        entry Signal;
        entry Reset;

    private
        Signals : Integer := 0;
    end Semaphore;

end Ada_Store.Support.IPC;
```

The specification for our mutual exclusion semaphore includes a Boolean discriminant which indicates whether the semaphore resets itself after a `Wait` call succeeds. The body of the `Semaphore` type shows what we do with the `Auto_Reset` flag.

```
package body Ada_Store.Support.IPC is

    protected body Mutex is

        entry Acquire when not Locked is
        begin
            Locked := True;
        end Acquire;

        procedure Release is
        begin
            Locked := False;
        end Release;

    end Mutex;

    protected body Semaphore is

        entry Wait when Signals > 0 is
        begin
            if Auto_Reset then
                requeue Reset;
            end if;
        end Wait;
```

```
    entry Signal when True is
    begin
        Signals := Signals + 1;
    end Signal;

    entry Reset when Signals > 0 is
    begin
        Signals := Signals - 1;
    end Reset;

end Semaphore;

end Ada_Store.Support.IPC;
```

If the semaphore is auto-resetting then we use the **requeue** statement to call the Reset entry from within the Wait entry. The **requeue** statement can only be used within one entry to pass control to another entry (or even to pass control back to the same entry).

You may also have noticed a difference between an entry statement in a task and the entry in a protected type:

- In a task we use **entry** in the specification and **accept** in the body. In a protected type **entry** is used for both specification and body.

- An **accept** statement in a task body takes the form

```
when expression accept Name(..) do
    statements
end Name;
```

whereas an **entry** in a protected type body takes the form

```
entry Name(..) when expression is
    declarations
begin
    statements
end Name;
```

- The **accept** in a task body is a compound statement; it does not introduce a new scope, and as you can see from the example above an **entry** in a protected type has its own declaration part.

7.5 Summary

A quick summary of the task and rendezvous syntax might be useful. First, a task specification:

```
task Example(discriminant) is

    entry First_Entry;
    entry Second_Entry(Params);

private
    entry Third_Example;
end Example;
```

The example below is simply a brief overview and reminder of the syntax brought up in this chapter; it will not compile!

```
task body Example is
    declarations
begin
    accept First_Entry do
        statements
    end First_Entry;

    loop
        select
            when expression =>
                accept Second_Example do
                    statements
                    requeue Third_Example;
                end Second_Example;
        or
            delay 5.0;
            statements
        or
            terminate;
        else
            select
                triggering_alternative
                statements
            then abort
                statements
            end select;
        end select;
    end loop;

    accept Third_Example do
        statements
    end Third_Example;
end Example;
```

The following is a brief review of protected types.

```
protected type Example(discriminant) is

   procedure proc_name  ..;
   function  func_name   ..;
   entry     entry_name ..;

private
   data : data_type;
end Example;

protected body Example is

   entry entry_name when expression is
      declarations
   begin
      statements
   end entry_name;
   ..
end Example;
```

The IPC package introduced in this chapter is taken from our example application and can be used wherever the built-in facilities of tasks and protected types are
not quite suitable. For example we spoke in Chapter 5 about the use of our linked list
package in Ada_Store.PoST.Input_Queue. Here is that package:

```
package Ada_Store.PoST.Input_Queue is

   type Input_Action is ( Unknown,
                           Enter, Cancel,
                           Sign_On, Sign_Off, Close_Down,
                           Item_Sale, Department_Sale,
                           Price_Enquiry, Subtract_Line,
                           Sub_Total,
                           Cash_Payment, Cheque_Payment,
                           Card_Payment );

   Max_Input_Text : constant Positive := 40;

   type Message is
      record
         Action : Input_Action := Unknown;
         Input  : String(1 .. Max_Input_Text);
         Length : Natural := 0;
      end record;

   type Message_Ptr is access all Message;

   procedure Append
      (Message : in Message_Ptr);
```

```
   function Get
     (Wait : in Boolean := False)
       return Message_Ptr;

   function Peek
     (Wait : in Boolean := False)
       return Message_Ptr;

 end Ada_Store.PoST.Input_Queue;
```

The input queue is used to sequence input from peripheral devices. The devices decode their input and construct a **Message** which is then stored in the input queue which the application reads. The body for this package is:

```
 with Ada_Store.Support.List;
 with Ada_Store.Support.IPC;

 package body Ada_Store.PoST.Input_Queue is

    package Unsafe_List is new Support.List(Message_Ptr);

    type List_Ptr is access Unsafe_List.Instance;

    Real_List : List_Ptr := new Unsafe_List.Instance;
    Semaphore : Support.IPC.Semaphore(False);
    Mutex     : Support.IPC.Mutex;

    procedure Append
      (Message : in Message_Ptr) is
    begin
       Mutex.Acquire;
       Unsafe_List.Append(Real_List, Message);
       Mutex.Release;

       Semaphore.Signal;
    end Append;

    function Get
      (Wait : in Boolean := False)
        return Message_Ptr is

       Message : Message_Ptr;
    begin
       Semaphore.Wait;
       Semaphore.Reset;

       Mutex.Acquire;
       Message := Unsafe_List.Get(Real_List);
       Mutex.Release;

       return Message;
    end Get;
```

```
function Peek
  (Wait : in Boolean := False)
   return Message_Ptr is

   Message : Message_Ptr;
begin
   Semaphore.Wait;

   Mutex.Acquire;
   Message := Unsafe_List.Peek(Real_List);
   Mutex.Release;

   return Message;
end Peek;

end Ada_Store.PoST.Input_Queue;
```

We have used both a semaphore and a mutex in the above example. The mutex protects the input queue from concurrent access by multiple tasks, the semaphore allows the reader to block on either Peek or Get until an item is placed on the queue.

Another use of tasking is found in the keyboard device; a task Keyboard_Reader reads characters from the PC keyboard and handles echoing the characters to the screen.

```
task Keyboard_Reader is
   pragma Priority(0);

   entry Start;
end Keyboard_Reader;

task body Keyboard_Reader is

   Read_Char  : Character;
   Ext_Char   : Character;
begin
   accept Start do
      null;
   end Start;

   loop
      Read_Char := Support.Screen.Get;

      case Read_Char is
         when Character'Val(0) =>
            Ext_Char := Support.Screen.Get;
            End_Echo(Configuration.Keyboard0, Ext_Char);

         when Character'Val(13) =>
            End_Echo(Configuration.Keyboard0, Read_Char);
```

```
        when others =>
             Echo_Char(Configuration.Keyboard0, Read_Char);
      end case;
   end loop;
end Keyboard_Reader;
```

The task above is quite simple: the main loop reads characters, identifies those that end a sequence, and calls the keyboard device. The interesting point is that the task does not start reading characters the moment it is created; it has a rendezvous `Start` that must be called first. The `Echo_Char` procedure puts the character read from the keyboard on the display, and buffers all characters until the `End_Echo` procedure is called. `End_Echo` then packages the keys so far and interprets their meaning.

Part 2

The Ada library and language annexes

You have now covered all the Ada language itself. Part 2 of this book will introduce you to Ada95's standard library and how the features found therein can be used to enhance the portability, maintainability, and safety of your Ada applications.

Ada uses its facility for creating hierarchical libraries in the definition of its own library. Three root packages have been defined, `Standard`, `Ada`, and `System`. Below these three a number of packages provide generic and flexible, yet remarkably comprehensive, facilities for character and string handling, numeric computation, input/output, system programming, and management of library issues such as storage management and task control.

The following diagram illustrates the hierarchy of the Ada95 library. Most packages are part of the core library, though some (in italics) are defined as part of the language annexes.

```
Ada
        Asynchronous_Task_Control
        Calendar
        Characters
                Handling
                Latin_1
        Command_Line
        Decimal
        Direct_IO
        Dynamic_Priorities
        Exceptions
        Finalization
        Interrupts
                Names
```

```
IO_Exceptions
Numerics
        Complex_Elementary_Functions
        Complex_Types
        Discrete_Random
        Elementary_Functions
        Float_Random
        Generic_Complex_Elementary_Functions
        Generic_Complex_Types
        Generic_Elementary_Functions
Real_Time
Sequential_IO
Storage_IO
Streams
        Stream_IO
Strings
        Bounded
        Fixed
        Maps
                Constants
        Unbounded
        Wide_Bounded
        Wide_Fixed
        Wide_Maps
                Wide_Constants
        Wide_Unbounded
Synchronous_Task_Control
Tags
Task_Attributes
Task_Identification
Text_IO
        Complex_IO
        Editing
        Text_Streams
Unchecked_Conversion
Unchecked_Deallocation
Wide_Text_IO
        Complex_IO
        Editing
        Text_Streams

Interfaces
    C
        Pointers
        Strings
```

```
COBOL
Fortran

System
    Address_To_Access_Conversions
    Machine_Code
    RPC
    Storage_Elements
    Storage_Pools
```

As we have said before there are seven annexes to the language:

- Interfaces to other programming languages.
- Support for systems programming.
- Support for real-time systems.
- Support for distributed systems.
- Support for information systems.
- Support for numerics.
- Safety and security.

The first annex, interfaces to other programming languages, is required of all Ada implementations. The other '*specialized needs annexes*' are optional, which means that compilers may achieve validation without them.

8 A standard library for portable programming

8.1	Type support	8.3	Miscellaneous
8.2	Input/output	8.4	Summary

We have briefly introduced some library packages already, `Ada.Text_IO` for example, and have hinted at more. This chapter covers the library in some detail with examples of package use.

8.1 Type support

This section covers library packages that provide additional operations on the Ada standard types.

8.1.1 Numeric support

The hierarchy of packages `Ada.Numerics` provides standard functions acting on numeric types. The most commonly used are the child packages `Discrete_Random`, `Float_Random`, and `Generic_Elementary_Functions`.

Library specification: **package** Ada.Numerics.Discrete_Random ─────────

```
generic
   type Result_Subtype is (<>);
package Ada.Numerics.Discrete_Random is

   -- Basic facilities.

   type Generator is limited private;
```

```
function Random (Gen        : Generator) return Result_Subtype;

procedure Reset (Gen        : in Generator;
                 Initiator : in Integer);
procedure Reset (Gen        : in Generator);

-- Advanced facilities.

type State is private;

procedure Save   (Gen        : in  Generator;
                  To_State  : out State);
procedure Reset (Gen        : in  Generator;
                 From_State : in  State);

Max_Image_Width : constant := -- Implementation defined

function Image (Of_State   : State)  return String;
function Value (Coded_State : String) return State;
```

```
end Ada.Numerics.Discrete_Random;
```

This first package provides a random number generator for discrete types, so it can be used with not only numeric but other discrete types such as enumerations.

Example 8.1   Using random numbers to shuffle a pack of cards ────────────

A simple example is a package which may be used in a game program to draw a card at random from a pack.

```
-- file: Card_Pack.ads
with Ada.Numerics.Discrete_Random;

package Card_Pack is

   type Suits is (Hearts, Spades, Diamonds, Clubs);
   type Cards is new Positive range 1 .. 13;

   Jack  : constant Cards := 11;
   Queen : constant Cards := 12;
   King  : constant Cards := 13;

   type Pack is limited private;

   procedure Shuffle(The_Pack : in out Pack);

   procedure Draw(The_Pack : in out Pack;
                  The_Suit :     out Suits;
                  The_Card :     out Cards);

   Pack_Empty : exception;
```

```ada
private
   type Index is new Positive range 1 .. 52;
   type Card_Array is array (Index) of Boolean;
   pragma Pack(Card_Array);

   package Random_Card is new Ada.Numerics.Discrete_Random (Index);

   type Pack is limited
      record
         All_Cards : Card_Array;
         Drawn     : Integer;
         Gen       : Random_Card.Generator;
      end record;

end Card_Pack;
```

The specification provides some useful types, a pack of cards, the suits, and the cards in a suit. The two subprograms Shuffle and Draw initialize a pack and draw a single card from the pack respectively.

The body of the package below shows how we initialize the pack by first setting the array of drawn cards to all false and resetting the random number generator:

```ada
-- file: Card_Pack.ads
package body Card_Pack is

   procedure Shuffle(The_Pack : in out Pack) is
   begin
      The_Pack.All_Cards := (others => False);
      The_Pack.Drawn     := 0;
      Random_Card.Reset(The_Pack.Gen);
   end Shuffle;

   procedure Draw(The_Pack : in out Pack;
                  The_Suit :    out Suits;
                  The_Card :    out Cards) is
      The_Index : Index;
   begin
      if The_Pack.Drawn = 52 then
         raise Pack_Empty;
      end if;

      loop
         The_Index := Random_Card.Random(The_Pack.Gen);

         if The_Pack.All_Cards(The_Index) = False then

            The_Pack.All_Cards(The_Index) := True;
            The_Suit := Suits'Val(The_Index mod 13 + 1);
            The_Card := Cards(The_Index / 13);
```

```
                The_Pack.Drawn := The_Pack.Drawn + 1;
                exit;
            end if;
        end loop;
    end Draw;

end Card_Pack;
```

The subprogram Draw selects a card by continuously selecting a random number until one is found that has not yet been drawn and then calculating the suit and number of the card.

Elementary_Functions

This package provides a set of standard mathematical functions (acting on floating point numbers) and is presented below:

```
package Ada.Numerics.Elementary_Functions is
    new Ada.Numerics.Generic_Elementary_Functions(Float);
```

As you can see, the standard package is actually just an instantiation of the generic package presented fully below. Note the use of the attribute 'Base which allows the subprograms to take a more varied set of types than indicated by the generic parameter.

Library specification:
```
package Ada.Numerics.Generic_Elementary_Functions _____

    generic
        type Float_Type is digits <>;

    package Ada.Numerics.Generic_Elementary_Functions is
        pragma Pure (Generic_Elementary_Functions);
        function Sqrt    (X            : Float_Type'Base)
            return Float_Type'Base;
        function Log     (X            : Float_Type'Base)
            return Float_Type'Base;
        function Log     (X, Base      : Float_Type'Base)
            return Float_Type'Base;
        function Exp     (X            : Float_Type'Base)
            return Float_Type'Base;
        function "**"    (Left, Right  : Float_Type'Base)
            return Float_Type'Base;

        function Sin     (X            : Float_Type'Base)
            return Float_Type'Base;
```

```
function Sin      (X, Cycle    : Float_Type'Base)
   return Float_Type'Base;
function Cos      (X           : Float_Type'Base)
   return Float_Type'Base;
function Cos      (X, Cycle    : Float_Type'Base)
   return Float_Type'Base;
function Tan      (X           : Float_Type'Base)
   return Float_Type'Base;
function Tan      (X, Cycle    : Float_Type'Base)
   return Float_Type'Base;
function Cot      (X           : Float_Type'Base)
   return Float_Type'Base;
function Cot      (X, Cycle    : Float_Type'Base)
   return Float_Type'Base;

function Arcsin  (X           : Float_Type'Base)
   return Float_Type'Base;
function Arcsin  (X, Cycle    : Float_Type'Base)
   return Float_Type'Base;
function Arccos  (X           : Float_Type'Base)
   return Float_Type'Base;
function Arccos  (X, Cycle    : Float_Type'Base)
   return Float_Type'Base;
function Arctan  (Y    : Float_Type'Base;
                  X    : Float_Type'Base := 1.0)
   return Float_Type'Base;
function Arctan  (Y     : Float_Type'Base;
                  X     : Float_Type'Base := 1.0;
                  Cycle : Float_Type'Base)
   return Float_Type'Base;
function Arccot  (X    : Float_Type'Base;
                  Y    : Float_Type'Base := 1.0)
   return Float_Type'Base;
function Arccot  (X     : Float_Type'Base;
                  Y     : Float_Type'Base := 1.0;
                  Cycle : Float_Type'Base)
   return Float_Type'Base;

function Sinh    (X : Float_Type'Base) return Float_Type'Base;
function Cosh    (X : Float_Type'Base) return Float_Type'Base;
function Tanh    (X : Float_Type'Base) return Float_Type'Base;
function Coth    (X : Float_Type'Base) return Float_Type'Base;
function Arcsinh (X : Float_Type'Base) return Float_Type'Base;
function Arccosh (X : Float_Type'Base) return Float_Type'Base;
function Arctanh (X : Float_Type'Base) return Float_Type'Base;
function Arccoth (X : Float_Type'Base) return Float_Type'Base;
```

end Ada.Numerics.Generic_Elementary_Functions;

The set of functions in the above package are similar to those defined in the standard C library header math.h with functions such as:

```
double acos(double);
double asin(double);
double atan(double);
```

The C library simply takes parameters and returns values of type float, so if your application deals with types which logically have a restricted set of values (say some coordinate type with values 0.0 .. 360.0) then you must check each call for violation of those bounds. The Ada example, being a generic, can be instantiated with your coordinate type and will then perform all the required checks for you.

```
with Ada.Numerics.Generic_Elementary_Functions;

procedure Co_Ordinate_Application is

    subtype Co_Ordinate is Float range ..;

    package Math is new Generic_Elementary_Functions (Co_Ordinate);

    Point_X, Point_Y : Co_Ordinate;
begin
    ..
    Point_X := Math.Sin(Point_Y);
    ..
end Co_Ordinate_Application;
```

8.1.2 Character support

Library specification: **package** Ada.Characters.Handling ⎯⎯⎯⎯⎯⎯

```
package Ada.Characters.Handling is
    pragma Preelaborate (Handling);

    function Is_Control      (Item : in Character) return Boolean;
    function Is_Graphic      (Item : in Character) return Boolean;
    function Is_Letter       (Item : in Character) return Boolean;
    function Is_Lower        (Item : in Character) return Boolean;
    function Is_Upper        (Item : in Character) return Boolean;
    function Is_Basic        (Item : in Character) return Boolean;
    function Is_Digit        (Item : in Character) return Boolean;
    function Is_Decimal_Digit (Item : in Character)
        return Boolean renames Is_Digit;
    function Is_Hexadecimal_Digit (Item : in Character)
        return Boolean;
```

```ada
function Is_Alphanumeric (Item : in Character) return Boolean;
function Is_Special      (Item : in Character) return Boolean;

function To_Lower (Item : in Character) return Character;
function To_Upper (Item : in Character) return Character;
function To_Basic (Item : in Character) return Character;

function To_Lower (Item : in String)    return String;
function To_Upper (Item : in String)    return String;
function To_Basic (Item : in String)    return String;

subtype ISO_646 is
   Character range Character'Val (0) .. Character'Val (127);

function Is_ISO_646 (Item : in Character) return Boolean;
function Is_ISO_646 (Item : in String)    return Boolean;

function To_ISO_646
  (Item       : in Character;
   Substitute : in ISO_646 := ' ')
   return       ISO_646;

function To_ISO_646
  (Item       : in String;
   Substitute : in ISO_646 := ' ')
   return       String;

function Is_Character (Item : in Wide_Character)
   return Boolean;
function Is_String    (Item : in Wide_String)
   return Boolean;

function To_Character
  (Item       : in Wide_Character;
   Substitute : in Character := ' ')
   return       Character;

function To_String
  (Item       : in Wide_String;
   Substitute : in Character := ' ')
   return       String;

function To_Wide_Character (Item : in Character)
   return Wide_Character;

function To_Wide_String    (Item : in String)
   return Wide_String;

end Ada.Characters.Handling;
```

The main package for character support is Ada.Characters.Handling, which does the job of the C functions defined in ctype.h. Two sets of functions exist, classification and conversion. Classification functions begin with `Is_` and return `Booleans`, conversion functions begin with `To_` and take characters and return characters or strings.

This package is used in our example, in the keyboard device package, to classify keys as they are read from the keyboard.

As well as the character-to-character conversions, this package also defines some string-to-string conversions, so you do not have to loop through the string converting each character. As well as conversions between ISO-8859-1 (Latin-1) and ISO-10646 (Wide) there are conversions to ISO-646, the original ASCII seven-bit character set.

8.1.3 String support

Ada95 has a very good set of string-handling functions which are much more flexible than the standard C library and provide most of the functionality of the proposed C++ standard `String` class and some more.

The root of these packages is `Ada.Strings`.

Library specification: package `Ada.Strings` ────────────

```
package Ada.Strings is
   pragma Pure (Strings);

   Space       : constant Character      := ' ';
   Wide_Space  : constant Wide_Character := ' ';

   Length_Error, Pattern_Error, Index_Error,
               Translation_Error : exception;

   type Alignment  is (Left, Right, Center);
   type Truncation is (Left, Right, Error);
   type Membership is (Inside, Outside);
   type Direction  is (Forward, Backward);
   type Trim_End   is (Left, Right, Both);

end Ada.Strings;
```

As you can see this package simply declares some standard objects used by child packages.

The Ada library defines three kinds of strings, `Fixed`, `Bounded`, and `Unbounded`. Fixed strings are the array-based string type `Standard.String` (see Section 3.4.2) which is simply an array of characters. `Bounded` and `Unbounded` strings are types used where `Fixed` strings are not flexible enough.

Library specification: package `Ada.Strings.Fixed` ────────────

```
package Ada.Strings.Fixed is
   pragma Preelaborate (Fixed);
```

```
-- "Copy" procedure for strings of possibly
-- different lengths
procedure Move
  (Source  : in   String;
   Target  : out  String;
   Drop    : in   Truncation := Error;
   Justify : in   Alignment  := Left;
   Pad     : in   Character  := Space);

-- Search subprograms
function Index
  (Source  : in String;
   Pattern : in String;
   Going   : in Direction := Forward;
   Mapping : in Maps.Character_Mapping
              := Maps.Identity)
   return    Natural;

function Index
  (Source  : in String;
   Pattern : in String;
   Going   : in Direction := Forward;
   Mapping : in Maps.Character_Mapping_Function)
   return    Natural;

function Index
  (Source : in String;
   Set    : in Maps.Character_Set;
   Test   : in Membership := Inside;
   Going  : in Direction  := Forward)
   return    Natural;

function Index_Non_Blank
  (Source : in String;
   Going  : in Direction := Forward)
   return    Natural;

function Count
  (Source  : in String;
   Pattern : in String;
   Mapping : in Maps.Character_Mapping
              := Maps.Identity)
   return    Natural;

function Count
  (Source  : in String;
   Pattern : in String;
   Mapping : in Maps.Character_Mapping_Function)
   return    Natural;
```

```
function Count
   (Source : in String;
    Set    : in Maps.Character_Set)
    return    Natural;

procedure Find_Token
   (Source : in String;
    Set    : in Maps.Character_Set;
    Test   : in Membership;
    First  : out Positive;
    Last   : out Natural);

-- String translation subprograms
function Translate
   (Source  : in String;
    Mapping : in Maps.Character_Mapping)
    return     String;

procedure Translate
   (Source  : in out String;
    Mapping : in Maps.Character_Mapping);

function Translate
   (Source  : in String;
    Mapping : in Maps.Character_Mapping_Function)
    return     String;

procedure Translate
   (Source  : in out String;
    Mapping : in Maps.Character_Mapping_Function);

function Replace_Slice
   (Source : in String;
    Low    : in Positive;
    High   : in Natural;
    By     : in String)
    return    String;

procedure Replace_Slice
   (Source  : in out String;
    Low     : in Positive;
    High    : in Natural;
    By      : in String;
    Drop    : in Truncation := Error;
    Justify : in Alignment  := Left;
    Pad     : in Character  := Space);
```

```
function Insert
  (Source   : in String;
   Before   : in Positive;
   New_Item : in String)
   return       String;

procedure Insert
  (Source   : in out String;
   Before   : in Positive;
   New_Item : in String;
   Drop     : in Truncation := Error);

function Overwrite
  (Source   : in String;
   Position : in Positive;
   New_Item : in String)
   return       String;

procedure Overwrite
  (Source   : in out String;
   Position : in Positive;
   New_Item : in String;
   Drop     : in Truncation := Right);

function Delete
  (Source   : in String;
   From     : in Positive;
   Through  : in Natural)
   return       String;

procedure Delete
  (Source  : in out String;
   From    : in Positive;
   Through : in Natural;
   Justify : in Alignment := Left;
   Pad     : in Character := Space);

-- String selector subprograms
function Trim
  (Source : in String;
   Side   : in Trim_End)
   return     String;

procedure Trim
  (Source  : in out String;
   Side    : in Trim_End;
   Justify : in Alignment := Left;
   Pad     : in Character := Space);
```

```ada
function Trim
  (Source : in String;
   Left   : in Maps.Character_Set;
   Right  : in Maps.Character_Set)
   return   String;

procedure Trim
  (Source  : in out String;
   Left    : in Maps.Character_Set;
   Right   : in Maps.Character_Set;
   Justify : in Alignment := Strings.Left;
   Pad     : in Character := Space);

function Head
  (Source : in String;
   Count  : in Natural;
   Pad    : in Character := Space)
   return   String;

procedure Head
  (Source  : in out String;
   Count   : in Natural;
   Justify : in Alignment := Left;
   Pad     : in Character := Space);

function Tail
  (Source : in String;
   Count  : in Natural;
   Pad    : in Character := Space)
   return   String;

procedure Tail
  (Source  : in out String;
   Count   : in Natural;
   Justify : in Alignment := Left;
   Pad     : in Character := Space);

-- string constructor functions
function "*"
  (Left  : in Natural;
   Right : in Character)
   return   String;

function "*"
  (Left  : in Natural;
   Right : in String)
   return   String;

end Ada.Strings.Fixed;
```

As you can see a wide range of subprograms and operations are available to operate on the standard string type. Most of the subprograms are self-explanatory, for example `Move`, `Replace_Slice`, `Insert`, `Overwrite`, `Delete`, `Trim`, `Head`, and `Tail` should all be fairly easy to understand although `Index`, `Index_Non_Blank`, `Count`, `Find_Token`, `Translate`, and "`*`" may not be so obvious.

Example 8.2   Using the `Ada.Strings` packages ———————————

Consider the following example which demonstrates most of the features of the basic string-handling package above. The `Translate` functions are covered later in this section.

```ada
-- file: String_Test.adb
with Ada.Strings; use Ada.Strings;
with Ada.Strings.Fixed; use Ada.Strings.Fixed;
with Ada.Text_IO; use Ada.Text_IO;

procedure String_Test is

    String_1 : String := "Hello";
    String_2 : String(1 .. 20);
    String_3 : String := "1234567890ABCDEFGHIJ";
    Result   : Natural;
begin

    Move(Source => String_1,
         Target => String_2,
         Justify => Left);
    Put_Line(" 1: " & String_2 & ".");

    Move(Source => String_1,
         Target => String_2,
         Justify => Right);
    Put_Line(" 2: " & String_2 & ".");

    Move(Source => String_1,
         Target => String_2,
         Justify => Left,
         Pad => '*');
    Put_Line(" 3: " & String_2 & ".");

    Replace_Slice(Source => String_2,
                  Low => String_1'First,
                  High => String_1'Last,
                  By => "HELLO");
    Put_Line(" 4: " & String_2 & ".");
```

```
begin
   Insert(Source => String_2,
          Before => 3,
          New_Item => "mum");

exception
   when Length_Error =>
      Put_Line(" 5: String is now too long!");
end;

Delete(Source => String_2,
       From => String_1'Last,
       Through => String_2'Last);
Put_Line(" 6: " & String_2 & ".");

New_Line;

Put_Line(" 7: " & Head(Source => String_3, Count => 5) & ".");

Put_Line(" 8: " & Tail(Source => String_3, Count => 5) & ".");

Put_Line(" 9: " & (20 * '+') & ".");

Put_Line("10: " & (5 * "Ada ") & ".");

String_3(11 .. 20) := String_3(1 .. 10);
New_Line;

Result := Index(Source => String_3;
                Pattern => "8");

Put_Line("11: First '8' in String_3 is " &
         Natural'Image(Result));

Result := Index(Source => String_3,
                Pattern => "8",
                Going => Backward);
Put_Line("12: Last '8' in String_3 is " &
         Natural'Image(Result));

Result := Ada.Strings.Fixed.Count(Source => String_3,
                                  Pattern => "8");
Put_Line("13: Number of '8' in String_3 is " &
         Natural'Image(Result));
-- full qualification due to a Count specified in
-- the package Ada.Text_IO.

end String_Test;
```

The output from this function looks like this (note the use of the period character to show the length of the strings).

```
 1: Hello              .
 2:                    Hello.
 3: Hello***************.
 4: HELLO***************.
 5: String is now too long!
 6: HELL               .

 7: 12345.
 8: FGHIJ.
 9: +++++++++++++++++++++.
10: Ada Ada Ada Ada Ada .

11: First '8' in String_3 is  8
12: Last '8' in String_3 is  18
13: Number of '8' in String_3 is  2
```

This string package is far superior to facilities specified by the ANSI C standard; the proposed standard for C++ does provide a standard string class. Whether the full facilities provided by the Ada library will be available with all C/C++ compilers is arguable.

Both packages `Ada.Strings.Bounded` and `Ada.Strings.Unbounded` contain declarations of subprograms equivalent to those in the above package and also conversion functions to and from the type `Standard.String`. The packages also have to provide operators `'='`, `'<'`, `'<='`, `'>'`, `'>='`, and `'&'` to match the functionality of the standard string type, as well as an append function to extend the size of the string.

The bounded-length string is instantiated with a maximum size beyond which the string cannot grow; however, the internal storage can be less than this size if the implementation matches storage requirements to the usage of the string. The unbounded-length string has a maximum size which is the largest value possible for the type `Natural` (`Natural'Last`).

Library specification: package Ada.Strings.Maps ⎯⎯⎯⎯⎯⎯⎯⎯⎯⎯⎯⎯

```
package Ada.Strings.Maps is
   pragma Preelaborate (Maps);
   -- Representation for a set of character values
   type Character_Set is private;

   Null_Set : constant Character_Set;

   type Character_Range is record
      Low  : Character;
      High : Character;
   end record;
   -- Represents Character range Low .. High

   type Character_Ranges is array (Positive range <>)
                              of Character_Range;
```

```ada
function To_Set     (Ranges : in Character_Ranges)
   return Character_Set;

function To_Set     (Span   : in Character_Ranges)
   return Character_Set;

function To_Ranges (Set    : in Character_Set)
   return Character_Ranges;

function "="    (Left, Right : in Character_Set)
   return Boolean;

function "not" (Right        : in Character_Set)
   return Character_Set;

function "and" (Left, Right : in Character_Set)
   return Character_Set;

function "or"  (Left, Right : in Character_Set)
   return Character_Set;

function "xor" (Left, Right : in Character_Set)
   return Character_Set;

function "−"    (Left, Right : in Character_Set)
   return Character_Set;

function Is_In
   (Element : in Character;
    Set     : in Character_Set)
    return      Boolean;

function Is_Subset
   (Elements : in Character_Set;
    Set      : in Character_Set)
    return      Boolean;

function "<="
   (Left  : in Character_Set;
    Right : in Character_Set)
    return   Boolean renames Is_Subset;

-- Alternative representation for a set of
-- character values
subtype Character_Sequence is String;

function To_Set (Sequence : in Character_Sequence)
   return Character_Set;

function To_Set (Singleton : in Character)
   return Character_Set;
```

```ada
function To_Sequence (Set : in Character_Set)
   return Character_Sequence;

-- Representation for a character-to-character
-- mapping:
type Character_Mapping is private;

function Value
   (Map     : in Character_Mapping;
    Element : in Character)
   return    Character;

Identity : constant Character_Mapping;

function To_Mapping
   (From, To : in Character_Sequence)
   return     Character_Mapping;

function To_Domain
   (Map : in Character_Mapping)
   return Character_Sequence;

function To_Range
   (Map : in Character_Mapping)
   return Character_Sequence;

type Character_Mapping_Function is
   access function (From : in Character)
      return Character;

private
   ..
end Ada.Strings.Maps;
```

This package allows you to change characters in a string using either a static map or a mapping function. The child package `Ada.Strings.Maps.Constant` provides a set of maps which covers the most common usage.

The create database program uses the map `Lower_Case_Map` to convert program arguments to lower case before comparing them against expected values, thus providing case-insensitive argument handling.

```ada
begin
   for Argument in 1 .. Ada.Command_Line.Argument_Count loop

      declare
         Arg_String : String :=
            Translate(Ada.Command_Line.Argument(Argument),
            Ada.Strings.Maps.Constants.Lower_Case_Map);
```

```
      begin
        if Arg_String = "all" then
        ..
```

The `Translate` function converts characters in a string using a translation table
(`Character_Set` type) and returns the resulting string.
      The handling of command line arguments and the above example are described
more fully in Section 8.3.1.

8.1.4   Access type support

We mentioned in Section 3.5.2 that we can achieve the equivalent of overloading the
new and `delete` operators in C++. In Ada95 dynamically allocated objects are called
pool-specific as they are allocated from a storage pool and so to implement our own
allocation strategy we require our own storage pool.

Library specification: package `System.Storage_Pools` ────────────

```
  with Ada.Finalization;
  with System.Storage_Elements;

  package System.Storage_Pools is
     pragma Preelaborate (System.Storage_Pools);

     type Root_Storage_Pool is abstract
        new Ada.Finalization.Limited_Controlled with private;

     procedure Allocate
        (Pool                        : in out Root_Storage_Pool;
         Storage_Address             : out Address;
         Size_In_Storage_Elements : in
                            System.Storage_Elements.Storage_Count;
         Alignment                   : in
                            System.Storage_Elements.Storage_Count)
        is abstract;

     procedure Deallocate
        (Pool                        : in out Root_Storage_Pool;
         Storage_Address             : in Address;
         Size_In_Storage_Elements : in
                            System.Storage_Elements.Storage_Count;
         Alignment                   : in
                            System.Storage_Elements.Storage_Count)
        is abstract;

     function Storage_Size
        (Pool : Root_Storage_Pool)
        return System.Storage_Elements.Storage_Count
        is abstract;
```

private
    ..
end System.Storage_Pools;

The package above provides an abstract tagged type called Root_Storage_Pool
which when extended allows us to implement a storage pool.

The following example demonstrates how to implement a storage pool and then
how to designate that types use a specific pool. The example is a storage pool which
allocates objects in some form of shared memory.
As the storage pool is descended from a controlled type (see Section 8.1.6
for a discussion of controlled types), not only the abstract operations of Root_
Storage_Pool but also the abstract operations of Limited_Controlled must
be implemented.

Example 8.3   Implementing a storage pool ────────────────────────────

```
-- file: Shared_Pool.ads
with System.Storage_Pools;
with System.Storage_Elements;
use  System;

package Shared_Pool is

   type Pool_Name is access constant String;

   type Pool(Size : Storage_Elements.Storage_Count;
             Name : Pool_Name) is
      new Storage_Pools.Root_Storage_Pool with private;

   procedure Allocate
      (The_Pool                  : in out Pool;
       Storage_Address           : out Address;
       Size_In_Storage_Elements: in Storage_Elements.Storage_Count;
       Alignment                 : in Storage_Elements.Storage_Count);

   procedure Deallocate
      (The_Pool                  : in out Pool;
       Storage_Address           : out Address;
       Size_In_Storage_Elements: in Storage_Elements.Storage_Count;
       Alignment                 : in Storage_Elements.Storage_Count);

   function Storage_Size
      (The_Pool : in Pool)
       return Storage_Elements.Storage_Count;
```

```
   private

      procedure Initialize (Object : in out Pool);
      procedure Finalize   (Object : in out Pool);

      type Pool(Size : Storage_Elements.Storage_Count;
                Name : Pool_Name) is
        new Storage_Pools.Root_Storage_Pool with
        record
              .. -- implementation defined.
        end record;

   end Shared_Pool;
```

Now that we have a storage pool we can use it to share some data between our application and any other application that can access the shared memory.

The following example declares an object of the new `Shared_Pool.Pool` type to manage our shared memory (the `Size` discriminant is in storage elements, and so must be big enough to cater for all objects we wish to allocate). The example then continues by declaring a structure `App_Statistics` and an access type `Statistics_Ptr` which will hold our shared data. Then we use the attribute `'storage_Pool` to inform the compiler that all allocation for the type `Statistics_Ptr` must be done through our new storage pool.

Example 8.4   Using a specific storage pool ————————————————

```
   -- file: Pool_Test.adb
   with Shared_Pool;

   procedure Pool_Test is

      Pool_Name       : aliased constant String := "stats";
      Statistics_Pool : Shared_Pool.Pool(1024,
                                         Pool_Name'Unchecked_Access);

      type App_Statistics is
        record
            ..
        end record;

      type Statistics_Ptr is access App_Statistics;
      for Statistics_Ptr'Storage_Pool use Statistics_Pool;

      Shared_Statistics : Statistics_Ptr;
   begin
      Shared_Statistics := new App_Statistics;
      -- the above is now satisfied from our shared memory
      -- storage pool Statistics_Pool.
      ..
   end Pool_Test;
```

This mechanism is not as elegant as the C++ solution, overriding `new` and `delete`, and because Ada does not allow you to overload de-reference operators, managing storage is not as easy as in C++. This said, the differing requirements of C++ and Ada make this inevitable.

8.1.5   Exception support

The co-dependency between the language itself (specifically attributes) and the library is also to be found when dealing with exceptions.

Library specification: package `Ada.Exceptions` ⎯⎯⎯⎯⎯⎯⎯⎯⎯⎯⎯⎯⎯

```
package Ada.Exceptions is

   type Exception_Id is private;

   Null_Id : constant Exception_Id;
   function Exception_Name (X : Exception_Id) return String;

   type Exception_Occurrence is limited private
   type Exception_Occurrence_Access is
      access all Exception_Occurrence;

   Null_Occurrence : constant Exception_Occurrence;

   procedure Raise_Exception
      (E       : in Exception_Id;
       Message : in String := "");

   function Exception_Message
      (X : Exception_Occurrence) return String;

   procedure Reraise_Occurrence
      (X : Exception_Occurrence);

   function Exception_Identity
      (X : Exception_Occurrence) return Exception_Id;

   function Exception_Name
      (X : Exception_Occurrence) return String;

   function Exception_Information
      (X : Exception_Occurrence) return String;

   procedure Save_Occurrence
      (Target :     out Exception_Occurrence;
       Source : in      Exception_Occurrence);

   function Save_Occurrence
      (Source : in Exception_Occurrence)
       return Exception_Occurrence_Access;
end Ada.Exceptions;
```

The type `Exception_Id` above is vitally important as it is returned by the attribute `'Identity` applied to an exception name.

This package has two important implications. Firstly by using the 'Identity attribute and the library subprogram Raise_Exception you can associate a message with the exception, providing diagnostic or context information. The example below shows how to associate a message with an exception and how to display the message in the exception handler.

```ada
with Ada.Exceptions; use Ada.Exceptions;
with Ada.Text_IO; use Ada.Text_IO;

procedure Exception_Test is

   My_Exception : exception;
begin

   Raise_Exception(My_Exception'Identity, "Whoops");

exception
   when An_Occurrence : My_Exception =>
      Put_Line("My_Exception raised, Message = " &
               Exception_Message(An_Occurrence));
end Exception_Test;
```

That part of the exception handler between the **when** and the => is now treated as a declaration with An_Occurrence an instance of the type Exception_ Occurrence declared in the library package above. This means that any of the sub-programs taking a parameter of type Exception_Occurrence can use the newly introduced object (note that the object is a constant and cannot be changed in any way).

This plays a big part in the second usage of this package – saving exceptions. For example consider a program where two tasks are running. The first is executing almost constantly, querying some resource and placing data in a protected type to be read by the second task. If the first task receives an exception while processing the resource, it needs to inform the reading task of an error. It could of course simply place an error record into the buffer, but it would not identify the actual exception, so we can save the exception and raise it when the client reads the buffer.

```ada
..
   protected body Shared_Buffer is
      type Actual_Node is limited
         record
            Is_Data      : Boolean := True;
            Data         : Data_Type;
            An_Exception : Exception_Occurrence;
         end record;

      Actual_Buffer : array(1 .. 1000) of Actual_Node;
      First, Last : Natural;
```

```
procedure Write_Exception(Actual : Exception_Occurrence) is
begin
    Actual_Buffer(Last).Is_Data := False;
    Save_Occurrence(Actual_Buffer(Last).An_Exception,
                    Actual);

    ..

end Write_Exception;

function Read return Data_Type is
begin
    if not Actual_Buffer(First).Is_Data then
        Reraise_Exception(Actual_Buffer(First).An_Exception);
    ..
end Read;
end Shared_Buffer;

task body Resource_Handler is
begin
    loop
        begin
            Buffer.Write_Data(..);
        exception
            when Actual : others =>
                Buffer.Write_Exception(Actual);
        end;
    end loop;
end Resource_Handler;

..
```

The incomplete example above shows how the buffer can store either data items or exceptions and can re-raise an exception to inform the client of the error indicated by the resource handler.

8.1.6   Tagged type support

Library specification: **package** Ada.Tags ─────────────────────────────

```
package Ada.Tags is

    type Tag is private;

    function Expanded_Name (T : Tag) return String;
    function External_Tag  (T : Tag) return String;
    function Internal_Tag  (External : String) return Tag;

    Tag_Error : exception;
```

```
private
  ..
end Ada.Tags;
```

The first package we introduce here is used to create internal and external tags for a tagged type.

Tagged types are another example of where the language and the library meet – an internal tag is the value returned by the attribute 'Tag and is of type Tag defined in this package. It is also the value used by the run-time to perform dispatched operations and so is an integral part of the language. An external tag is a human readable string containing the fully qualified name of the type (we introduced this idea in Section 6.3.2).

The following text is the output from a hex dump program which inspected the log file managed by the Ada_Store.Log package. The block of text on the right clearly shows the name of the tagged type which was written to the file, the stream IO package obviously uses the external tag of the type as part of the identification when read back in.

```
00000000 010000002A000000 — 4144415F53544F52 : ....*...ADA_STOR
00000016 452E504F53542E41 — 50504C4943415449 : E.POST.APPLICATI
00000032 4F4E2E4150504C49 — 434154494F4E5F4C : ON.APPLICATION_L
00000048 4F47000200000000 — A73C8D21FF750B01 : OG.......<.!.u..
```

The next package was hinted at in Section 6.4.5 as a way of synthesizing constructors and destructors for tagged types.

Library specification: package Ada.Finalization ⎯⎯⎯⎯⎯⎯⎯⎯⎯⎯

```
package Ada.Finalization is
pragma Preelaborate (Finalization);

    type Controlled is abstract tagged private;

    procedure Initialize (Object : in out Controlled);
    procedure Adjust     (Object : in out Controlled);
    procedure Finalize   (Object : in out Controlled);

    type Limited_Controlled is abstract tagged limited private;

    procedure Initialize (Object : in out Limited_Controlled);
    procedure Finalize   (Object : in out Limited_Controlled);

private
  ..
end Ada.Finalization;
```

When a tagged type is derived from one of the two types in this package certain *facilities* are provided.

The reason for the two types in this package is that if the derived type is declared as limited private then there is no need for an `Adjust` operator and so you can derive from the `Limited Controlled` type for limited derived types.

Let us consider a simple example first. We will construct a dummy package called `Final` which declares a type derived from `Controlled` and where each of the operators is overloaded to print its name.

Example 8.5 Using finalization ————————————————————————————

```
-- file: Final.ads
with Ada.Finalization;

package Final is

    type Example is new Ada.Finalization.Controlled with
        null record;

private
    procedure Initialize (Object : in out Example);
    procedure Adjust      (Object : in out Example);
    procedure Finalize    (Object : in out Example);
end Final;

-- file: Final.adb
with Ada.Text_IO;
use Ada;

package body Final is

    procedure Initialize (Object : in out Example) is
    begin
        Text_IO.Put_Line("Initialize");
    end Initialize;

    procedure Adjust      (Object : in out Example) is
    begin
        Text_IO.Put_Line("Adjust");
    end Adjust;

    procedure Finalize    (Object : in out Example) is
    begin
        Text_IO.Put_Line("Finalize");
    end Finalize;

end Final;
```

Note: the operators inherited from the type `Controlled` are put into the private part of our package by convention only.

We can now look at an example program to see what the effect of all this is. You will see that the example tries to use many ways to create objects, simply at lines 7 and 8, as an access type at line 13 and with an initializer at line 18.

```
 1 with Final;
 2
 3 procedure Final_Test is
 4
 5     type Example_Ptr is access Final.Example;
 6
 7     Ex_1 : Final.Example;
 8     Ex_2 : Final.Example;
 9     Ex_3 : Example_Ptr;
10 begin
11     Ex_1 := Ex_2;
12
13     Ex_3 := new Final.Example;
14
15     Ex_3.all := Ex_2;
16
17     declare
18         Ex_4 : Final.Example := Ex_2;
19     begin
20         null;
21     end;
22
23 end Final_Test;
```

The following is the output from running the test above (the line number information on the right was added afterwards):

```
F:\SRC\ADA\TEST>final_test
Initialize                        <= Line 7
Initialize                        <= Line 8
Finalize                          <= Line 11
Adjust                            <= Line 11
Initialize                        <= Line 13
Finalize                          <= Line 15
Adjust                            <= Line 15
Adjust                            <= Line 18
Finalize                          <= Line 21
Finalize                          <= Line 23
Finalize                          <= Line 23
Finalize                          <= Line 23
```

Lines 7 and 8 provide few surprises; the `Initialize` operation is called when the object is constructed as it is when we create an object dynamically at line 13. If we look at the assignments, however (lines 11 and 15), we see that before the `Adjust` operator is called, the `Finalize` is called. This last point is important when we look at line 18 where we declare a new object and immediately assign to it; no `Initialize` was called. Because the `Adjust` operator can make no assumption about the state of the operator it can be called without an explicit `Initialize`.

In C++ constructors may take parameters; in Ada if we declare a type derived from either `Controlled` or `Limited_Controlled` then we have a constructor/ destructor-like mechanism and if we declare our type with discriminants then we can in effect pass parameters that are available to the operators above.

8.1.7   Decimal type support

Although decimal types are part of the language itself the support packages specified for them are part of Annex F – Information Systems (Section 9.5).

8.2   Input/output

A common area for confusion is the Ada IO model. This has been shaped by the nature of the language itself and specifically the strong typing which has a direct impact on the model used to construct the IO libraries. If you think about it briefly it is quite clear that with the typing rules we have introduced above you cannot write a function such as the C `write()` which takes anything and puts it out to a file. How can you write a function that will take any parameter, even types that will be introduced after it has been completed? Ada83 took a two-pronged approach to IO, with the package `Text_IO` for simple, textual input/output, and the packages `Sequential_IO` and `Direct_IO` which are generic packages for binary output of structured data.

The most common problem for C and C++ programmers is the lack of the `printf` family of IO functions. There is a good reason for their absence in Ada. C uses variable arguments, the '...' at the end of the `printf` function specification. Ada cannot support such a construct since the type of each parameter is unknown.

8.2.1   Ada.Text_IO

The common way to do console-like IO, similar to C's `printf()`, `puts()`, and `putchar()` is to use **package** `Ada.Text_IO`.

Library specification: package `Ada.Text_IO` ───────────────────

```
package Ada.Text_IO is

    type File_Type is limited private;

    type File_Mode is (In_File, Out_File, Append_File);
```

```
type Count is range 0 .. -- implementation defined
subtype Positive_Count is Count range 1 .. Count'Last;
Unbounded : constant Count := 0;

subtype Field is Integer range 0 .. -- implementation
subtype Number_Base is Integer range 2 .. 16;

type Type_Set is (Lower_Case, Upper_Case);

-- File Management

procedure Create
  (File : in out File_Type;
   Mode : in File_Mode := Out_File;
   Name : in String := "";
   Form : in String := "");

procedure Open
  (File : in out File_Type;
   Mode : in File_Mode;
   Name : in String;
   Form : in String := "");

procedure Close  (File : in out File_Type);
procedure Delete (File : in out File_Type);
procedure Reset  (File : in out File_Type;
                  Mode : in File_Mode);
procedure Reset  (File : in out File_Type);

function Mode (File : in File_Type) return File_Mode;
function Name (File : in File_Type) return String;
function Form (File : in File_Type) return String;

function Is_Open (File : in File_Type) return Boolean;

-- Control of default input, output and error files

procedure Set_Input  (File : in File_Type);
procedure Set_Output (File : in File_Type);
procedure Set_Error  (File : in File_Type);

function Standard_Input   return File_Type;
function Standard_Output  return File_Type;
function Standard_Error   return File_Type;

function Current_Input   return File_Type;
function Current_Output  return File_Type;
function Current_Error   return File_Type;

type File_Access is access constant File_Type;

function Standard_Input   return File_Access;
```

```
function Standard_Output return File_Access;
function Standard_Error  return File_Access;

function Current_Input  return File_Access;
function Current_Output return File_Access;
function Current_Error  return File_Access;

-- Buffer control

procedure Flush (File : in File_Type);
procedure Flush;

-- Specification of line and page lengths

procedure Set_Line_Length (File : in File_Type; To : in Count);
procedure Set_Line_Length (To : in Count);

procedure Set_Page_Length (File : in File_Type; To : in Count);
procedure Set_Page_Length (To : in Count);

function Line_Length (File : in File_Type) return Count;
function Line_Length return Count;

function Page_Length (File : in File_Type) return Count;
function Page_Length return Count;

-- Column, Line, and Page Control

procedure New_Line (File    : in File_Type;
                    Spacing : in Positive_Count := 1);
procedure New_Line (Spacing : in Positive_Count := 1);

procedure Skip_Line (File    : in File_Type;
                     Spacing : in Positive_Count := 1);
procedure Skip_Line (Spacing : in Positive_Count := 1);

function End_Of_Line (File : in File_Type) return Boolean;
function End_Of_Line return Boolean;

procedure New_Page (File : in File_Type);
procedure New_Page;

procedure Skip_Page (File : in File_Type);
procedure Skip_Page;

function End_Of_Page (File : in File_Type) return Boolean;
function End_Of_Page return Boolean;

function End_Of_File (File : in File_Type) return Boolean;
function End_Of_File return Boolean;

procedure Set_Col (File : in File_Type;
                   To   : in Positive_Count);
```

```
procedure Set_Col (To : in Positive_Count);

procedure Set_Line (File : in File_Type;
                    To   : in Positive_Count);
procedure Set_Line (To   : in Positive_Count);

function Col (File : in File_Type) return Positive_Count;
function Col return Positive_Count;

function Line (File : in File_Type) return Positive_Count;
function Line return Positive_Count;

function Page (File : in File_Type) return Positive_Count;
function Page return Positive_Count;

-- Characters Input-Output

procedure Get (File : in File_Type; Item : out Character);
procedure Get (Item : out Character);

procedure Put (File : in File_Type; Item : in Character);
procedure Put (Item : in Character);

procedure Look_Ahead (File        : in File_Type;
                      Item        : out Character;
                      End_Of_Line : out Boolean);
procedure Look_Ahead (Item        : out Character;
                      End_Of_Line : out Boolean);

procedure Get_Immediate (File      : in File_Type;
                         Item      : out Character);
procedure Get_Immediate (Item      : out Character);
procedure Get_Immediate (File      : in File_Type;
                         Item      : out Character;
                         Available : out Boolean);
procedure Get_Immediate (Item      : out Character;
                         Available : out Boolean);

-- String Input-Output

procedure Get (File : in File_Type; Item : out String);
procedure Get (Item : out String);

procedure Put (File : in File_Type; Item : in String);
procedure Put (Item : in String);

procedure Get_Line (File : in File_Type;
                    Item : out String;
                    Last : out Natural);
procedure Get_Line (Item : out String;
                    Last : out Natural);
```

```
procedure Put_Line (File : in File_Type;
                    Item : in String);
procedure Put_Line (Item : in String);

generic
   type Num is range <>;
package Integer_IO is
   ..
end Integer_IO;

generic
   type Num is mod <>;
package Modular_IO is
   ..
end Modular_IO;

generic
   type Num is digits <>;
package Float_IO is
   ..
end Float_IO;

generic
   type Num is delta <>;
package Fixed_IO is
   ..
end Fixed_IO;

generic
   type Num is delta <> digits <>;
package Decimal_IO is
   ..
end Decimal_IO;

generic
   type Enum is (<>);
package Enumeration_IO is
   ..
end Enumeration_IO;

-- Exceptions

Status_Error : exception renames IO_Exceptions.Status_Error;
Mode_Error   : exception renames IO_Exceptions.Mode_Error;
Name_Error   : exception renames IO_Exceptions.Name_Error;
Use_Error    : exception renames IO_Exceptions.Use_Error;
Device_Error : exception renames IO_Exceptions.Device_Error;
End_Error    : exception renames IO_Exceptions.End_Error;
Data_Error   : exception renames IO_Exceptions.Data_Error;
Layout_Error : exception renames IO_Exceptions.Layout_Error;
```

end Ada.Text_IO;

This provides a set of overloaded functions called Put and Get to read and write to the screen or to simple text files. There are also functions to open and close such files, to check end of file conditions, and to do line and page management. The basic text input and output is far more comprehensive than that provided by the C library *package* stdio though possibly not as flexible as the C++ stream's input/output facility.

One point not covered by any of the Ada library input/output packages is file concurrency, i.e. share modes on open and create, and file and record locking. Because Ada is designed to work in environments such as small embedded computers where such facilities are not required, the library has left them out.

Note: I have left out the specifications for the nested generic packages as they are all the same, providing Get and Put functions.

Below is the obligatory *hello world* example program again:

```
with Ada.Text_IO;
use   Ada.Text_IO;

procedure Hello_World is
begin
    Put_Line("Hello Brave New World!");
end Hello_World;
```

It is also possible to use one of the generic child packages of Ada.Text_IO such as Ada.Text_IO.Integer_IO which can be instantiated with a particular type to provide type safe textual IO for numerics.

Example 8.6   Simple test of the Ada.Text_IO package ─────────────

```
-- file: IO_Test1.adb
with Ada.Text_IO;
use   Ada.Text_IO;

procedure IO_Test1 is

    package My_Integer_IO is new Integer_IO(Integer);
    use My_Integer_IO;

    package My_Float_IO is new Float_IO(Float);
    use My_Float_IO;
begin
    Put_Line("Test Starts Here >");
    Put("Integer is ");
    Put(2);
    New_Line;
    Put("Float is    ");
    Put(2.0);
```

```
      New_Line;
      Put_Line("Test Ends Here");
   end IO_Test1;
```

The program below uses the attribute `'Image` defined for all scalar types which gives back a `String` representation of a value to achieve the same as above:

```
   -- file: IO_Test2.adb
   with Ada.Text_IO;
   use  Ada.Text_IO;

   procedure IO_Test2 is
   begin
      Put_Line("Test Starts Here >");
      Put_Line("Integer is " & Integer'Image(2));
      Put_Line("Float is   " & Float'Image(2.0));
      Put_Line("Test Ends Here");
   end IO_Test2;
```

8.2.2   Ada.Sequential_IO and Ada.Direct_IO

These two generic packages provide input/output facilities for files that contain mult-iple records of a single type.

Library specification: package Ada.Sequential_IO ————————————

```
   generic
      type Element_Type (<>) is private;

   package Ada.Sequential_IO is

      type File_Type is limited private;

      type File_Mode is (In_File, Out_File, Append_File);

      procedure Create
        (File : in out File_Type;
         Mode : in File_Mode := Out_File;
         Name : in String := "";
         Form : in String := "");

      procedure Open
        (File : in out File_Type;
         Mode : in File_Mode;
         Name : in String;
         Form : in String := "");

      procedure Close  (File : in out File_Type);
      procedure Delete (File : in out File_Type);
```

```
procedure Reset
  (File : in out File_Type;
   Mode : in File_Mode);
procedure Reset  (File : in out File_Type);

function Mode     (File : in File_Type) return File_Mode;
function Name     (File : in File_Type) return String;
function Form     (File : in File_Type) return String;

function Is_Open (File : in File_Type) return Boolean;

procedure Read   (File : in File_Type; Item : out Element_Type);
procedure Write  (File : in File_Type; Item : in Element_Type);

function End_Of_File (File : in File_Type) return Boolean;

Status_Error : exception renames IO_Exceptions.Status_Error;
Mode_Error   : exception renames IO_Exceptions.Mode_Error;
Name_Error   : exception renames IO_Exceptions.Name_Error;
Use_Error    : exception renames IO_Exceptions.Use_Error;
Device_Error : exception renames IO_Exceptions.Device_Error;
End_Error    : exception renames IO_Exceptions.End_Error;
Data_Error   : exception renames IO_Exceptions.Data_Error;

end Ada.Sequential_IO;
```

This package provides access to the records in the file in a sequential manner. The implication of this is that other than the obvious open, create, and close operations there are only read and write operations, and no seek or find operations.

Library specification: package Ada.Direct_IO —————————————————

```
generic
   type Element_Type is private;

package Ada.Direct_IO is

   type File_Type is limited private;

   type File_Mode is (In_File, Inout_File, Out_File);

   type Count is range 0 .. implementation_defined;

   subtype Positive_Count is Count range
                          1 .. Count'Last;

   -- File management
   procedure Create
     (File : in out File_Type;
      Mode : in File_Mode := Inout_File;
      Name : in String := "";
      Form : in String := "");
```

```
procedure Open
  (File : in out File_Type;
   Mode : in File_Mode;
   Name : in String;
   Form : in String := "");

procedure Close  (File : in out File_Type);
procedure Delete (File : in out File_Type);
procedure Reset
  (File : in out File_Type;
   Mode : in File_Mode);
procedure Reset  (File : in out File_Type);

function Mode (File : in File_Type) return File_Mode;
function Name (File : in File_Type) return String;
function Form (File : in File_Type) return String;

function Is_Open (File : in File_Type) return Boolean;

-- Input and output operations
procedure Read
  (File : in File_Type;
   Item : out Element_Type;
   From : in Positive_Count);
procedure Read
  (File : in File_Type;
   Item : out Element_Type);

procedure Write
  (File : in File_Type;
   Item : in Element_Type;
   To   : in Positive_Count);
procedure Write
  (File : in File_Type;
   Item : in Element_Type);

procedure Set_Index
  (File : in File_Type;
   To   : in Positive_Count);

function Index (File : in File_Type) return Positive_Count;
function Size  (File : in File_Type) return Count;

function End_Of_File (File : in File_Type) return Boolean;

Status_Error : exception renames IO_Exceptions.Status_Error;
Mode_Error   : exception renames IO_Exceptions.Mode_Error;
Name_Error   : exception renames IO_Exceptions.Name_Error;
Use_Error    : exception renames IO_Exceptions.Use_Error;
```

```
      Device_Error : exception renames IO_Exceptions.Device_Error;
      End_Error    : exception renames IO_Exceptions.End_Error;
      Data_Error   : exception renames IO_Exceptions.Data_Error;

   end Ada.Direct_IO;
```

This package provides far more flexibility over the management of the records in the
file as it provides true random access. To support random access to the file the
concept of an index, or record number, is introduced with the additional operations
`Set_Index` which moves you to the specified record and `Index` which returns your
current position in the file. Both the `Read` and `Write` operations are also overloaded with operations that provide the index of the record to operate on.

These two packages can be instantiated in a similar way to the generic text IO
packages above; consider the following, for example.

Example 8.7   Using direct IO

```
-- file: Direct_Test.adb
with Ada.Direct_IO;

procedure Direct_Test is

   type File_Header is
      record
         Magic_Number      : Special_Stamp;
         Number_Of_Records : Record_Number;
         First_Deleted     : Record_Number;
      end record;

   type Row is
      record
         Key  : String(1 .. 80);
         Data : String(1 .. 255);
      end record;

   package Header_IO is new Direct_IO (File_Header);

   package Row_IO    is new Direct_IO (Row);
   ..
end Direct_Test;
```

Now that we have some instantiated packages we can read and write records
and headers to and from a file. However, we want each database file to consist of a
header followed by a number of rows, so we try the following:

```
declare
   Handle   : Header_IO.File_Type;
   A_Header : File_Header;
   A_Row    : Row;
```

```
  begin
     Header_IO.Open(File => Handle, Name => "Test");

     Header_IO.Write(Handle, A_Header);

     Row_IO.Write(Handle, A_Row);

     Header_IO.Close(Handle);
  end;
```

The error in the code above is that `Handle` is defined as a type exported from the `Header_IO` package and so cannot be passed to the procedure `Write` from the package `Row_IO`. This strong typing means that both `Sequential_IO` and `Direct_IO` are designed only to work on files containing all elements of the same type.

When designing a package, if you want to avoid this sort of problem (the designers of these packages did intend this restriction) then you could embed the generic part within an enclosing package, thus:

```
  package generic_IO is

     type File_Type is limited private;

     procedure Create(File : File_Type ....
     procedure Close .....

     generic
        type Element_Type is private;
     package Read_Write is

        procedure Read
          (File : File_Type;
           Element : Element_Type ...
        procedure Write .....
     end Read_Write;

  end generic_IO;
```

This would make our database package look something like:

```
  with generic_IO;
  package body A_Database is

     type File_Header is
        record
           Magic_Number   : Special_Stamp;
           Number_Of_Records : Record_Number;
           First_Deleted : Record_Number;
        end record;
```

```
type Row is
   record
      Key              : String(1 .. 80);
      Data             : String(1 .. 255);
   end record;

package Header_IO is new generic_IO.Read_Write (File_Header);

package Row_IO    is new generic_IO.Read_Write (Row);

Handle    : generic_IO.File_Type;
A_Header  : File_Header;
A_Row     : Row;
begin
   generic_IO.Open(File => Handle, Name => "Test");

   Header_IO.Write(Handle, A_Header);

   Row_IO.Write(Handle, A_Row);

   generic_IO.Close(Handle);
end A_Database;
```

8.2.3   Streams

Streams are a new feature of Ada95 added to counter the need for input/output based on heterogeneous data structures made from tagged types. Ada streams are superficially similar to the stream library in C++ and as we have found in a number of cases both have advantages and disadvantages.

C++ IO streams

The C++ stream library provides the basic functionality for opening, closing, and moving around streams and for setting input and output flags. If you then want to write an object of a user-defined type into a stream, you must add specific code to that user-defined type to allow it to be written to or read from a stream.

Example 8.8   Using C++ streams ————————————————————————

For example we may wish to be able to use streams to manage our database of users, based around the following class definition.

```
class User {
public:
   ..
private:
   String Name;
   String Address;
   int    Security;
};
```

We cannot simply use the stream operators to write out an instance of `User` as the stream does not know what the user looks like. We have to write overloaded stream operators explicitly to read and write a user.

```
class User {
public:
    ..
    friend ostream& operator<< (ostream& strm, const User& usr);
    friend istream& operator>> (istream& strm, User& usr);
private:
    ..
};

inline ostream& operator<< (ostream& strm, const User& usr)
{
    strm << Name << Address << Security;

    return strm;
}

inline istream& operator>> (istream& strm, User& usr)
{
    strm >> Name >> Address >> Security;

    return strm;
}
```

We can now write out a user object into a stream:

```
{
    ostream  usrstrm("Users.dat");
    User     Manager("Simon Johnston", "..", 1);

    usrstrm << Manager;
}
```

The C++ stream library is extremely important, though it does require some work of the object designer to decide which objects require stream operators and so forth.

Library specification: package `Ada.Streams` ─────────────

```
package Ada.Streams is
    pragma Pure (Streams);

    type Root_Stream_Type is abstract tagged limited private;

    type Stream_Element is mod    -- implementation defined

    type Stream_Element_Offset is range    -- implementation defined
```

```
subtype Stream_Element_Count is
   Stream_Element_Offset range 0 .. Stream_Element_Offset'Last;
type Stream_Element_Array is
   array (Stream_Element_Offset range <>) of Stream_Element;

procedure Read
   (Stream : in out Root_Stream_Type;
    Item   : out Stream_Element_Array;
    Last   : out Stream_Element_Offset) is abstract;

procedure Write
   (Stream : in out Root_Stream_Type;
    Item   : in Stream_Element_Array) is abstract;

end Ada.Streams;
```

This package provides the abstract `Root_Stream_Type` which is analogous to the `ios` part of the C++ stream library. All stream types must support both the `Read` and `Write` operations as specified in the abstract above.

Library specification: package Ada.Streams.Stream_IO ──────────

```
with Ada.IO_Exceptions;

package Ada.Streams.Stream_IO is

   type Stream_Access is access all Root_Stream_Type'Class;

   type File_Type is limited private;

   type File_Mode is (In_File, Out_File, Append_File);

   type Count is range 0 .. -- implementation defined

   subtype Positive_Count is Count range 1 .. Count'Last;

   -- Index into file, in stream elements

   procedure Create
      (File : in out File_Type;
       Mode : in File_Mode := Out_File;
       Name : in String := "";
       Form : in String := "");

   procedure Open
      (File : in out File_Type;
       Mode : in File_Mode;
       Name : in String;
       Form : in String := "");

   procedure Close  (File : in out File_Type);
   procedure Delete (File : in out File_Type);
```

```ada
procedure Reset
  (File : in out File_Type;
   Mode : in File_Mode);

procedure Reset (File : in out File_Type);

function Mode (File : in File_Type) return File_Mode;
function Name (File : in File_Type) return String;
function Form (File : in File_Type) return String;

function Is_Open    (File : in File_Type) return Boolean;
function End_Of_File (File : in File_Type) return Boolean;

function Stream (File : in File_Type) return Stream_Access;
   -- Return stream access for use with T'Input and T'Output

-- Read array of stream elements from file
procedure Read
  (File : in File_Type;
   Item : out Stream_Element_Array;
   Last : out Stream_Element_Offset;
   From : in Positive_Count);

procedure Read
  (File : in File_Type;
   Item : out Stream_Element_Array;
   Last : out Stream_Element_Offset);

-- Write array of stream elements into file
procedure Write
  (File : in File_Type;
   Item : in Stream_Element_Array;
   To   : in Positive_Count);

procedure Write
  (File : in File_Type;
   Item : in Stream_Element_Array);

-- Operations on Position within File
procedure Set_Index
  (File : in File_Type;
   To   : in Positive_Count);

function Index (File : in File_Type) return Positive_Count;
function Size  (File : in File_Type) return Count;

procedure Set_Mode
   (File : in out File_Type;
    Mode : in File_Mode);

procedure Flush (File : in out File_Type);
```

```
-- Exceptions
Status_Error : exception renames IO_Exceptions.Status_Error;
Mode_Error   : exception renames IO_Exceptions.Mode_Error;
Name_Error   : exception renames IO_Exceptions.Name_Error;
Use_Error    : exception renames IO_Exceptions.Use_Error;
Device_Error : exception renames IO_Exceptions.Device_Error;
End_Error    : exception renames IO_Exceptions.End_Error;
Data_Error   : exception renames IO_Exceptions.Data_Error;
```

end Ada.Streams.Stream_IO;

This is the main stream package, and has all the operations required to open or create the file and convert the file type to a stream type. The operations on streams defined here are supplemented by a set of important stream attributes.

Library specification: **package** Ada.Text_IO.Text_Streams

with Ada.Streams;

package Ada.Text_IO.Text_Streams **is**

    type Stream_Access **is access all**
                              Streams.Root_Streams_Type'Class;

    function Stream(File : **in** File_Type) **return** Stream_Access;
end Ada.Text_IO.Text_Streams;

The library package above provides a constructor for a stream that is text-based; the previous package supports only binary streams.

Stream attributes

The following stream attributes are defined for all types, which means that unlike C++ any type can be written to a stream or read from one.

```
procedure A_Type'Write
  (S_Stream : access Ada.Streams.Root_Stream_Type'Class;
   An_Item  : A_Type);

function A_Type'Read
  (S_Stream : access Ada.Streams.Root_Stream_Type'Class)
   return A_Type;

procedure A_Type'Class'Write
  (S_Stream : access Ada.Streams.Root_Stream_Type'Class;
   An_Item  : A_Type'Class);

function A_Type'Class'Read
  (S_Stream : access Ada.Streams.Root_Stream_Type'Class)
   return A_Type'Class;
```

```
procedure A_Type'Output
   (S_Stream : access Ada.Streams.Root_Stream_Type'Class;
    An_Item   : A_Type);

function A_Type'Input
   (S_Stream : access Ada.Streams.Root_Stream_Type'Class)
    return A_Type;

procedure A_Type'Class'Output
   (S_Stream : access Ada.Streams.Root_Stream_Type'Class;
    An_Item   : A_Type'Class);

function A_Type'Class'Input
   (S_Stream : access Ada.Streams.Root_Stream_Type'Class)
    return A_Type'Class;
```

So by simply writing (from the example above) `User'Write (Output_Stream, Manager);` we can send an object to a stream; no further work is required. The class-based stream attributes allow us to dispatch the read/write operations, which we will see below.

The difference between `Write` and `Output` or `Read` and `Input` is that the former simply write a representation of the object itself, whereas the latter forms also write out additional information, such as the bounds for an array type, or the tag for a tagged type.

Example 8.9   Using Ada95 streams _____

```
with Ada.Calendar;
with Ada_Store.Station;

package Ada_Store.Log is

   type Element is tagged private;

   procedure Open_Log;

   procedure Put (Element_In  : in out Element'Class);

private
   type Sequence_Number is new Long_Integer
      range 1 .. Long_Integer'Last;

   type Element is tagged
      record
         Sequence       : Sequence_Number;
         Calendar_Time : Ada.Calendar.Time;
         Station_ID     : Station.Identifier;
      end record;

end Ada_Store.Log;
```

The log package above allows subsystems in the **Ada_Store** application to write information into a log file. The way the logging works is that a client must extend the **Element** type and then call the **Put** operation. The following is the body of the log package and demonstrates the writing of the log records:

```
with Ada.Streams.Stream_IO;
use  Ada.Streams.Stream_IO;
with Ada.IO.Exceptions;

package body Ada_Store.Log is

   -- internal

   Current_Sequence : Sequence_Number := 1;

   type Log_File is
      record
         Open       : Boolean := False;
         As_File    : File_Type;
         As_Stream  : Stream_Access;
      end record;

   Current_Log : Log_File;

   -- public

   procedure Open_Log is
      Log_File_Name    : constant String := "Ada_Store.log";
   begin
      begin
         Open(File => Current_Log.As_File,
              Mode => Append_File,
              Name => Log_File_Name);

      exception
      when Ada.IO_Exceptions.Name_Error =>
         Create(File => Current_Log.As_File,
                Mode => Append_File,
                Name => Log_File_Name);

      end;
      Current_Log.As_Stream := Stream(Current_Log.As_File);
   end Open_Log;

   procedure Put
     (Element_In : in out Element'Class) is
   begin
      Current_Sequence := Current_Sequence + 1;

      Element(Element_In).Sequence       := Current_Sequence;
      Element(Element_In).Calendar_Time := Ada.Calendar.Clock;
```

```
      Element(Element_In).Station_ID    :=
         Ada_Store.Station.This_Station;

      Element'Class'Output(Current_Log.As_Stream, Element_In);
      Flush(Current_Log.As_File);
   end Put;

end Ada_Store.Log;
```

The operation `Open_Log` performs the required `Open` or `Create` and then calls `Stream` to obtain a stream type to operate on. The `Put` procedure is the more important here, as it actually writes a record to the stream using the dispatching version of the `Write` attribute so that the correct operation on the actual type is called, not the `Write` defined for the `Element` type.

The following procedure shows how we can read elements from the resulting log file:

```
procedure Log_View is

   Log_File_Name : constant String := "Ada_Store.log";
   As_File       : Streams.Stream_IO.File_Type;
   As_Stream     : Streams.Stream_IO.Stream_Access;
begin
   Streams.Stream_IO.Open(File => As_File,
                          Mode => Streams.Stream_IO.In_File,
                          Name => Log_File_Name);
   As_Stream := Streams.Stream_IO.Stream(As_File);
   Text_IO.Put_Line("Log View v.1.0 Started");

   loop
      declare
         An_Element : Log.Element'Class :=
            Log.Element'Class'Input(As_Stream);

      begin
         Text_IO.Put_Line(Tags.Expanded_Name(An_Element'Tag) &
                          " read");

      end;
   end loop;

   Text_IO.Put_Line("Log View Completed");
   Streams.Stream_IO.Close(As_File);

exception
   when IO_Exceptions.Name_Error =>
      Text_IO.Put_Line("Could not open log file");

   when IO_Exceptions.Data_Error =>
      Text_IO.Put_Line("Error reading log file");
end Log_View;
```

The most important line in the example above is the declaration of `An_Element` within the loop. As we saw in Chapter 6 a type declared as `Log.Element'Class` is unconstrained and must be explicitly initialized, so the reading from the stream using `'Class'Input` fixes the type of `An_Element` to the type of the element read from the file. It is important that this declaration is within the loop so that the type of the object is evaluated for each element.

We can now create streams, read elements from a stream, and write elements to a stream, and Ada95 does almost everything for us; at least it does more than the C++ streams library.

However, there are times when it is important to be able to exert more direct control over how a type is put into a stream. To this end Ada95 allows you to override the default `Read` and `Write` attributes with your own.

Example 8.10   User-defined `Read/Write` attributes

```
with Ada.Streams;

with Ada_Store.Log;

package Ada_Store.Complex_Type is

   type Instance is new Log.Element with private;
   ..
private
   type Instance is new Log.Element with
      ..

   function Complex_Input
     (S_Stream : access Ada.Streams.Root_Stream_Type'Class)
      return Instance;

   procedure Complex_Output
     (S_Stream : access Ada.Streams.Root_Stream_Type'Class;
      An_Item  : Instance);

   for Instance'Input use Complex_Input;
   for Instance'Output use Complex_Output;

end Ada_Store.Complex_Type;
```

The representation clauses tell the compiler always to use the two user-defined subprograms whenever the attributes are used in the application.

Example 8.11   Implementing a stream type

The following example demonstrates how to implement a new stream type. In this example a package manages network connections, and uses streams to send data across connections.

```
-- file: Network_IO.ads
with Ada.Streams;

package Network_IO is

   type Stream_Access is access all
      Ada.Streams.Root_Stream_Type'Class;

   type Connection_Type is private;

   -- This will be extended in time to include
   -- other protocols as support becomes
   -- available.
   type Connection_Protocol is ( Tcp, Udp );

   -- Create_Connection initializes a server port.
   -- A server port can only be created on this
   -- host so no host parameter is required.
   function Create_Connection
     (Service      : in String;
      Protocol     : in Connection_Protocol;
      Max_Clients  : in Positive := 4)
      return Connection_Type;

   -- This call is used by a server after
   -- calling the Create_Connection above, it
   -- waits for a connection and returns the client.
   function Wait_For_Client
     (Server_Connection : in Connection_Type)
      return Connection_Type;

   -- Connect_To initializes a client port, and
   -- as such requires the host on which the server
   -- port resides.
   function Connect_To
     (Service  : in String;
      Protocol : in Connection_Protocol;
      Host     : in String := "localhost")
      return Connection_Type;

   -- close a connection and all associated streams
   -- completely.
   procedure Close
     (Connection          : in out Connection_Type);

   -- This returns a stream type which can be used
   -- with the Read, Write, Input, and Output
   -- attributes.
   function Stream(Connection : in Connection_Type)
      return Stream_Access;
```

```
-- exceptions.
Connection_Creation_Error : exception;
Connection_Invalid        : exception;
Connection_Closed         : exception;
Operating_System_Error    : exception;
Parameter_In_Error        : exception;
private
   use Ada.Streams;

   type Network_Stream_Type is new Root_Stream_Type with
      record
         Connection : Connection_Type;
      end record;

   type Network_Stream_Access is access all Network_Stream_Type;

   type Connection_Type is new Integer;

   procedure Read
     (Stream : in out Network_Stream_Type;
      Item   : out    Stream_Element_Array;
      Last   : out    Stream_Element_Offset);

   procedure Write
     (Stream : in out Network_Stream_Type;
      Item   : in     Stream_Element_Array);

end Network_IO;
```

The package specification provides the ability to create a connection (the server side of the connection) and connect to the server. Once connections have been made the Stream function is used to convert a connection to a stream for reading and writing. The private part of this package demonstrates how the stream type itself is implemented. The type is derived from Root_Stream_Type and implements the Read and Write abstract operations. The body below demonstrates how the Read and Write operations work, not how the network connections are managed.

```
-- file: Network_IO.adb
with Ada.Text_IO;

package body Network_IO is

   ..
   function Stream
     (Connection : in Connection_Type)
     return Stream_Access is

      The_Stream : Network_Stream_Access;
   begin
      The_Stream := new Network_Stream_Type;
```

```
      The_Stream.Connection := Connection;

      return Stream_Access(The_Stream);
   end Stream;

   procedure Read
      (Stream : in out Network_Stream_Type;
       Item   : out     Stream_Element_Array;
       Last   : out     Stream_Element_Offset) is
   begin
      Ada.Text_IO.Put_Line("Socket'Read ( 1 .. " &
                           Stream_Element_Offset'Image(Last) &
                           " )");
   end Read;

   procedure Write
      (Stream : in out Network_Stream_Type;
       Item   : in     Stream_Element_Array) is
   begin
      Ada.Text_IO.Put_Line("Socket'Write (" &
                           Stream_Element_Offset'Image(Item'First) &
                           " .. " &
                           Stream_Element_Offset'Image(Item'Last) &
                           " ) :=");
      for I in Item'Range loop
         Ada.Text_IO.Put(Stream_Element'Image(Item(I)));
      end loop;
      Ada.Text_IO.New_Line;
   end Write;

end Network_IO;
```

The Read operation is passed an array in which the data is to be put, and the Write operation is passed an array containing the data to be written.

8.3   Miscellaneous

The following section describes packages that are part of the core language but are not specifically for type support.

8.3.1   Command line handling

You will have noticed that in Ada the concept of main () as a special entity does not exist. In Ada the start point of an application is whatever you tell the binder/linker it is. This main subprogram is usually a parameterless procedure, so where are argc and argv? The answer is that you get your parameters from a library package.

Library specification: package Ada.Command_Line _____

```
package Ada.Command_Line is
    pragma Preelaborate (Command_Line);

    function Argument_Count return Natural;

    function Argument (Number : in Positive) return String;

    function Command_Name return String;

    type Exit_Status is .. -- implementation defined

    Success : constant Exit_Status;
    Failure : constant Exit_Status;

    procedure Set_Exit_Status (Code : in Exit_Status);
private
    ..
end Ada.Command_Line;
```

As you can see, not only can you get your start-up parameters but also you can set your exit status, the equivalent of C's `exit ( )` function.

The following example shows how to use the command line facilities. It simply writes out the name of the program and its arguments. Before completion it sets the exit status to Success to indicate that nothing untoward has happened.

```
-- file: Echo_Args.adb
with Ada.Text_IO;
with Ada.Command_Line;

procedure Echo_Args is
begin
    Ada.Text_IO.Put_Line("Program " &
                    Ada.Command_Line.Command_Name &
                    " called with " &
                    Natural'Image(Ada.Command_Line.Argument_Count) &
                    " arguments:");

    for I in 1 .. Ada.Command_Line.Argument_Count loop

        Ada.Text_IO.Put_Line("    " & Ada.Command_Line.Argument(I));
    end loop;

    Ada.Command_Line.Set_Exit_Status(Ada.Command_Line.Success);
end Echo_Args;
```

The following is an extract from `create_database.adb` which is a utility to populate the database files with example records. The resulting program can be used to create any individual file or all files depending on the Boolean variables declared at the top.

Each command line argument is read and converted to lower case so that a case-insensitive comparison can take place:

```ada
..
Tenders     : Boolean := False;
Departments : Boolean := False;
Items       : Boolean := False;
Users       : Boolean := False;
Config      : Boolean := False;
begin

    for Argument in 1 .. Ada.Command_Line.Argument_Count loop

        declare
            Arg_String : String :=
                Translate(Ada.Command_Line.Argument(Argument),
                          Ada.Strings.Maps.Constants.Lower_Case_Map);

        begin
            if Arg_String = "all" then

                Tenders     := True;
                Departments := True;
                Items       := True;
                Users       := True;
                Config      := True;
                exit;
            elsif Arg_String = "tenders" then

                Tenders := True;
            elsif Arg_String = "departments" then

                Departments := True;
            elsif Arg_String = "items" then

                Items := True;
            elsif Arg_String = "users" then

                Users := True;
            elsif Arg_String = "config" then

                Config := True;
            else
                Ada.Text_IO.Put_Line("Error: argument " &
                             Ada.Command_Line.Argument(Argument) &
                             " is invalid");
            end if;
        end;
    end loop;
    ..
```

8.3.2   `Ada.Calendar`

We introduced this package when dealing with delayed entry calls in Chapter 7. The **delay until** statement requires an argument of type `Time` declared in the package `Ada.Calendar`.

Library specification: **package** `Ada.Calendar` ————————————————

```
package Ada.Calendar is

   type Time is private;

   subtype Year_Number  is Integer range 1901 .. 2099;
   subtype Month_Number is Integer range 1 .. 12;
   subtype Day_Number   is Integer range 1 .. 31;
   subtype Day_Duration is Duration range 0.0 .. 86_400.0;

   function Clock return Time;

   function Year    (Date : Time) return Year_Number;
   function Month   (Date : Time) return Month_Number;
   function Day     (Date : Time) return Day_Number;
   function Seconds (Date : Time) return Day_Duration;

   procedure Split
     (Date    : Time;
      Year    : out Year_Number;
      Month   : out Month_Number;
      Day     : out Day_Number;
      Seconds : out Day_Duration);

   function Time_Of
     (Year    : Year_Number;
      Month   : Month_Number;
      Day     : Day_Number;
      Seconds : Day_Duration := 0.0)
      return    Time;

   function "+" (Left : Time;     Right : Duration) return Time;
   function "+" (Left : Duration; Right : Time)     return Time;
   function "-" (Left : Time;     Right : Duration) return Time;
   function "-" (Left : Time;     Right : Time) return Duration;

   function "<"  (Left, Right : Time) return Boolean;
   function "<=" (Left, Right : Time) return Boolean;
   function ">"  (Left, Right : Time) return Boolean;
   function ">=" (Left, Right : Time) return Boolean;

   Time_Error : exception;
private
   ..
end Ada.Calendar;
```

This package is much more useful than its requirement for the delay statement; as you can see date and time values can be obtained from the type `Time` and a `Time` object can be constructed from date and time values. In this respect it is similar to the facilities provided by the standard C header `time.h` which are centered around the `struct tm` type presented below.

```
struct tm {
        int tm_sec;      /* seconds after the minute — [0,59]*/
        int tm_min;      /* minutes after the hour — [0,59] */
        int tm_hour;     /* hours since midnight — [0,23] */
        int tm_mday;     /* day of the month — [1,31] */
        int tm_mon;      /* months since January — [0,11] */
        int tm_year;     /* years since 1900 */
        int tm_wday;     /* days since Sunday — [0,6] */
        int tm_yday;     /* days since January 1 — [0,365] */
        int tm_isdst;    /* daylight savings time flag */
        };
```

If you now compare the fields in the structure above to the data available from the `Time` type then you are missing `tm_min` and `tm_hour` which can be calculated from the `Seconds` operator in the `Calendar` package and `tm_wday`, `tm_yday`, `tm_isdst` which cannot.

We use `Ada.Calendar` in a couple of places in our example. In the two packages `Ada_Store.Log` and `Ada_Store.Support.Trace` we use objects of type `Time` as time-stamps to mark when events occurred. More interesting though is the `Start` procedure in `Ada_Store.Trading`:

```
package body Ada_Store.Trading is

    subtype Trading_Time is Ada.Calendar.Day_Duration
        range 30_600.0 .. 66_600.0;
    —— range 8:30am .. 6:30pm

    Trading_State : State := Not_Trading;

    procedure Start is
        Time_Now : Day_Duration := Seconds (Clock);
    begin
        if Time_Now in Trading_Time'Range then
            Trading_State := Trading;
        else
            raise Invalid_Trading_Time;
        end if;
    end Start;

    ..
```

The subtype `Trading_Time` specifies the time during which calls to `Start` are valid; the procedure itself uses the `Clock` function in the `Calendar` package to get the current time and the `Seconds` function to return the actual time.

8.3.3   System package

The following is **package** `System`, the root of a rather important set of packages (section 13.7 of the language reference manual).

Library specification: package `System` ────────────────────────

```
package System is
   pragma Pure (System);

   type Name is -- Implementation-dependent enumeration
   System_Name : constant Name := -- Implementation-dependent

   -- System-dependent Named Numbers

   Min_Int                 : constant := -- Root_Integer'First
   Max_Int                 : constant := -- Root_Integer'Last;

   Max_Binary_Modulus      : constant := -- Implementation-dep.
   Max_Nonbinary_Modulus   : constant := -- Implementation-dep.

   Max_Base_Digits         : constant := -- Root_Real'Digits;
   Max_Digits              : constant := -- Implementation-dep.

   Max_Mantissa            : constant := -- Implementation-dep.
   Fine_Delta              : constant := -- Implementation-dep.

   Tick                    : constant := -- Implementation-dep.

   -- Storage-related declarations

   type Address is -- Implementation-dep.
   Null_Address : constant Address;

   Storage_Unit            : constant := -- Implementation-dep.
   Word_Size               : constant := -- Implementation-dep.
   Memory_Size             : constant := -- Implementation-dep.

   -- Address comparison

   function "<"  (Left, Right : Address) return Boolean;
   function "<=" (Left, Right : Address) return Boolean;
   function ">"  (Left, Right : Address) return Boolean;
   function ">=" (Left, Right : Address) return Boolean;
   function "="  (Left, Right : Address) return Boolean;

   pragma Convention(Intrinsic, "<");
   pragma Convention(Intrinsic, "<=");
```

```
pragma Convention(Intrinsic, ">");
pragma Convention(Intrinsic, ">=");
pragma Convention(Intrinsic, "=");

-- Other System-dependent Declarations

type Bit_Order is (High_Order_First, Low_Order_First);
Default_Bit_Order : constant Bit_Order;

-- Priority-related Declarations (RM D.1)

subtype Any_Priority is Integer range -- Implementation-dep.
subtype Priority is Any_Priority
    range Any_Priority'First .. -- Implementation-dep.
subtype Interrupt_Priority is Any_Priority
    range Priority'Last+1 .. Any_Priority'Last;

Default_Priority : constant Priority :=
    (Priority'First + Priority'Last) / 2;

end System;
```

As you can see it declares such things as the maximum and minimum values for base types, the type `Address`, and constants defining the system storage size and word size. It is also important for the systems programming and real-time systems annexes described in the next chapter.

8.4 Summary

Now that we have introduced the language itself and the core library you can see how well-rounded the Ada95 general purpose programming language is.

Some features seem to be missing at first glance – for instance the lack of sharing operations on files or the fact there is no library routine to get environment variables. However, you must always remember that one of the prime objectives of the Ada programming language is portability, from small embedded programs in machines as small as a toaster through massive multi-million line, multi-platform applications on main-frame computers.

To help this situation the ability to interface with code written in other languages allows you to access routines not available in the core library or vendor/platform-specific libraries.

Ada_Store

This chapter has introduced a number of examples from the `Ada_Store` application, though of course the library is used in more places than mentioned here. For example the string-handling routines are heavily used in the package `Ada_Store.PoST. Application.Operations` to format text for output to the displays or printers.

Language annexes

The annexes to the Ada95 programming language provide additional packages and in some cases attributes and pragmas to cover special application areas.

Compiler vendors do not have to provide implementations for the optional annexes (only the interfacing annex is not optional); the validation process will identify which of the annexes are supported in a compiler. It is also likely that vendors will supply partial implementations of packages specified in the optional annexes; these can be legitimately ignored during validation. This chapter will rely heavily on examples to illustrate the features provided by the annexes and their associated packages.

Note that the following section is entitled Annex B; this is because in the language reference manual Annex A describes the *pre-defined language environment*, the material we covered in the previous chapter.

9.1   Annex B: language interfaces annex

Part of the process of revising the language standard was the realization that Ada code is very rarely developed in isolation, that calls to libraries were not developed in Ada, and that the ability for that code to make calls to subprograms written in Ada was required. In Ada83 specifying the calling convention of a subprogram or storage convention for objects was, for instance, difficult.

This resulted in the first, non-optional, annex 'Interface to other languages'. This primarily consists of a specific set of packages that declare features, types, and primitive operations useful to interface to libraries of code not written in Ada.

In Ada the specifications of interfaces to code written in non-Ada are known as *bindings*. Most Ada compilers will be provided with bindings to the underlying operating system; in our point of sale example we use a set of bindings to the Win32 API used on Windows NT.

The library **package** Interfaces is the parent to a number of other library packages and contains a number of useful types and operations. Note that although 8, 16, 32, and 64-bit numeric types are specified in this package only those supported by the hardware for an implementation are required.

Library specification: package Interfaces ⎯⎯⎯⎯⎯⎯⎯⎯⎯⎯⎯⎯⎯⎯⎯

```
package Interfaces is
   pragma Pure (Interfaces);

   type Integer_8  is range -2 **  7 .. 2 ** 7 - 1;
   for  Integer_8'Size use  8;

   type Integer_16 is range -2 ** 15 .. 2 ** 15 - 1;
   for  Integer_16'Size use 16;

   type Integer_32 is range -2 ** 31 .. 2 ** 31 - 1;
   for  Integer_32'Size use 32;

   type Integer_64 is range -2 ** 63 .. 2 ** 63 - 1;
   for  Integer_64'Size use 64;

   type Unsigned_8  is mod 2 ** 8;
   for  Unsigned_8'Size use  8;

   type Unsigned_16 is mod 2 ** 16;
   for  Unsigned_16'Size use 16;

   type Unsigned_32 is mod 2 ** 32;
   for  Unsigned_32'Size use 32;

   type Unsigned_64 is mod 2 ** 64;
   for  Unsigned_64'Size use 64;

   function Shift_Left
     (Value  : Unsigned_8;
      Amount : Natural)
      return Unsigned_8;

   function Shift_Right
     (Value  : Unsigned_8;
      Amount : Natural)
      return Unsigned_8;
```

```
function Shift_Right_Arithmetic
  (Value  : Unsigned_8;
   Amount : Natural)
   return Unsigned_8;

function Rotate_Left
  (Value  : Unsigned_8;
   Amount : Natural)
   return Unsigned_8;

function Rotate_Right
  (Value  : Unsigned_8;
   Amount : Natural)
   return Unsigned_8;

function Shift_Left
  (Value  : Unsigned_16;
   Amount : Natural)
   return Unsigned_16;

function Shift_Right
  (Value  : Unsigned_16;
   Amount : Natural)
   return Unsigned_16;

function Shift_Right_Arithmetic
  (Value  : Unsigned_16;
   Amount : Natural)
   return Unsigned_16;

function Rotate_Left
  (Value  : Unsigned_16;
   Amount : Natural)
   return Unsigned_16;

function Rotate_Right
  (Value  : Unsigned_16;
   Amount : Natural)
   return Unsigned_16;

function Shift_Left
  (Value  : Unsigned_32;
   Amount : Natural)
   return Unsigned_32;

function Shift_Right
  (Value  : Unsigned_32;
   Amount : Natural)
   return Unsigned_32;
```

```
function Shift_Right_Arithmetic
  (Value  : Unsigned_32;
   Amount : Natural)
   return Unsigned_32;

function Rotate_Left
  (Value  : Unsigned_32;
   Amount : Natural)
   return Unsigned_32;

function Rotate_Right
  (Value  : Unsigned_32;
   Amount : Natural)
   return Unsigned_32;

function Shift_Left
  (Value  : Unsigned_64;
   Amount : Natural)
   return Unsigned_64;

function Shift_Right
  (Value  : Unsigned_64;
   Amount : Natural)
   return Unsigned_64;

function Shift_Right_Arithmetic
  (Value  : Unsigned_64;
   Amount : Natural)
   return Unsigned_64;

function Rotate_Left
  (Value  : Unsigned_64;
   Amount : Natural)
   return Unsigned_64;

function Rotate_Right
  (Value  : Unsigned_64;
   Amount : Natural)
   return Unsigned_64;

end Interfaces;
```

Such low-level types are useful when converting date types between an Ada program and external language routines.

9.1.1 Pragmas

Four additional pragmas are introduced by this annex, Import, Export, Convention, and Linker_Options. These allow fine control over access to subprograms and objects between Ada and other languages. The following example shows the use of all these pragmas and is explained below.

```ada
-- file: Import_Test1.adb
with Interfaces;

package Import_Test1 is

   function  C_Get_Data return Interfaces.Unsigned_64;

   procedure C_Set_Data(Data : Interfaces.Unsigned_64);

   pragma Import(Convention    => C,
                 Entity        => C_Get_Data,
                 External_Name => "getdata",
                 Link_Name     => "_getdata");

   pragma Import(Convention    => C,
                 Entity        => C_Set_Data,
                 External_Name => "setdata");

   procedure Data_Changed;

   pragma Export(Convention    => C,
                 Entity        => Data_Changed,
                 External_Name => "datachanged",
                 Link_Name     => "_datachanged");

   type Data_2 is
      record
         A : Integer;
      end record;

   pragma Convention(Convention => C,
                     Entity => Data_2);

   pragma Linker_Options("data.obj");
   ..
end Import_Test1;
```

The pragmas `Import` and `Export` both take four parameters, firstly an identifier for the calling convention, in this case C. The second parameter identifies the local entity, that is the subprogram or object being operated on. The third and fourth parameters are optional, and specify the external name and linker name for the entity. The compiler should be able to work out the name of the subprogram or entity if no change is required (in the example above the entity name and external names are different, though for `setdata` we have left it up to the compiler to work out the linker name). The only conventions specified by the language itself are `Ada` and `Intrinsic`; if the full annex is supported then additional conventions `C`, `FORTRAN`, and `COBOL` are also supported.

The `Convention` pragma is similar to `Export` in that it specifies the convention for a subprogram or object declared in the Ada code. The obvious difference between `Convention` and `Export` is that `Convention` does not support the parameters `External_Name` and `Link_Name`.

Finally `Linker_Options` specifies a completely implementation-dependent string of options and directives for the linker.

9.1.2   Interfacing to C

Library specification: package `Interfaces.C` ─────────────────────────

```
package Interfaces.C is
pragma Pure (C);

   -- Declarations based on C's <limits.h>
   CHAR_BIT  : constant := 8;
   SCHAR_MIN : constant := -128;
   SCHAR_MAX : constant := 127;
   UCHAR_MAX : constant := 255;

   -- Signed and Unsigned Integers
   type int   is new Integer;
   type short is new Short_Integer;
   type long  is new Long_Integer;

   type signed_char is range SCHAR_MIN .. SCHAR_MAX;
   for  signed_char'Size use CHAR_BIT;

   type unsigned       is mod 2 ** Integer'Size;
   type unsigned_short is mod 2 ** Short_Integer'Size;
   type unsigned_long  is mod 2 ** Long_Integer'Size;

   type unsigned_char is mod (UCHAR_MAX + 1);
   for  unsigned_char'Size use CHAR_BIT;

   type ptrdiff_t is
     range -(2 ** (Standard'Address_Size - 1)) ..
           +(2 ** (Standard'Address_Size - 1) - 1);

   type size_t is mod 2 ** Standard'Address_Size;

   -- Floating point
   type C_float      is new Float;
   type double       is new Standard.Long_Float;
   type long_double  is new Standard.Long_Long_Float;

   -- Characters and Strings
   type char is new Character;
```

```
nul : constant char := char'First;

function To_C
   (Item : Character) return char;
function To_Ada
   (Item : char) return Character;

type char_array is array (size_t range <>)
   of aliased char;
for  char_array'Component_Size use CHAR_BIT;

function Is_Nul_Terminated
   (Item : in char_array) return Boolean;

function To_C
   (Item       : in String;
    Append_Nul : in Boolean := True)
    return char_array;

function To_Ada
   (Item     : in char_array;
    Trim_Nul : in Boolean := True)
    return String;

procedure To_C
   (Item       : in  String;
    Target     : out char_array;
    Count      : out size_t;
    Append_Nul : in  Boolean := True);

procedure To_Ada
   (Item     : in  char_array;
    Target   : out String;
    Count    : out Natural;
    Trim_Nul : in  Boolean := True);


-- Wide Character and Wide String
type wchar_t is new Wide_Character;
wide_nul : constant wchar_t := wchar_t'First;

function To_C
   (Item : in Wide_Character) return wchar_t;
function To_Ada
   (Item : in wchar_t) return Wide_Character;

type wchar_array is array (size_t range <>)
   of aliased wchar_t;

function Is_Nul_Terminated
   (Item : in wchar_array) return Boolean;
```

```
function To_C
   (Item        : in Wide_String;
    Append_Nul : in Boolean := True)
    return wchar_array;

function To_Ada
   (Item       : in wchar_array;
    Trim_Nul : in Boolean := True)
    return Wide_String;

procedure To_C
   (Item         : in  Wide_String;
    Target      : out wchar_array;
    Count       : out size_t;
    Append_Nul : in   Boolean := True);

procedure To_Ada
   (Item       : in   wchar_array;
    Target    : out Wide_String;
    Count     : out Natural;
    Trim_Nul : in   Boolean := True);

Terminator_Error : exception;

private
   ..
end Interfaces.C;
```

This child package of `Interfaces` provides additional, C language-specific types and subprograms. It provides types `char`, `int`, `short`, `long`, `float`, `double`, `size_t`, and other C standard types, and it provides functions `To_C` and `To_Ada` for many of these types.

This package is backed up by two child packages itself, `Interfaces.C.Strings` and `Interface.C.Pointers`, which together form a real ability to work with C code.

As an example of the use of the C interfacing package, consider the following C module: it declares a single function which will output a string. We will use the C interface packages to call this routine a number of ways.

```
/* file: ctest.c */
#include <stdio.h>

void putstring(char* str)
{
   puts(str);
}
```

First we will use the `char_array` type introduced in the package above to represent our string type:

```
-- file: C_Test1.adb
with Interfaces.C;
use type Interfaces.C.char_array;

procedure C_Test1 is

    procedure PutString(S : Interfaces.C.char_array);

    pragma Import(C, PutString, "putstring");

    C_Str : Interfaces.C.char_array := "hello world" &
                                        Interfaces.C.nul;
begin

    PutString(C_Str);

end C_Test1;
```

Library specification: package `Interfaces.C.Strings` ――――――――――

```
package Interfaces.C.Strings is
pragma Preelaborate (Strings);

    type char_array_access is access all char_array;

    type chars_ptr is private;

    type chars_ptr_array is array (size_t range <>)
       of chars_ptr;

    Null_Ptr : constant chars_ptr;

    function To_Chars_Ptr
       (Item       : in char_array_access;
        Nul_Check : in Boolean := False)
        return chars_ptr;

    function New_Char_Array
       (Chars : in char_array) return chars_ptr;

    function New_String
       (Str : in String) return chars_ptr;

    procedure Free
       (Item : in out chars_ptr);

    Dereference_Error : exception;

    function Value
       (Item : in chars_ptr) return char_array;
```

```ada
   function Value
      (Item   : in chars_ptr;
       Length : in size_t)
       return char_array;
   function Value
      (Item : in chars_ptr) return String;

   function Value
      (Item   : in chars_ptr;
       Length : in size_t)
       return String;

   function Strlen
      (Item : in chars_ptr) return size_t;

   procedure Update
      (Item   : in chars_ptr;
       Offset : in size_t;
       Chars  : in char_array;
       Check  : Boolean := True);

   procedure Update
      (Item   : in chars_ptr;
       Offset : in size_t;
       Str    : in String;
       Check  : in Boolean := True);

   Update_Error : exception;

private
   ..
end Interfaces.C.Strings;
```

This package provides support for C style null-terminated strings and conversion routines from arrays of characters and from Ada style strings.

The following shows our `PutString` example again, using the type `chars_ptr` from the strings package above:

```ada
-- file: C_Test2.adb
with Interfaces.C.Strings;

procedure C_Test2 is

   procedure PutString(S : Interfaces.C.Strings.chars_ptr);

   pragma Import(C, PutString, "putstring");

   Pass_This : String := "hello world";
   C_Str     : Interfaces.C.Strings.chars_ptr;
```

```
begin

   C_Str := Interfaces.C.Strings.New_String(Pass_This);

   PutString(C_Str);

   Interfaces.C.Strings.Free(C_Str);

end C_Test2;
```

Bindings again

The example above is known as a *thin* binding: a procedure is declared and all clients must use the conversion routines before calling the binding. The alternative *thick* binding approach is to provide subprograms which take more natural Ada parameters and do any conversion internally, so we might re-write the above as:

```
-- file: PutString_Binding.ads
package PutString_Binding is

   procedure Put(S : String);
end PutString_Binding;
```

```
-- file: PutString_Binding.adb
with Interfaces.C.Strings;

package body PutString_Binding is

   procedure PutString(S : Interfaces.C.Strings.chars_ptr);

   pragma Import(C, PutString, "putstring");

   procedure Put(S : String) is
      C_Str      : Interfaces.C.Strings.chars_ptr;
   begin
      C_Str := Interfaces.C.Strings.New_String(S);
      PutString(C_Str);
      Interfaces.C.Strings.Free(C_Str);
   end Put;

end PutString_Binding;
```

```
-- file: C_Test3.adb
with PutString_Binding;
procedure C_Test3 is
begin
   PutString_Binding.Put("hello world");
end C_Test3;
```

The types of binding which you may have to work with will depend on how much overhead is introduced by the thick approach, and what the application you are binding to provides in the way of services.

Library specification: package `Interfaces.C.Pointers` _____

```
generic
   type Index is (<>);
   type Element is private;
   type Element_Array is array (Index range <>)
      of aliased Element;
   Default_Terminator : Element;

package Interfaces.C.Pointers is
pragma Preelaborate (Pointers);

   type Pointer is access all Element;

   function Value
     (Ref        : in Pointer;
      Terminator : in Element := Default_Terminator)
      return Element_Array;

   function Value
     (Ref    : in Pointer;
      Length : in ptrdiff_t)
      return Element_Array;

   Pointer_Error : exception;

   -- C-style Pointer Arithmetic
   function "+"
     (Left  : in Pointer;
      Right : in ptrdiff_t)
      return Pointer;
   function "+"
     (Left  : in ptrdiff_t;
      Right : in Pointer)
      return Pointer;
   function "-"
     (Left  : in Pointer;
      Right : in ptrdiff_t)
      return Pointer;
   function "-"
     (Left  : in Pointer;
      Right : in Pointer)
      return ptrdiff_t;

   procedure Increment (Ref : in out Pointer);
   procedure Decrement (Ref : in out Pointer);

   pragma Convention (Intrinsic, "+");
   pragma Convention (Intrinsic, "-");
```

```
pragma Convention (Intrinsic, Increment);
pragma Convention (Intrinsic, Decrement);

function Virtual_Length
   (Ref           : in Pointer;
    Terminator    : in Element := Default_Terminator)
    return ptrdiff_t;

procedure Copy_Terminated_Array
   (Source      : in Pointer;
    Target      : in Pointer;
    Limit       : in ptrdiff_t := ptrdiff_t'Last;
    Terminator  : in Element   := Default_Terminator);

procedure Copy_Array
   (Source   : in Pointer;
    Target   : in Pointer;
    Length   : in ptrdiff_t);

end Interfaces.C.Pointers;
```

This final package is a generic package that provides facilities to create a pointer to any type, and handles the conversion between an array of that type and a pointer.

The following example shows how we can use the pointers generic package to instantiate a package which takes a character array and allows us to treat it as a C style pointer:

```
-- file: C_Test4.adb
with Interfaces.C;
use type Interfaces.C.char_array;
with Interfaces.C.Pointers;

procedure C_Test4 is

   package C_char is
      new Interfaces.C.Pointers(Interfaces.C.size_T,
                                Interfaces.C.char,
                                Interfaces.C.char_array,
                                Interfaces.C.nul);

   procedure PutString(S : C_char.Pointer);

   pragma Import(C, PutString, "putstring");

   C_Str : Interfaces.C.char_array := "hello world 3" &
                                Interfaces.C.nul;
begin

   PutString(C_Str(C_Str'First)'Access);

end C_Test4;
```

The effect of the generic package is to provide a new type, `Pointer`, which is a C style pointer to the type `Element`. This type is used to manage C code where pointers are used to represent arrays and the generic allows you to work with terminated arrays, or arrays of fixed length. Once the package has been instantiated then you can even do a form of pointer arithmetic on the resulting `Pointer` type.

If we return briefly to our point of sale example, we have been provided by the vendor of our peripherals a C library we can call to drive them. The vendor has provided us with the link time, run-time libraries and a C header file. We have to develop a binding to the peripheral API so that we can successfully work with the provided peripherals.

Below is the C header file provided to us by the peripheral vendor:

```
/**********************************************
 * API Version, used to check calls.
 */
#define POS_API_VERSION 255

/**********************************************
 * Devices.
 */
typedef enum {
  POS_UNIT_NONE = -1,
  POS_UNIT_ALL = 0,
  POS_UNIT_POS_KEYBOARD,
  POS_UNIT_PC_KEYBOARD,
  POS_UNIT_ALARM,
  POS_UNIT_MSR,
  POS_UNIT_KEYLOCK,
  POS_UNIT_MAIN_SCANNER,
  POS_UNIT_HH_SCANNER,
  POS_UNIT_SCALE,
  POS_UNIT_OPER_DISPLAY,
  POS_UNIT_CUST_DISPLAY,
  POS_UNIT_BOTH_DISPLAYS,
  POS_UNIT_RCPT_PRINTER,
  POS_UNIT_AUDT_PRINTER,
  POS_UNIT_BOTH_PRINTERS,
  POS_UNIT_SLIP_PRINTER,
  POS_UNIT_FIRST_CASHDRAWER,
  POS_UNIT_SECOND_CASHDRAWER
} POS_UNIT_ID;

/**********************************************
 * Error codes.
 */
typedef enum {
```

```
   POSERROR_OK = 0,
   POSERROR_NOT_INITIALIZED,
   POSERROR_ALREADY_INITIALIZED,
   POSERROR_OS_ERROR,
   POSERROR_COMMAND_INVALID,
   POSERROR_COMMAND_DATA_ERROR,
   POSERROR_DEVICE_INVALID,
   POSERROR_DEVICE_WRITE_FAILED,
   POSERROR_DEVICE_FAILURE,
   POSERROR_DEVICE_OFFLINE,
   POSERROR_DEVICE_SEQUENCE_ERR,
   POSERROR_DEVICE_STATUS_CHANGED,
   POSERROR_KEYBOARD_MULTIPLE_KEYS,
   POSERROR_MSR_INVALID_TRACK,
   POSERROR_MSR_MULTIPLE_TRACKS,
   POSERROR_PRINTER_FORMAT_ERR,
   POSERROR_SCALE_ILLEGAL_WEIGHT,
   POSERROR_SCALE_ZERO_DETECTED,
   POSERROR_SCALE_NOT_ZEROED,
   POSERROR_SCALE_WEIGHT_NOT_REMOVED,
   POSERROR_SCALE_VERIFY_FAILED,
   POSERROR_SCALE_WEIGHT_NOT_STABLE,
   POSERROR_SLIP_SEQUENCE_ERR
} POS_ERROR_CODE;

/********************************************
 * API Control Functions.
 */
POS_ERROR_CODE POSAPI
PosInitialize(PUSHORT  PosApiVersion);

VOID POSAPI
PosTerminate(USHORT    TermCode);

POS_ERROR_CODE POSAPI
PosSystemError(VOID);

/********************************************
 * The API Read Function.
 */
#define POS_MAX_BUFFER_LENGTH 512

POS_ERROR_CODE POSAPI
PosRead (BYTE          Buffer[]
         USHORT        BufferLength,
         POS_UNIT_ID*  ReturnedUnit,
         PUSHORT       ReturnedLength);
```

```
/************************************************
 * General Device Functions.
 */
typedef enum {
  DEVICE_RESET = 0,
  DEVICE_INITIALIZE,
  DEVICE_FLUSH,
  DEVICE_ONLINE,
} POS_DEVICE_CMD;

POS_ERROR_CODE POSAPI
PosDeviceControl(POS_UNIT_ID    Unit,
                 POS_DEVICE_CMD Command);

typedef struct {
  BYTE DeviceAvailable : 1;
  BYTE DeviceOnLine    : 1;
  BYTE HandlerEnabled  : 1;
  BYTE ExDeviceStatus;
} POS_DEVICE_STATUS;

POS_ERROR_CODE POSAPI
PosDeviceStatus(POS_UNIT_ID        Unit,
                POS_DEVICE_STATUS* Command);

/************************************************
 * Alarm Device Functions.
 */
typedef struct {
  USHORT Duration;
  USHORT Pitch;
  USHORT Volume;
} POS_ALARM_TONE;

typedef struct {
  POS_ALARM_TONE Tone1;
  POS_ALARM_TONE Tone2;
  BYTE           SupportsTone2    : 1;
  BYTE           SupportsInterrupt : 1;
} POS_ALARM_CONFIG;

POS_ERROR_CODE POSAPI
PosAlarmConfig(POS_UNIT_ID       Unit,
               POS_ALARM_CONFIG* ConfigRecord);

POS_ERROR_CODE POSAPI
PosAlarmSound(POS_UNIT_ID Unit,
              USHORT      RepeatValue);
```

```
/*********************************************
 * Display Device Functions.
 */
#define STATUS_FADE_ON  1
#define STATUS_FADE_OFF 0

typedef struct {
  USHORT NumberOfLines;
  USHORT CharactersPerLine;
  USHORT NumberOfLEDs;
  BYTE   SupportsScrolling : 1;
  BYTE   SupportsFade      : 1;
} POS_DISPLAY_CONFIG;

POS_ERROR_CODE POSAPI
PosDisplayConfig(POS_UNIT_ID          Unit,
                 POS_DISPLAY_CONFIG* ConfigRecord);

POS_ERROR_CODE POSAPI
PosDisplayText(POS_UNIT_ID Unit,
               USHORT      LineNumber,
               USHORT      ColumnNumber,
               PSZ         TextBuffer);

POS_ERROR_CODE POSAPI
PosDisplayLed(POS_UNIT_ID Unit,
              USHORT      LedState);

/*********************************************
 * Cashdrawer Device Functions.
 */
#define STATUS_DRAWER_OPEN   1
#define STATUS_DRAWER_CLOSED 0

POS_ERROR_CODE POSAPI
PosCashdrawerOpen(POS_UNIT_ID Unit);

POS_ERROR_CODE POSAPI
PosCashdrawerLock(POS_UNIT_ID Unit,
                  BOOLEAN     On);

/*********************************************
 * MSR Device Functions.
 */
POS_ERROR_CODE POSAPI
PosMsrTrackEnable(POS_UNIT_ID Unit,
                  BYTE        TrackBitMap);

/*********************************************
 * General Port Device Functions.
```

```
 */
typedef enum {
  INACTIVE    = 0,
  CTS_ACTIVE = 1,
  DSR_ACTIVE = 2,
  DCD_ACTIVE = 4,
  RTS_ACTIVE = 8,
  DTR_ACTIVE = 16
} POS_PORT_STATUS;
POS_ERROR_CODE POSAPI
PosPortRead(POS_UNIT_ID       Unit,
            USHORT            BufferLength,
            BYTE              Buffer[],
            PUSHORT           ReturnedLength,
            POS_PORT_STATUS*  ReturnedStatus);


POS_ERROR_CODE POSAPI
PosPortWrite(POS_UNIT_ID      Unit,
            USHORT            BufferLength,
            BYTE              Buffer[],
            PUSHORT           ReturnedLength,
            POS_PORT_STATUS*  ReturnedStatus);


/*********************************************
 * Printer Device Functions.
 */
#define STATUS_PAPER_LOW        1
#define STATUS_PAPER_BACK       0
#define STATUS_SLIP_PAPER_IN    2
#define STATUS_SLIP_PAPER_OUT   0
typedef enum {
  EPC_WIDE_ON = 16,
  EPC_WIDE_OFF,
  EPC_TALL_ON,
  EPC_TALL_OFF,
  EPC_BOLD_ON,
  EPC_BOLD_OFF,
  EPC_ITALICS_ON,
  EPC_ITALICS_OFF,
  EPC_SIDEWAYS_ON,
  EPC_SIDEWAYS_OFF,
  EPC_INVERTED_ON,
  EPC_INVERTED_OFF,
} POS_PRINTER_CAPS;
```

```
typedef struct {
  USHORT NumberOfLines;
  USHORT CharactersPerLine;
  USHORT CutMargin;
  BYTE    SupportsPaperCut       : 1;
  BYTE    SupportsPaperPerforate : 1;
  BYTE    SupportsWide     : 1;
  BYTE    SupportsTall     : 1;
  BYTE    SupportsBold     : 1;
  BYTE    SupportsItalic   : 1;
  BYTE    SupportsSideways : 1;
  BYTE    SupportsInverted : 1;
} POS_PRINTER_CONFIG;

POS_ERROR_CODE POSAPI
PosPrinterConfig(POS_UNIT_ID          Unit,
                 POS_PRINTER_CONFIG* ConfigRecord);

POS_ERROR_CODE POSAPI
PosPrintText(POS_UNIT_ID Unit,
             USHORT       linefeedsBefore,
             USHORT       linefeedsAfter,
             PSZ          textBufferLine1);

POS_ERROR_CODE POSAPI
PosPrinterAdvance(POS_UNIT_ID Unit,
                  BYTE           numberOfLines);
POS_ERROR_CODE POSAPI
PosPrinterCut(POS_UNIT_ID Unit,
              BOOLEAN     PerforateOnly);

typedef enum {
  OPEN_JAWS,
  CLOSE_JAWS,
  ROLL_PAPER_IN,
  EJECT_PAPER
} POS_SLIPPRINTER_CMD;

POS_ERROR_CODE POSAPI
PosSlipPrinterCommand(POS_UNIT_ID          Unit,
                      POS_SLIPPRINTER_CMD Command);

/*********************************************
 * Weigh Scale Device Functions.
 */
#define STATUS_SCALE_ZEROED 1

typedef struct {
```

```
    BYTE InMetric : 1;
} POS_SCALE_CONFIG;

POS_ERROR_CODE POSAPI
PosScaleConfig(POS_UNIT_ID        Unit,
               POS_SCALE_CONFIG* ConfigRecord);

POS_ERROR_CODE POSAPI
PosScaleVerify(POS_DEVICE_ID  deviceID);

POS_ERROR_CODE POSAPI
PosScaleRead(POS_DEVICE_ID deviceID,
             USHORT*        grossWeight);
```

Below is the Ada (thin) binding to the peripheral library. Note the use of the `Import` pragma of the pointers generic package and extensive use of the representation clauses introduced in Section 3.7.

```
-- file: Pos.ads
with Interfaces.C;
with Interfaces.C.Pointers;

package Pos is

    type     BYTE    is new Interfaces.C.Unsigned_Char;
    type     PBYTE   is access all BYTE;
    subtype  USHORT  is Interfaces.C.Unsigned_Short;
    type     PUSHORT is access all USHORT;

    type BYTEARRAY1 is array (USHORT range <>) of aliased BYTE;
    package BYTEARRAY2 is
       new Interfaces.C.Pointers(USHORT,
                                 BYTE,
                                 BYTEARRAY1,
                                 BYTE(0));

    subtype BYTEARRAY is BYTEARRAY2.Pointer;

    package CHARARRAY is
       new Interfaces.C.Pointers(Interfaces.C.size_t,
                                 Interfaces.C.char,
                                 Interfaces.C.char_array,
                                 Interfaces.C.nul);
    subtype PSZ is CHARARRAY.Pointer;
    -- ---------------------------------------------
    -- API Version, used to check calls.
    --
    API_VERSION : constant := 255;

    -- ---------------------------------------------
```

```
-- Devices.
--
type UNIT_ID is (UNIT_NONE = -1,
                 UNIT_ALL = 0,
                 UNIT_POS_KEYBOARD,
                 UNIT_PC_KEYBOARD,
                 UNIT_ALARM,
                 UNIT_MSR,
                 UNIT_KEYLOCK,
                 UNIT_MAIN_SCANNER,
                 UNIT_HH_SCANNER,
                 UNIT_SCALE,
                 UNIT_OPER_DISPLAY,
                 UNIT_CUST_DISPLAY,
                 UNIT_BOTH_DISPLAYS,
                 UNIT_RCPT_PRINTER,
                 UNIT_AUDT_PRINTER,
                 UNIT_BOTH_PRINTERS,
                 UNIT_SLIP_PRINTER,
                 UNIT_FIRST_CASHDRAWER,
                 UNIT_SECOND_CASHDRAWER);

for UNIT_ID use (UNIT_NONE => -1,
                 UNIT_ALL => 0,
                 UNIT_POS_KEYBOARD => 1,
                 UNIT_PC_KEYBOARD => 2,
                 UNIT_ALARM => 3,
                 UNIT_MSR => 4,
                 UNIT_KEYLOCK => 5,
                 UNIT_MAIN_SCANNER => 6,
                 UNIT_HH_SCANNER => 7,
                 UNIT_SCALE => 8,
                 UNIT_OPER_DISPLAY => 9,
                 UNIT_CUST_DISPLAY => 10,
                 UNIT_BOTH_DISPLAYS => 11,
                 UNIT_RCPT_PRINTER => 12,
                 UNIT_AUDT_PRINTER => 13,
                 UNIT_BOTH_PRINTERS => 14,
                 UNIT_SLIP_PRINTER => 15,
                 UNIT_FIRST_CASHDRAWER => 16,
                 UNIT_SECOND_CASHDRAWER => 17);

for UNIT_ID'Size use USHORT'Size;

type PUNIT_ID is access all UNIT_ID;

-- --------------------------------------------
```

```
-- Error codes.
--
type ERROR_CODE is (ERROR_OK = 0,
                    ERROR_NOT_INITIALIZED,
                    ERROR_ALREADY_INITIALIZED,
                    ERROR_OS_ERROR,
                    ERROR_COMMAND_INVALID,
                    ERROR_COMMAND_DATA_ERROR,
                    ERROR_DEVICE_INVALID,
                    ERROR_DEVICE_WRITE_FAILED,
                    ERROR_DEVICE_FAILURE,
                    ERROR_DEVICE_OFFLINE,
                    ERROR_DEVICE_SEQUENCE_ERR,
                    ERROR_DEVICE_STATUS_CHANGED,
                    ERROR_KEYBOARD_MULTIPLE_KEYS,
                    ERROR_MSR_INVALID_TRACK,
                    ERROR_MSR_MULTIPLE_TRACKS,
                    ERROR_PRINTER_FORMAT_ERR,
                    ERROR_SCALE_ILLEGAL_WEIGHT,
                    ERROR_SCALE_ZERO_DETECTED,
                    ERROR_SCALE_NOT_ZEROED,
                    ERROR_SCALE_WEIGHT_NOT_REMOVED,
                    ERROR_SCALE_VERIFY_FAILED,
                    ERROR_SCALE_WEIGHT_NOT_STABLE,
                    ERROR_SLIP_SEQUENCE_ERR);

for ERROR_CODE use (ERROR_OK => 0,
                    ERROR_NOT_INITIALIZED => 1,
                    ERROR_ALREADY_INITIALIZED => 2,
                    ERROR_OS_ERROR => 3,
                    ERROR_COMMAND_INVALID => 4,
                    ERROR_COMMAND_DATA_ERROR => 5,
                    ERROR_DEVICE_INVALID => 6,
                    ERROR_DEVICE_WRITE_FAILED => 7,
                    ERROR_DEVICE_FAILURE => 8,
                    ERROR_DEVICE_OFFLINE => 9,
                    ERROR_DEVICE_SEQUENCE_ERR => 10,
                    ERROR_DEVICE_STATUS_CHANGED => 11,
                    ERROR_KEYBOARD_MULTIPLE_KEYS => 12,
                    ERROR_MSR_INVALID_TRACK => 13,
                    ERROR_MSR_MULTIPLE_TRACKS => 14,
                    ERROR_PRINTER_FORMAT_ERR => 15,
                    ERROR_SCALE_ILLEGAL_WEIGHT => 16,
                    ERROR_SCALE_ZERO_DETECTED => 17,
                    ERROR_SCALE_NOT_ZEROED => 18,
```

```
                          ERROR_SCALE_WEIGHT_NOT_REMOVED => 19,
                          ERROR_SCALE_VERIFY_FAILED => 20,
                          ERROR_SCALE_WEIGHT_NOT_STABLE => 21,
                          ERROR_SLIP_SEQUENCE_ERR => 22);

   for ERROR_CODE'Size use USHORT'Size;

   type PERROR_CODE is access all ERROR_CODE;

   -- -------------------------------------------
   -- API Control Functions.
   --
   function Initialize
     (ApiVersion : PUSHORT)
      return ERROR_CODE;

   pragma Import(Stdcall, Initialize, "PosInitialize");

   procedure TerminatePoS
     (TermCode : in USHORT);

   pragma Import(Stdcall, TerminatePoS, "PosTerminate");

   function SystemError
      return ERROR_CODE;

   pragma Import(Stdcall, SystemError, "PosSystemError");

   -- -------------------------------------------
   -- The API Read Function.
   --
   MAX_BUFFER_LENGTH : constant USHORT := 512;

   function Read
     (Buffer         : in BYTEARRAY;
      BufferLength   : in USHORT;
      ReturnedUnit   : in PUNIT_ID;
      ReturnedLength : in PUSHORT)
      return ERROR_CODE;

   pragma Import(Stdcall, Read, "PosRead");

   -- -------------------------------------------
   -- General Device Functions.
   --
   type DEVICE_CMD is (RESET,
                       INITIALIZE,
                       FLUSH,
                       ONLINE);
```

```
for DEVICE_CMD use (RESET => 0,
                    INITIALIZE => 1,
                    FLUSH => 2,
                    ONLINE => 3);

function DeviceControl
   (Unit    : in UNIT_ID;
    Command : in DEVICE_CMD)
    return ERROR_CODE;

pragma Import(Stdcall, DeviceControl, "PosDeviceControl");

type DEVICE_STATUS is
   record
      DeviceAvailable : Boolean;
      DeviceOnLine    : Boolean;
      HandlerEnabled  : Boolean;
      ExDeviceStatus  : BYTE;
   end record;
pragma Convention(C, DEVICE_STATUS);

type PDEVICE_STATUS is access all DEVICE_STATUS;

for DEVICE_STATUS use
   record
      DeviceAvailable at 0 range 0 .. 1;
      DeviceOnLine    at 0 range 1 .. 2;
      HandlerEnabled  at 0 range 2 .. 3;
      ExDeviceStatus  at 1 range 0 .. 7;
   end record;

function DeviceStatus
   (Unit    : in UNIT_ID;
    Command : in PDEVICE_STATUS)
    return ERROR_CODE;

pragma Import(Stdcall, DeviceStatus, "PosDeviceStatus");

-- ----------------------------------------------
-- Alarm Device Functions.
--
type ALARM_TONE is
   record
      Duration : USHORT;
      Pitch    : USHORT;
      Volume   : USHORT;
   end record;
pragma Convention(C, ALARM_TONE);
```

```
type ALARM_CONFIG is
   record
      Tone1            : ALARM_TONE;
      Tone2            : ALARM_TONE;
      SupportsTone2    : Boolean;
      SupportsInterrupt : Boolean;
   end record;
pragma Convention(C, ALARM_CONFIG);
type PALARM_CONFIG is access all ALARM_CONFIG;

for ALARM_CONFIG use
   record
      Tone1            at 0  range 0 .. 47;
      Tone2            at 6  range 0 .. 47;
      SupportsTone2    at 12 range 0 .. 1;
      SupportsInterrupt at 12 range 1 .. 2;
   end record;

function AlarmConfig
  (Unit         : in UNIT_ID;
   ConfigRecord : in PALARM_CONFIG)
   return ERROR_CODE;

pragma Import(Stdcall, AlarmConfig, "PosAlarmConfig");

function AlarmSound
  (Unit         : in UNIT_ID;
   RepeatValue : in USHORT)
   return ERROR_CODE;

pragma Import(Stdcall, AlarmSound, "PosAlarmSound");

-- ----------------------------------------------
-- Display Device Functions.
--
FADE_ON  : constant := 1;
FADE_OFF : constant := 0;

type DISPLAY_CONFIG is
   record
      NumberOfLines     : USHORT;
      CharactersPerLine : USHORT;
      NumberOfLEDs      : USHORT;
      SupportsScrolling : Boolean;
      SupportsFade      : Boolean;
   end record;
pragma Convention(C, DISPLAY_CONFIG);
type PDISPLAY_CONFIG is access all DISPLAY_CONFIG;
```

```
for DISPLAY_CONFIG use
   record
      NumberOfLines       at 0 range 0 .. 15;
      CharactersPerLine  at 2 range 0 .. 15;
      NumberOfLEDs        at 4 range 0 .. 15;
      SupportsScrolling  at 6 range 0 .. 1;
      SupportsFade        at 6 range 1 .. 2;
   end record;

function DisplayConfig
  (Unit         : in UNIT_ID;
   ConfigRecord : in PDISPLAY_CONFIG)
   return ERROR_CODE;

pragma Import(Stdcall, DisplayConfig, "PosDisplayConfig");

function DisplayText
  (Unit         : in UNIT_ID;
   LineNumber   : in USHORT;
   ColumnNumber : in USHORT;
   TextBuffer   : in PSZ)
   return ERROR_CODE;

pragma Import(Stdcall, DisplayText, "PosDisplayText");

function DisplayLed
  (Unit     : in UNIT_ID;
   LedState : in USHORT)
   return ERROR_CODE;

pragma Import(Stdcall, DisplayLed, "PosDisplayLed");

-- --------------------------------------------
-- Display Device Functions.
--

DRAWER_OPEN   : constant := 1;
DRAWER_CLOSED : constant := 0;

function OpenDrawer
  (Unit : in UNIT_ID)
   return ERROR_CODE;

pragma Import(Stdcall, OpenDrawer, "PosCashdrawerOpen");

function LockDrawer
  (Unit : in UNIT_ID;
   On   : in Boolean)
   return ERROR_CODE;

pragma Import(Stdcall, LockDrawer, "PosCashdrawerLock");
```

```
-- ------------------------------------------
-- MSR not used, binding not included
--

-- ------------------------------------------
-- Port handler not used, binding not included
--

-- ------------------------------------------
-- Display Device Functions.
--
PAPER_LOW        : constant := 1;
PAPER_BACK       : constant := 0;
SLIP_PAPER_IN    : constant := 2;
SLIP_PAPER_OUT   : constant := 0;

type PRINTER_CAPS is (EPC_WIDE_ON,
                      EPC_WIDE_OFF,
                      EPC_TALL_ON,
                      EPC_TALL_OFF,
                      EPC_BOLD_ON,
                      EPC_BOLD_OFF,
                      EPC_ITALICS_ON,
                      EPC_ITALICS_OFF,
                      EPC_SIDEWAYS_ON,
                      EPC_SIDEWAYS_OFF,
                      EPC_INVERTED_ON,
                      EPC_INVERTED_OFF);

for PRINTER_CAPS use (EPC_WIDE_ON => 16,
                      EPC_WIDE_OFF => 17,
                      EPC_TALL_ON => 18,
                      EPC_TALL_OFF => 19,
                      EPC_BOLD_ON => 20,
                      EPC_BOLD_OFF => 21,
                      EPC_ITALICS_ON => 22,
                      EPC_ITALICS_OFF => 23,
                      EPC_SIDEWAYS_ON => 24,
                      EPC_SIDEWAYS_OFF => 25,
                      EPC_INVERTED_ON => 26,
                      EPC_INVERTED_OFF => 27);

type PRINTER_CONFIG is
   record
      NumberOfLines          : USHORT;
      CharactersPerLine      : USHORT;
      CutMargin              : USHORT;
```

```ada
      SupportsPaperCut        : Boolean;
      SupportsPaperPerforate  : Boolean;
      SupportsWide            : Boolean;
      SupportsTall            : Boolean;
      SupportsBold            : Boolean;
      SupportsItalic          : Boolean;
      SupportsSideways        : Boolean;
      SupportsInverted        : Boolean;
   end record;
pragma Convention(C, PRINTER_CONFIG);
type PPRINTER_CONFIG is access all PRINTER_CONFIG;

for PRINTER_CONFIG use
   record
      NumberOfLines          at 0 range 0 .. 15;
      CharactersPerLine      at 2 range 0 .. 15;
      CutMargin              at 4 range 0 .. 15;
      SupportsPaperCut       at 6 range 0 .. 1;
      SupportsPaperPerforate at 6 range 1 .. 2;
      SupportsWide           at 6 range 2 .. 3;
      SupportsTall           at 6 range 3 .. 4;
      SupportsBold           at 6 range 4 .. 5;
      SupportsItalic         at 6 range 5 .. 6;
      SupportsSideways       at 6 range 6 .. 7;
      SupportsInverted       at 6 range 7 .. 8;
   end record;

function PrinterConfig
   (Unit         : in UNIT_ID;
    ConfigRecord : in PPRINTER_CONFIG)
    return ERROR_CODE;

pragma Import(Stdcall, PrinterConfig, "PosPrinterConfig");

function PrintText
   (Unit            : in UNIT_ID;
    LinefeedsBefore : in USHORT;
    LinefeedsAfter  : in USHORT;
    TextBuffer      : in PSZ)
    return ERROR_CODE;

pragma Import(Stdcall, PrintText, "PosPrintText");

function PrinterAdvance
   (Unit          : in UNIT_ID;
    NumberOfLines : in BYTE)
    return ERROR_CODE;
```

```
pragma Import(Stdcall, PrinterAdvance, "PosPrinterAdvance");

function PrinterCut
  (Unit          : in UNIT_ID;
   PerforateOnly : in Boolean)
   return ERROR_CODE;

pragma Import(Stdcall, PrinterCut, "PosPrinterCut");

type SLIPPRINTER_CMD is (OPEN_JAWS,
                         CLOSE_JAWS,
                         ROLL_PAPER_IN,
                         EJECT_PAPER);

for SLIPPRINTER_CMD use (OPEN_JAWS => 0,
                         CLOSE_JAWS => 1,
                         ROLL_PAPER_IN => 2,
                         EJECT_PAPER => 3);

function SlipPrinterCommand
  (Unit    : in UNIT_ID;
   Command : in SLIPPRINTER_CMD)
   return ERROR_CODE;

pragma Import(Stdcall, SlipPrinterCommand,
                       "PosSlipPrinterCommand");

-- -------------------------------------------
-- Weigh Scale not used, binding not included
--

end Pos;
```

9.1.3 Interfacing to COBOL

This package provides very similar facilities to the `Interfaces.C` package standard types, and subprograms to pass them between the two languages. Another goal of the COBOL interfaces section is the ability for each language to produce compatible data in files, that is to write a record from COBOL and be able to read it in an Ada program.

Library specification: package `Interfaces.COBOL` ⎯⎯⎯⎯⎯⎯⎯⎯

```
package Interfaces.COBOL is

  -- Types and operations for internal
  -- data representation
  type Floating      is new Float;
  type Long_Floating is new Long_Float;

  type Binary        is new Integer;
  type Long_Binary   is new Long_Long_Integer;
```

```
Max_Digits_Binary      : constant := 9;
Max_Digits_Long_Binary : constant := 18;

type Decimal_Element is mod 16;

type Packed_Decimal is array (Positive range <>)
   of Decimal_Element;
pragma Pack (Packed_Decimal);

type COBOL_Character is new Character;

Ada_To_COBOL : array (Standard.Character)
   of COBOL_Character := (
      COBOL_Character'Val (000),
      COBOL_Character'Val (001),

      ..

      COBOL_Character'Val (255));

COBOL_To_Ada : array (COBOL_Character)
   of Standard.Character := (
      Standard.Character'Val (000),
      Standard.Character'Val (001),

      ..

      Standard.Character'Val (255));

type Alphanumeric is array (Positive range <>)
   of COBOL_Character;

function To_COBOL
   (Item   : String) return Alphanumeric;

function To_Ada
   (Item   : Alphanumeric) return String;

procedure To_COBOL
   (Item   :      String;
    Target : out Alphanumeric;
    Last   : out Natural);

procedure To_Ada
   (Item   :      Alphanumeric;
    Target : out String;
    Last   : out Natural);

type Numeric is array (Positive range <>)
   of COBOL_CHARACTER;

-- Formats for COBOL data representations
type Display_Format is private;
```

```
Unsigned               : constant Display_Format;
Leading_Separate       : constant Display_Format;
Trailing_Separate      : constant Display_Format;
Leading_Nonseparate    : constant Display_Format;
Trailing_Nonseparate   : constant Display_Format;

type Binary_Format is private;

High_Order_First            : constant Binary_Format;
Low_Order_First             : constant Binary_Format;
Native_Binary               : constant Binary_Format;
High_Order_First_Unsigned   : constant Binary_Format;
Low_Order_First_Unsigned    : constant Binary_Format;
Native_Binary_Unsigned      : constant Binary_Format;

type Packed_Format is private;

Packed_Unsigned    : constant Packed_Format;
Packed_Signed      : constant Packed_Format;


-- Types for external representation of
-- COBOL binary data
type Byte is mod 2 ** COBOL_Character'Size;
type Byte_Array is array (Positive range <>)
   of Byte;

Conversion_Error : exception;

generic
   type Num is delta <> digits <>;

package Decimal_Conversions is

   -- Display formats: data values as Numerics
   function Valid
     (Item   : Numeric;
      Format : Display_Format)
      return Boolean;

   function Length
     (Format : Display_Format)
      return Natural;

   function To_Decimal
     (Item   : Numeric;
      Format : Display_Format)
      return Num;

   function To_Display
     (Item   : Num;
```

```
   Format : Display_Format)
     return Numeric;

-- Display formats: data values as Packed_Decimal
function Valid
  (Item    : Packed_Decimal;
   Format : Packed_Format)
     return Boolean;

function Length
  (Format : Packed_Format)
     return Natural;

function To_Decimal
  (Item    : Packed_Decimal;
   Format : Packed_Format)
     return Num;

function To_Packed
  (Item    : Num;
   Format : Packed_Format)
     return Packed_Decimal;

-- Display formats: data values as Byte_Array
function Valid
  (Item    : Byte_Array;
   Format : Binary_Format)
     return Boolean;

function Length
  (Format : Binary_Format)
     return Natural;

function To_Decimal
  (Item    : Byte_Array;
   Format : Binary_Format)
     return Num;

function To_Binary
  (Item    : Num;
   Format : Binary_Format)
     return Byte_Array;

-- Display formats: data values as Long_Binary
function To_Decimal
  (Item : Binary) return Num;

function To_Decimal
  (Item : Long_Binary) return Num;
```

```
    function To_Binary
       (Item : Num) return Binary;

    function To_Long_Binary
       (Item : Num) return Long_Binary;

  private
     ..
  end Decimal_Conversions;

private
  ..
end Interfaces.COBOL;
```

Discussion and examples of the use of this package are beyond the scope of this book.

9.1.4   Interfacing to FORTRAN

```
package Interfaces.Fortran is
   pragma Pure (Fortran);

   type Fortran_Integer  is new Integer;
   type Real             is new Float;
   type Double_Precision is new Long_Float;
   type Logical          is new Boolean;

   package Single_Precision_Complex_Types is
      new Ada.Numerics.Generic_Complex_Types (Real);

   type Complex is new
      Single_Precision_Complex_Types.Complex;

   type Imaginary is new
      Single_Precision_Complex_Types.Imaginary;
   i : constant Imaginary := Imaginary
      (Single_Precision_Complex_Types.i);
   j : constant Imaginary := Imaginary
      (Single_Precision_Complex_Types.j);

   type Character_Set is new Character;

   type Fortran_Character is array(Positive range <>)
      of Character_Set;

   function To_Fortran
      (Item : in Character) return Character_Set;
```

```
function To_Ada
  (Item : in Character_Set) return Character;
function To_Fortran
  (Item : in String) return Fortran_Character;
function To_Ada
  (Item : in Fortran_Character) return String;
procedure To_Fortran
  (Item   : in  String;
   Target : out Fortran_Character;
   Last   : out Natural);
procedure To_Ada
  (Item   : in  Fortran_Character;
   Target : out String;
   Last   : out Natural);

end Interfaces.Fortran;
```

Discussion and examples of this package are beyond the scope of this book.

9.2 Annex C: systems programming annex

This annex provides facilities for programming at a very low level; for instance it introduces a new language convention `Assembler` for use with the interface pragmas in Section 9.1.1 to allow Ada to call assembly language routines.

The facilities here are usually included in any implementation. There are some very useful features, not just for systems level programming, but for more day-to-day concerns.

9.2.1 Interrupt handling

This optional annex introduces two new library packages `Ada.Interrupts` and its child `Ada.Interrupts.Names` which provide the ability to use Ada subprograms as interrupt handlers. Actual interrupt handler subprograms must be *protected procedures*, procedures declared within a protected type. This has one major benefit in that such a procedure cannot be called more than once simultaneously.

To assist the packages below two additional pragmas are also included in this annex.

- **pragma** `Interrupt_Handler(Handler_Name);` This pragma identifies a protected procedure which is to be used as an interrupt handler. It is not installed as a handler; this has to be done using the facilities in the packages below.

- **pragma** Attach_Handler(Handler_Name, expression); This pragma directly associates a protected procedure with a given interrupt to act as an interrupt handler.

Library specification: package Ada.Interrupts ⎯⎯⎯⎯⎯⎯⎯⎯⎯

```
with System;

package Ada.Interrupts is

    type Interrupt_ID is .. -- implementation defined.
    type Parameterless_Handler is
       access protected procedure;

    function Is_Reserved (Interrupt : Interrupt_ID)
       return Boolean;

    function Is_Attached (Interrupt : Interrupt_ID)
       return Boolean;

    function Current_Handler (Interrupt : Interrupt_ID)
       return Parameterless_Handler;

    procedure Attach_Handler
       (New_Handler : in Parameterless_Handler;
        Interrupt   : in Interrupt_ID);

    procedure Exchange_Handler
       (Old_Handler : out Parameterless_Handler;
        New_Handler : in  Parameterless_Handler;
        Interrupt   : in  Interrupt_ID);

    procedure Detach_Handler
       (Interrupt : in Interrupt_ID);

    function Reference (Interrupt : Interrupt_ID)
       return System.Address;
private
    ..
end Ada.Interrupts;
```

This provides the ability to attach a protected procedure to an interrupt identifier. The subprograms Is_Reserved and Is_Attached can also be used to find out the state of an interrupt and its associated handler.

Library specification: example package Ada.Interrupts.Names ⎯⎯⎯⎯⎯

```
package Ada.Interrupts.Names is

    Keyboard_Controller : constant Interrupt_ID := 1;
    Unused02            : constant Interrupt_ID := 2;
    Serial_Port01       : constant Interrupt_ID := 3;
```

```
Mouse_Port            : constant Interrupt_ID := 4;
Unused05              : constant Interrupt_ID := 5;
Floppy_Controller     : constant Interrupt_ID := 6;
Unused07              : constant Interrupt_ID := 7;
Unused08              : constant Interrupt_ID := 8;
Unused09              : constant Interrupt_ID := 9;
Unused10              : constant Interrupt_ID := 10;
Unused11              : constant Interrupt_ID := 11;
Unused12              : constant Interrupt_ID := 12;
Unused13              : constant Interrupt_ID := 13;
Unused14              : constant Interrupt_ID := 14;
Unused15              : constant Interrupt_ID := 15;
end Ada.Interrupts.Names;
```

This child package simply provides a list of symbolic names and their interrupt IDs; the package is completely implementation-dependent. The example above is *completely contrived* and denotes a standard configuration for a PC.

Now we can take all this information and develop an interrupt handler for some arbitrary device attached to our first PC serial port.

Example 9.1   Compile-time interrupt handler _____

```
with Ada.Interrupts;

package body Our_Device is

    -- internal

    protected type Device_Handler is

        entry Read(Char  : out Character);
        entry Write(Char : in  Character);
    private

        procedure Handler;
        pragma Attach_Handler(Handler,
                              Ada.Interrupts.Names.Serial_Port01);
    end Device_Handler;

    ..

end Our_Device;
```

In this example you can see that we have used the pragma `Attach_Handler` to map the handler for our device statically to the serial port interrupt.

This solution, although perfectly legal, may not be acceptable in some environments. For example, if we run the resulting application we take possession of the interrupt, but what happens when our application terminates? Does the operating system return the original handler?

If this is an embedded application, or part of the operating system itself, then such code is perfectly acceptable. If not then we need a way to manage the interrupt handlers more flexibly.

Example 9.2   Run-time interrupt handler ─────────────────────────

```ada
with Ada.Interrupts;
use Ada;

package body Our_Device is

   -- internal

   protected type Device_Handler is

       entry Read(Char  : out Character);
       entry Write(Char : in  Character);
   private

       procedure Handler;
       pragma Interrupt_Handler(Handler);
   end Device_Handler;

   ..

   Our_Interrupt : Interrupts.Interrupt_ID;
   Old_Handler   : Interrupts.Parameterless_Handler:=null;
begin

   Get_Our_Interrupt(Our_Interrupt);

   if Interrupts.Is_Attached(Our_Interrupt) then
       Interrupts.Exchange_Handler(Old_Handler,
                                Device_Handler.Handler'Access,
                                Our_Interrupt);

   else
       Interrupts.Attach_Handler(Device_Handler.Handler'Access,
                                Our_Interrupt);

   end if;

   ..

   if Old_Handler = null then
       Interrupts.Detach_Handler(Our_Interrupt);
   else
       Interrupts.Attach_Handler(Old_Interrupt,
                                Our_Interrupt);
```

```
   end if;
end Our_Device;
```

In the example above we have used the more general facilities provided by the library **package** Ada.Interrupts to accomplish the same result. Note that if the interrupt we wish to use already has a handler then we carefully save it and restore it later.

9.2.2   Additional tasking support

The first part of the tasking support provided by this annex is the ability to obtain a unique identifier for any task. This facility is useful in many cases: it allows you to acquire an identifier for a running task, store it, and even compare it at a later stage.

Library specification: package Ada.Task_Identification ⎯⎯⎯⎯⎯⎯⎯⎯

```
package Ada.Task_Identification is

   type Task_ID is private;
   Null_Task_ID : constant Task_ID;

   function "=" (Left, Right : Task_ID) return Boolean;

   function Image (T : Task_ID) return String;

   function Current_Task return Task_ID;

   procedure Abort_Task (T : in out Task_ID);

   function Is_Terminated (T : Task_ID) return Boolean;
   function Is_Callable (T : Task_ID)    return Boolean;

private
   ..
end Ada.Task_Identification;
```

As well as using the Current_Task function to acquire a Task_ID, you can use the attribute 'Identity on a running task. Also a task can use the attribute 'Caller to receive the identifier of the task which called a given entry.

The ability to determine the identity of a task can be very useful; for example, in an application where a task is used to perform some asynchronous operation that the caller wishes to check the state of, or where a pool of tasks is used then the Task_ID can be used as a look-up mechanism for clients to determine which task may be free.

Example 9.3   Using Task_IDs ⎯⎯⎯⎯⎯⎯⎯⎯⎯⎯⎯⎯⎯⎯

```
procedure Taskpool_Test is

   task type Test is
      entry Do_It;
      entry Done(Res : in out Boolean);
   end Test;
```

```
      ..
   Test_Task : Test;
   Test_Ok   : Boolean;
begin
   Test_Task.Do_It;
   Test_Task.Done(Test_Ok);
end Taskpool_Test;
```

The entry `Do_It` initiates some asynchronous operation so that the caller can continue; however, the caller cannot continue beyond some point without knowing whether the asynchronous operation has completed, so the `Done` entry returns a completed flag. The `Do_It` entry can use attribute `'Caller` to get the `Task_ID` of the task calling the entry. It could then use this as a key into a data structure containing results.

```
task body Test is
   package Results is new Map(Task_ID, Boolean);
begin
   Results.ExcludeAll;
   loop
      accept Do_It do
         if Results.Includes(Do_It'Caller) then
            raise Already_Working_For_You;
         else
            Results.Include(Do_It'Caller, False);
            .. -- start operation.
         end if;
      end Do_It;

      accept Done(Result : in out Boolean) do
         if Results.Includes(Do_It'Caller) then
            Result := Results.Value(Do_It'Caller);
            if Result then
               Results.Exclude(Do_It'Caller);
            end if;
         else
            raise Not_Working_For_You;
         end if;
      end Done;
   end loop;
end Test;
```

The body of the task relies on a package `Map` which associates a key (`Task_ID`) with a value (`Boolean`) which we set in the `Do_It` entry and which we query, and possibly clear, in the `Done` entry.

Library specification: package `Ada.Task_Attributes` _____

```
with Ada.Task_Identification;
use  Ada.Task_Identification;

generic
   type Attribute is private;
   Initial_Value : in Attribute;
package Ada.Task_Attributes is

   type Attribute_Handle is access all Attribute;

   function Value (T : Task_Id := Current_Task)
      return Attribute;

   function Reference (T : Task_Id := Current_Task)
      return Attribute_Handle;

   procedure Set_Value (Val : Attribute;
                        T   : Task_Id := Current_Task);

   procedure Reinitialize (T : Task_Id := Current_Task);

end Ada.Task_Attributes;
```

This package is provided for tasking support and allows you to create a package that acts like an attribute for each and every task in an application. This generic package is quite difficult to describe, but its use can be seen with a small example (though we will present the library package itself first).

_____

Our example creates a new attribute called `Threaded` which can then be set/queried on a per task basis. The attribute type is `Boolean` and the initial value is `True`. The body of the procedure itself will print out the value of the attribute for the main task and for the dependent task `An_X`.

```
-- file: Task_Test.adb
with Ada.Task_Attributes;
with Ada.Text_IO;
use  Ada;

procedure Task_Test is

   package Threaded is new Task_Attributes(Boolean,
                                           True);

   task type X is
      entry Start;
   end X;

   task body X is
   begin
```

```
        Threaded.Set_Value(False);
        accept Start do
            null;
        end Start;
    end X;

    An_X : X;
begin
    Text_IO.Put_Line("Current Task Value = " &
                    Boolean'Image(Threaded.Value));

    Text_IO.Put_Line("An_X Value = " &
                    Boolean'Image(Threaded.Value(An_X'Identity)));

end Task_Test;
```

9.2.3 Additional pragmas

This annex also provides some additional pragmas specifically for informing the compiler of specific code generation requirements.

- **pragma** Discard_Names   This is an important pragma for people trying to optimize applications for size. The pragma instructs the compiler to remove information about the name of certain types of objects, enumerations, new types, new subtypes, or exceptions. The exclusion of the name of these objects at run-time can be a considerable space saving; however, for enumerations and exceptions it is important to note that certain previously available features are no longer available.

  For example, the use of 'Image on an object of an enumerated type specified in a pragma Discard_Names is implementation-defined; the compiler should have removed the name information so what is displayed? Also for exceptions, the functions in Ada.Exceptions which provide the name of an exception from its 'Identity may no longer work.
  This pragma may also be used with no parameter specified, in which case it applies to all declarations following it to the end of the current declarative region.

- **pragma** Atomic
- **pragma** Atomic_Components

These two pragmas denote that an object must be read and written in an indivisible operation if the underlying implementation supports it for that type. The second pragma is used for an array or record to denote that all components are assumed to be atomic.
  It important to note the fact that the reference manual does specify that the underlying implementation must support atomic reads and writes for the specified type, means that no unnecessary overheads are introduced to support atomicity where it is not warranted.

- **pragma** Volatile
- **pragma** Volatile_Components

These pragmas specify that an object may not be under the full control of the Ada program; it may be an object shared with system code, so all reads and writes must be done direct to memory, and no register optimization should be performed by the compiler.

```
with System;
with System.Storage_Elements;

package Main is

    Test_Address : constant System.Address :=
    System.Storage_Elements.To_Address(16#0340#);

    Test : Integer;
    for Test'Address use Test_Address;
    pragma Volatile(Test);
    ..
```

The example above shows an object `Test` which has an address representation clause specifying its physical location. We can assume this is some operating system or hardware storage area, so we use the `Volatile` pragma to make sure that if the object is passed as a parameter to a subprogram, the compiler will not use smart optimizations which would mean that updates are not committed directly to memory.

9.3   Annex D: real-time systems annex

This annex provides additional facilities for programming in either a hard or soft real-time environment. The implementation of this annex requires the facilities of the system's programming annex, so validation of this annex is dependent on validation of the previous one.

The main thrust of this annex is to provide programmers of real-time systems with an environment which provides fixed, predictable scheduling of tasks and interrupts within an application.

9.3.1   Tasking and scheduling

Scheduling model

This annex describes the tasking model of the Ada run-time environment in much greater detail and covers a priority scheduling model required for real-time systems. The basic model is for pre-emptive scheduling within a priority mechanism; each task within the application has a priority and state where the state can be used to indicate whether it is ready to be run. Each ready to run task is placed in the ready queue in order of priority. The point at which scheduling decisions are made is called a task dispatching point, and may be, for example, the completion of an **accept** statement when the scheduler decides which task is activated next.

We will cover first the priority part of this model, the range of priorities and the mechanisms for assigning them, and will then move on to the facilities for altering the scheduling model itself.

Priority types

The complete range of priorities is denoted by the type `Any_Priority` in the package `System`.

```
subtype Any_Priority is Integer range -- Implementation defined.
```

This is used as the base type for two further range types indicating actual priority values. The first, `Priority`, holds the actual range of values for tasking priorities and must have at least 30 discrete values. The second, `Interrupt_Priority`, is used to schedule interrupts and must have at least one discrete value.

```
subtype Priority is Any_Priority
    range Any_Priority'First .. -- Implementation defined
subtype Interrupt_Priority is Any_Priority
    range Priority'First+1 .. Any_Priority'Last;
```

The scheduler also declares a default priority in the package `System` which is used when no priorities are set by the programmer.

```
Default_Priority : constant Priority :=
    (Priority'First + Priority'Last)/2;
```

Priority pragmas

To set a priority for a task or interrupt handler the following two pragmas are used. The first may only appear as the first declaration within a task or protected type specification or the declarative part of a subprogram body, the second cannot be used in a subprogram body.

- **pragma** Priority(expr)
- **pragma** Interrupt_Priority(expr)

These set the priority of a task, protected type or subprogram and take an integer expression as an argument.

Library specification: package Ada.Dynamic_Priorities _____

```
with System;
with Ada.Task_Identification;

package Ada.Dynamic_Priorities is

   procedure Set_Priority
     (Priority : System.Any_Priority;
      T        : Ada.Task_Identification.Task_Id :=
                   Ada.Task_Identification.Current_Task);

   function Get_Priority
     (T        : Ada.Task_Identification.Task_Id :=
                   Ada.Task_Identification.Current_Task)
     return System.Any_Priority;

end Ada.Dynamic_Priorities;
```

This package allows the programmer to alter the priorities of tasks in a running application. This can, when used carefully and with experience, enable an application to monitor its environment and change its performance to match external events. However, it can also lead to a real mess if not used wisely. For example, it is not always obvious when the change in priority takes place in a running system.

Scheduling pragmas

The following configuration pragmas are used to alter the scheduling model itself.

- **pragma** Task_Dispatching_Policy() This pragma informs the scheduler of the way in which the ready queue is interpreted. The only language-defined parameter is FIFO_Within_Priorities which indicates the default model; the ready queue is read in first-in first-out order where tasks are grouped by priority. Other parameters may be specified by an implementation.

- **pragma** Locking_Policy() This pragma alters the way protected object locking is interpreted. The only language-defined parameter for this pragma is Ceiling_Locking which uses the priority of the protected type to indicate a ceiling priority for callers of the protected type. Other parameters may be specified by an implementation.

Note: if the Task_Dispatching_Policy is FIFO_Within_Priorities then the Locking_Policy must be Ceiling_Locking.

- **pragma** Queing_Policy() FIFO_Queing, Priority_Queing This pragma alters the way the queue associated with task or protected type entry points is managed. This pragma has two language-defined arguments, FIFO_Queing which queues calls on a strictly first-in first-out order and

Priority_Queing which orders on a strictly priority basis. The default queuing policy is FIFO_Queing. Other parameters may be specified by an implementation.

9.3.2   Timing

One important aspect of real-time systems is, not surprisingly, timing. Real-time systems rely heavily on knowing when events occurred and when events are to be scheduled to occur. To this end this annex includes two new features which it is hoped will address the requirement for better time information. The first is a replacement to the Ada.Calendar package which specifies more precise time values, and the second is a clarification of the accuracy of the **delay** statement.

Library specification: package Ada.Real_Time ─────────────────

```
package Ada.Real_Time is

    type Time is private;
    Time_First : constant Time;
    Time_Last  : constant Time;
    Time_Unit  : constant := -- Implementation defined.

    type Time_Span is private;
    Time_Span_First : constant Time_Span;
    Time_Span_Last  : constant Time_Span;
    Time_Span_Zero  : constant Time_Span;
    Time_Span_Unit  : constant Time_Span;

    Tick : constant Time_Span;
    function Clock return Time;

    function "+" (Left : Time; Right : Time_Span) return Time;
    function "+" (Left : Time_Span; Right : Time) return Time;
    function "-" (Left : Time; Right : Time_Span) return Time;
    function "-" (Left : Time; Right : Time) return Time_Span;

    function "<"  (Left, Right : Time) return Boolean;
    function "<=" (Left, Right : Time) return Boolean;
    function ">"  (Left, Right : Time) return Boolean;
    function ">=" (Left, Right : Time) return Boolean;

    function "+" (Left, Right : Time_Span)         return Time_Span;
    function "-" (Left, Right : Time_Span)         return Time_Span;
    function "-" (Right : Time_Span)               return Time_Span;
    function "*" (Left : Time_Span; Right : Integer)
       return Time_Span;
    function "*" (Left : Integer;   Right : Time_Span)
       return Time_Span;
```

```
function "/" (Left, Right : Time_Span)        return Integer;
function "/" (Left : Time_Span; Right : Integer)
   return Time_Span;

function "abs" (Right : Time_Span) return Time_Span;

function "<"  (Left, Right : Time_Span) return Boolean;
function "<=" (Left, Right : Time_Span) return Boolean;
function ">"  (Left, Right : Time_Span) return Boolean;
function ">=" (Left, Right : Time_Span) return Boolean;

function To_Duration  (TS : Time_Span) return Duration;
function To_Time_Span (D  : Duration)  return Time_Span;

function Nanoseconds  (NS : integer) return Time_Span;
function Microseconds (US : integer) return Time_Span;
function Milliseconds (MS : integer) return Time_Span;

type Seconds_Count is new integer
   range -integer'Last .. integer'Last;

procedure Split
  (T  : Time;
   SC : out Seconds_Count;
   TS : out Time_Span);
function Time_Of
  (SC : Seconds_Count;
   TS : Time_Span)
   return Time;

private
  ..
end Ada.Real_Time;
```

This package provides, as you can see, more precise time functions than those provided by the `Ada.Calendar` package. Note that the `Time_Unit` and `Time_Span_Unit` constants define the smallest interval represented in a given implementation.

The clarification of the **delay until** statement includes its operation with arguments of type `Ada.Real_Time.Time` instead of the more normal `Standard.Duration`.

9.3.3   Synchronous and asynchronous task control

This section describes two packages that provide some fine-grained control over task synchronization.

Library specification: **package** Ada.Synchronous_Task_Control ————

```
package Ada.Synchronous_Task_Control is

    type Suspension_Object is limited private;
    procedure Set_True (S : in out Suspension_Object);
    procedure Set_False (S : in out Suspension_Object);
    function  Current_State (S : Suspension_Object) return Boolean;
    procedure Suspend_Until_True (S : in out Suspension_Object);

private

    ..

end Ada.Synchronous_Task_Control;
```

This package in effect presents us a binary semaphore, with which we could replace the Mutex defined in Section 7.4.1.

Library specification: **package** Ada.Asynchronous_Task_Control ————

```
with Ada.Task_Identification;
package Ada.Asynchronous_Task_Control is

    procedure Hold (T : Ada.Task_Identification.Task_Id);
    procedure Continue (T : Ada.Task_Identification.Task_Id);
    function  Is_Held (T : Ada.Task_Identification.Task_Id)
        return Boolean;

end Ada.Asynchronous_Task_Control;
```

This package provides facilities to change the state of any task for which we can get the Task_ID. Note, when you call the Continue procedure the task in question may not immediately run; the scheduler will simply re-evaluate the state of that task and if it is eligible it will be placed on the ready queue.

These two packages differ greatly; the first is a true synchronization mechanism, as we have said in Section 7.4.1, and provides a facility which the normal rendezvous mechanisms do not. The second package provides not true synchronization operations, but some rather dramatic facilities to stop another task.

9.3.4 Restrictions

This annex defines some additional parameters for the pragma Restrictions. Below is a brief list of the new parameters:

```
Max_Asynchronous_Select_Nesting
Max_Protected_Entries
Max_Select_Alternatives
Max_Storage_At_Blocking
```

```
Max_Task_Entries
Max_Tasks
No_Abort_Statements
No_Dynamic_Priorities
No_Implicit_Heap_Allocators
No_Nested_Finalization
No_Task_Allocators
No_Task_Hierarchy
No_Terminate_Alternatives
```

These all assist the programmer in reducing unwanted effects and minimizing the size and requirements of the run-time environment.

9.4 Annex E: distributed systems annex

Ada95 has added support for distributed systems, where the application is distributed across a number of separate computation systems. The model for this is based around the idea of a number of cooperating *partitions* available across a number of cooperating processing nodes. The language specification defines how these partitions are to look, what restrictions are to be placed on distributed programs and how the run-time system manages calls between partitions. The specification does not, however, describe how one configures the distributed system, how partitions identify themselves to other active partitions, and how partitions manage a number of concurrent connections.

9.4.1 Partitions and library units

So far we have always talked about an Ada program or an Ada application, a single entity you can see. This view breaks down in a distributed system, so for example we have so far assumed the following:

- Our Ada program is a linked set of units starting with a specified entry procedure and consisting of units we have developed and units linked in from external libraries.
- Our Ada program runs as one or more cooperating tasks within a single address space.

In a distributed system there are many such programs working in cooperation. In such a system each distinct component is called a *partition*. An Ada95 distributed system is therefore a collection of one or more partitions cooperating across process and machine boundaries to provide a complete application.

Partitions exist in two forms, active and passive, to facilitate both distributed processing and shared data within the application. Active partitions equate to our current definition of an application and communicate by using remote procedure calls (RPC). Passive partitions provide shared types and shared data which can be shared between active partitions.

All communication between active partitions is through the language-specified partition communication subsystem (PCS) of which the package `System.RPC` is a part. The PCS defines the way in which remote calls are made, but does not specify what physical medium is used to transmit the messages.

9.4.2 Passive partitions and shared data

A package that acts as a passive partition provides global data for a distributed application and as such has to include the `Shared_Passive` pragma to denote the fact, and must conform to certain rules.

```
package Database_Names is
   pragma Shared_Passive(Database_Names);
   ..
```

The rules are that as this is a passive partition with no associated code then no elaboration is possible. This means that any such package must be pre-elaboratable, so that the inclusion of the additional pragma `Preelaborate(Database_Names)` is assumed. Also this package can only depend on packages that are also `Shared_Passive` or are pure (pragma `Pure` applies).

There is another form of passive partition, the `Remote_Types` partition, which provides type declarations used in communicating between active partitions. A remote types package may only depend on other remote types packages, shared passive packages, or pure packages.

9.4.3 Active partitions and remote subprograms

An active partition is one that contains packages whose specification includes the pragma `Remote_Call_Interface` or the pragma `All_Call_Remote`. Such a package exposes subprograms which may be called by remote partitions and has most of the restrictions of the shared passive and remote types packages lifted. Your package specification cannot, however, declare variables, limited types, nested generics, and inline subprograms.

If a package has specified `Remote_Call_Interface` then remote callers are routed through the PCS; if they are within the same partition then the call is a normal subprogram call. If, however, the pragma `All_Calls_Remote` is specified then even local callers are routed through the PCS.

Example 9.4   Remote call package ────────────────────────────────

```
-- file: Remote_Test.ads
package Remote_Test is

   pragma Remote_Call_Interface(Remote_Test);
```

```
procedure First_Remote;
function Second_Remote return Integer;

procedure Third_Remote;
pragma Asynchronous(Third_Remote);

type Remote_Type is tagged private;
subtype Remote_Type_Class is Remote_Type'Class;

procedure Fourth_Remote(Operand : access Remote_Type_Class);

end Remote_Test;
```

What is clear is that the first two subprograms are remote subprograms; the third is remote and asynchronous, which also means that it must be a procedure where all parameters are **in** mode only. What is also interesting is that we can dispatch calls to remote methods on a tagged type, and we can also use an access to subprogram type and execute remote subprograms by de-referencing them.

9.4.4   Communication and `System.RPC`

The PCS is that part of the Ada95 run-time that enables calls to be made between partitions. When a remote call package is compiled the compiler must produce *stubs* for the sender (or client) and receiver (or server) which manage the packaging of parameters, consistency checks, and establishment of the RPC call itself.

The PCS manages parameters by opening a stream between sender and receiver and using the stream attributes `'Read` and `'Write` on the parameters. As we said above the PCS also handles asynchronous calls and this is handled by the `Do_APC` instead of the usual `Do_RPC` in the package below.

Library specification: package `System.RPC` ——————————————————

```
with Ada.Streams;
with System.Storage_Elements;

package System.RPC is

   type Partition_ID is range 0 .. 63;

   Communication_Error : exception;

   type Params_Stream_Type
     (Initial_Size : Ada.Streams.Stream_Element_Count) is new
       Ada.Streams.Root_Stream_Type with private;

   procedure Read
     (Stream : in out Params_Stream_Type;
      Item    : out Ada.Streams.Stream_Element_Array;
      Last    : out Ada.Streams.Stream_Element_Offset);
```

```
procedure Write
  (Stream : in out Params_Stream_Type;
   Item   : in Ada.Streams.Stream_Element_Array);

-- Synchronous call
procedure Do_RPC
  (Partition : in Partition_ID;
   Params    : access Params_Stream_Type;
   Result    : access Params_Stream_Type);

-- Asynchronous call
procedure Do_APC
  (Partition : in Partition_ID;
   Params    : access Params_Stream_Type);

-- The handler for incoming RPCs.
type RPC_Receiver is
  access procedure
    (Params : access Params_Stream_Type;
     Result : access Params_Stream_Type);

procedure Establish_RPC_Receiver (
   Partition : in Partition_ID;
   Receiver  : in RPC_Receiver);
private
  ..
end System.RPC;
```

This package is a vital part of the PCS. The package defines both ends of the RPC mechanism and also declares the parameter stream type which is used to transmit the parameters between partitions.

9.4.5 Final details

The distributed system has to be built in a number of stages:

- Define the interfaces between partitions by selecting packages to be shared – passive, remote types, and remote call interface.

- Assign the packages specified above to partitions. The language standard does not cover this stage, known as configuration, but it is expected that some meta-language would be used to act as additional input to the build stage.

- Build the partitions, compiling and linking in the manner specified by your vendor. Note that compiling a remote call package will also create the client and server side of the RPC mechanism.

- Distribution, or the task of starting the various partitions on the relevant processing nodes and allowing partitions to find each other possibly over a network. Again the language standard does not cover this stage.

As you can see the language standard provides little more than the framework and some low-level support packages to assist in providing a distributed system, but it does also provide some assistance for the application programmers. For example to provide consistency in the resulting application the sender and receiver for an RPC must be expecting the same number and type of parameters, so versioning becomes important. In Ada95 this is accomplished with two new attributes, `'Version` and `'Body_Version`, which when applied to a package name supply the compiler-generated version number (of type integer).

Another useful attribute is `'Partition_ID` which when applied to any library level object will return the integer partition identifier of the partition in which the object was elaborated.

9.5   Annex F: information systems annex

This annex provides support for decimal types. Although the decimal type itself is part of the core language, the use of it was deemed to be mainly in information systems, and so any further details were put into this annex.

Information systems sounds at first like an area in which Ada was little used; however, a number of banks and other financial institutions world-wide have decided to use Ada because of its safety and the perceived lower cost of maintenance. It was therefore deemed important to add support for this large and relatively poorly supported industry within the language revision.

9.5.1   Additional decimal details

Machine radix

To facilitate conversion and cooperation with existing systems written in COBOL it is noted in the language reference manual that where the machine radix for a decimal type (specified with the attribute `'Machine_Radix`) is 10 then packaged decimal representation is to be used.

```
package Ada_Store is
    type Currency is delta 0.01 digits 8;
    for Currency'Machine_Radix use 10;
    ..
```

This would make passing an object of type `Currency` to a COBOL procedure which takes a packed decimal object easier and more efficient.

Division

The language has provided a specific division subprogram for exact handling of decimal types.

Library specification: package Ada.Decimal ─────────────────

```
package Ada.Decimal is
   pragma Pure (Decimal);

   Max_Scale : constant := -- Implementation-dependent
   Min_Scale : constant := -- Implementation-dependent

   Min_Delta : constant := 1.0E-18;
   Max_Delta : constant := 1.0E+18;

   Max_Decimal_Digits : constant := -- Implementation-dependent

   generic
      type Dividend_Type  is delta <> digits <>;
      type Divisor_Type   is delta <> digits <>;
      type Quotient_Type  is delta <> digits <>;
      type Remainder_Type is delta <> digits <>;
   procedure Divide
      (Dividend  : in  Dividend_Type;
       Divisor   : in  Divisor_Type;
       Quotient  : out Quotient_Type;
       Remainder : out Remainder_Type);
   pragma Convention(Intrinsic, Divide);

end Ada.Decimal;
```

This package provides a generic divide function for decimal types which provides both the quotient and remainder.

───

9.5.2 Edited output

Library specification: package Ada.Text_IO.Editing ─────────

```
package Ada.Text_IO.Editing is

   type Picture is private;

   function Valid
      (Pic_String      : in String;
       Blank_When_Zero : in Boolean := False)
       return             Boolean;

   function To_Picture
      (Pic_String      : in String;
       Blank_When_Zero : in Boolean := False)
       return             Picture;

   function Pic_String      (Pic : in Picture) return String;
   function Blank_When_Zero (Pic : in Picture) return Boolean;
```

```ada
Max_Picture_Length : constant := 64;

Picture_Error      : exception;

Default_Currency     : constant String    := "$";
Default_Fill         : constant Character := ' ';
Default_Separator    : constant Character := ',';
Default_Radix_Mark   : constant Character := '.';

generic
   type Num is delta <> digits <>;
   Default_Currency    : in String :=
      Text_IO.Editing.Default_Currency;
   Default_Fill        : in Character :=
      Text_IO.Editing.Default_Fill;
   Default_Separator   : in Character :=
      Text_IO.Editing.Default_Separator;
   Default_Radix_Mark : in Character :=
      Text_IO.Editing.Default_Radix_Mark;

package Decimal_Output is

   function Length
     (Pic      : in Picture;
      Currency : in String := Default_Currency)
      return     Natural;

   function Valid
     (Item     : Num;
      Pic      : in Picture;
      Currency : in String := Default_Currency)
      return     Boolean;

   function Image
     (Item       : Num;
      Pic        : in Picture;
      Currency   : in String    := Default_Currency;
      Fill       : in Character := Default_Fill;
      Separator  : in Character := Default_Separator;
      Radix_Mark : in Character := Default_Radix_Mark)
      return       String;

   procedure Put
     (File       : in File_Type;
      Item       : Num;
      Pic        : in Picture;
      Currency   : in String    := Default_Currency;
      Fill       : in Character := Default_Fill;
      Separator  : in Character := Default_Separator;
      Radix_Mark : in Character := Default_Radix_Mark);
```

```
procedure Put
   (Item        : Num;
    Pic         : in Picture;
    Currency    : in String    := Default_Currency;
    Fill        : in Character := Default_Fill;
    Separator   : in Character := Default_Separator;
    Radix_Mark  : in Character := Default_Radix_Mark);

procedure Put
   (To          : out String;
    Item        : Num;
    Pic         : in Picture;
    Currency    : in String    := Default_Currency;
    Fill        : in Character := Default_Fill;
    Separator   : in Character := Default_Separator;
    Radix_Mark  : in Character := Default_Radix_Mark);

end Decimal_Output;

private

   ..

end Ada.Text_IO.Editing;
```

This package provides the sort of flexible decimal-related output required for information systems. The actual use of the editing facilities will be familiar to anyone who has worked with COBOL for it is based on the idea of a picture string.

As you may have guessed our `Ada_Store` application uses the facilities provided above quite a bit. The following shows extracts from the package that provides operations for the application itself.

```
package body Ada_Store.PoST.Application.Operations is

   ..

   package Editing renames Ada.Text_IO.Editing;
   package Currency_EO is
      new Editing.Decimal_Output(Num => Currency,
                                 Default_Currency => "£");
   Currency_Pic : constant Editing.Picture :=
      Editing.To_Picture("$$$$_$$9.99");

   ..

   procedure Transaction_Item
      (Sales_Transaction : in out Transaction.Sale.Instance;
       Item_As_String    : in        String) is

      An_Item : Trading.Item.Instance;
      Item_No : Trading.Item.Identifier;
```

Decimal digit:	`'9'`					
Radix control:	`'.'`	`'V'`				
Sign control:	`'+'`	`'-'`	`'<'`	`'>'`	`"CR"`	`"DB"`
Currency control:	`'$'`	`'#'`				
Zero suppression:	`'Z'`	`'*'`				
Simple insertion:	`'_'`	`'B'`	`'0'`	`'/'`		

Figure 9.1   Formatting characters for picture strings.

```
   Line_Out : String(1 .. 20) := (others => ' ');
   Line_Prn : String(1 .. 40) := (others => ' ');
begin
   Item_No := Trading.Item.Identifier'Value(Item_As_String);
   An_Item := Trading.Item.Lookup(Item_No);

   declare
      Price : String :=
         Currency_EO.Image(Trading.Item.Price(An_Item),
                        Currency_Pic);
      Description : String :=
         String(Trading.Item.Display_Description(An_Item));
   begin
      Trading.Transaction.Sale.Add_Item(Sales_Transaction,
                                 An_Item);

      Display.Clear(Displays(Customer));
      Display.Write(Displays(Customer), 1, Description);
      Ada.Strings.Fixed.Replace_Slice(Line_Out,
                                 21 - Price'Length,
                                 20,
                                 Price);
      Display.Write(Displays(Customer), 2, Line_Out);

      ..
```

The object `Currency_Pic` is a picture that describes the way we want to display decimal values and that is subsequently used to dispaly price information in the procedure `Transaction_Item`.

For those without a background in COBOL programming here is a brief overview of picture strings. Firstly the picture string contains a mask into which the decimal value is placed with some special formatting. The formatting characters are specified in Figure 9.1.

The digit, radix, and currency characters simply denote where to place the corresponding input character in the output string. The sign control characters are slightly more complex; those that represent negative values ('-', '>', "DB") do not simply denote the position of a negative sign, they position the corresponding sign if the value is negative and space characters if the value is positive. If you use the positive characters ('+', '<', "CR") then the positive sign is used if the value is positive and the corresponding negative sign is used if the value is negative. The zero suppression characters are used to suppress leading and/or trailing zeros in the output.

Example 9.5 Use of Ada.Text_IO.Editing ——————————————

Input Decimal	Picture String	Output
−1.0	"−9.99"	"−1.00"
	"+9.99"	"−1.00"
+1.0	"−9.99"	" 1.00"
	"+9.99"	"+1.00"
1234.56	"99999.99"	"01234.56"
	"9_999.99"	"1,234.56"
1.99	"$_$$9.99−"	" $1.99 "
.50	"$_$$9.99−"	" $0.50 "
−2.99	"$_$$9.99−"	" $2.99−"
1.99	"$*_**9.99"	"$*,**1.99"
123456.99"	"$*_**9.99"	exception

As you can see the flexibility of the picture string aids financial applications a great deal (this table is available as a program Decimal_Test.adb).

9.6 Annex G: numerics annex

This annex is provided to support those developing compute-intensive applications, particularly scientific computing. This annex will probably be used in conjunction with the FORTRAN interface package to work with numeric applications written in FORTRAN.

9.6.1 Complex numbers

Library specification: **package** Ada.Numerics.Generic_Complex_Types ——

```
generic
   type Real is digits <>;

package Ada.Numerics.Generic_Complex_Types is
   pragma Pure (Generic_Complex_Types);

   type Complex is record
      Re, Im : Real'Base;
   end record;
```

```
type Imaginary is private;

i : constant Imaginary;
j : constant Imaginary;

function Re (X : Complex)    return Real'Base;
function Im (X : Complex)    return Real'Base;
function Im (X : Imaginary) return Real'Base;

procedure Set_Re (X : in out Complex;   Re : in Real'Base);
procedure Set_Im (X : in out Complex;   Im : in Real'Base);
procedure Set_Im (X :    out Imaginary; Im : in Real'Base);

function Compose_From_Cartesian (Re, Im : Real'Base)
   return Complex;
function Compose_From_Cartesian (Re     : Real'Base)
   return Complex;
function Compose_From_Cartesian (Im     : Imaginary)
   return Complex;

function Modulus (X     : Complex) return Real'Base;
function "abs"   (Right : Complex) return Real'Base
   renames Modulus;

function Argument (X : Complex)
   return Real'Base;
function Argument (X : Complex; Cycle : Real'Base)
   return Real'Base;

function Compose_From_Polar (Modulus, Argument : Real'Base)
   return Complex;

function Compose_From_Polar
   (Modulus, Argument, Cycle : Real'Base)
   return Complex;

function "+"       (Right : Complex) return Complex;
function "-"       (Right : Complex) return Complex;
function Conjugate (X     : Complex) return Complex;

function "+"       (Left, Right : Complex) return Complex;
function "-"       (Left, Right : Complex) return Complex;
function "*"       (Left, Right : Complex) return Complex;
function "/"       (Left, Right : Complex) return Complex;

function "**"      (Left : Complex; Right : Integer)
   return Complex;

function "+"       (Right : Imaginary) return Imaginary;
function "-"       (Right : Imaginary) return Imaginary;
```

```
function Conjugate (X      : Imaginary) return Imaginary
    renames "–";
function "abs"      (Right : Imaginary) return Real'Base;

function "+"        (Left, Right : Imaginary) return Imaginary;
function "–"        (Left, Right : Imaginary) return Imaginary;
function "*"        (Left, Right : Imaginary) return Real'Base;
function "/"        (Left, Right : Imaginary) return Real'Base;

function "**"       (Left : Imaginary; Right : Integer)
    return Complex;

function "<"        (Left, Right : Imaginary) return Boolean;
function "<="       (Left, Right : Imaginary) return Boolean;
function ">"        (Left, Right : Imaginary) return Boolean;
function ">="       (Left, Right : Imaginary) return Boolean;

function "+"        (Left : Complex;   Right : Real'Base)
    return Complex;
function "+"        (Left : Real'Base; Right : Complex)
    return Complex;
function "–"        (Left : Complex;   Right : Real'Base)
    return Complex;
function "–"        (Left : Real'Base; Right : Complex)
    return Complex;
function "*"        (Left : Complex;   Right : Real'Base)
    return Complex;
function "*"        (Left : Real'Base; Right : Complex)
    return Complex;
function "/"        (Left : Complex;   Right : Real'Base)
    return Complex;
function "/"        (Left : Real'Base; Right : Complex)
    return Complex;

function "+"        (Left : Complex;   Right : Imaginary)
    return Complex;
function "+"        (Left : Imaginary; Right : Complex)
    return Complex;
function "–"        (Left : Complex;   Right : Imaginary)
    return Complex;
function "–"        (Left : Imaginary; Right : Complex)
    return Complex;
function "*"        (Left : Complex;   Right : Imaginary)
    return Complex;
function "*"        (Left : Imaginary; Right : Complex)
    return Complex;
function "/"        (Left : Complex;   Right : Imaginary)
    return Complex;
```

```
function "/"        (Left : Imaginary; Right : Complex)
   return Complex;

function "+"        (Left : Imaginary; Right : Real'Base)
   return Complex;
function "+"        (Left : Real'Base; Right : Imaginary)
   return Complex;
function "-"        (Left : Imaginary; Right : Real'Base)
   return Complex;
function "-"        (Left : Real'Base; Right : Imaginary)
   return Complex;

function "*"        (Left : Imaginary; Right : Real'Base)
   return Imaginary;
function "*"        (Left : Real'Base; Right : Imaginary)
   return Imaginary;
function "/"        (Left : Imaginary; Right : Real'Base)
   return Imaginary;
function "/"        (Left : Real'Base; Right : Imaginary)
   return Imaginary;

private
   ..
end Ada.Numerics.Generic_Complex_Types;
```

This package provides Ada programmers with a standard complex number type for numeric-intensive computing requirements.

Elementary functions

To mirror the standard elementary functions package introduced in Section 8.1.1 a package of elementary functions, `Ada.Numerics.Generic_Complex_Elementary_Functions`, is also defined. Because of its similarity to already introduced facilities, this package is not shown here.

As with the discrete elementary functions non-generic forms of both complex packages are declared for the predefined `Float` type:

```
with Ada.Numerics.Generic_Complex_Types;

package Ada.Numerics.Complex_Types is
   new Ada.Numerics.Generic_Complex_Types (Float);

with Ada.Numerics.Complex_Types;
with Ada.Numerics.Generic_Complex_Elementary_Functions;

package Ada.Numerics.Complex_Elementary_Functions is
   new Ada.Numerics.Generic_Complex_Elementary_Functions
                        (Ada.Numerics.Complex_Types);
```

Complex IO

The annex also defines a child package of `Ada.Text_IO` called `Complex_IO` which allows you to write complex numbers to a text IO file. The set of functions in `Complex_IO` is very similar to the definition of the standard packages nested within `Text_IO` itself.

9.6.2   Floating and fixed point numbers

This annex defines attributes for floating point types which provide precise descriptions of the machine representation of the type. Using this precise description of floating point representation the annex then goes on to describe in great detail the exact manner in which arithmetic must be performed, under what circumstances `Constraint_Error` is raised, the accuracy required of arithmetic operations, and even the performance of these operations.

For further information on these issues the best source, as usual, is the language reference manual annex G.

9.7   Annex H: safety and security annex

This annex is primarily concerned with the ability to prove statically that an Ada program is correct.

9.7.1   Pragmas

A set of additional pragmas is included in this annex.

- **pragma** `Normalize_Scalars;`   This pragma ensures that all scalar objects are initialized by the compiler if not explicitly by the programmer. It is required by the language standard that the initial value chosen by the compiler be out of range (preferably an invalid representation) so that use of such an object will raise an exception.

    The pragma acts as a configuration pragma and applies to all compilation units in the application.

- **pragma** `Reviewable;`   This configuration pragma instructs the compiler to produce enough information for a review team to tie together the original Ada source code and the compiler-generated machine code. For example the language standard says that the information must include information on run-time checks and any possible run-time exceptions due to uninitialized objects. The compiler must also produce an annotated object code listing.

- **pragma** `Inspection_Point(object_name, ..);`   This pragma can be placed anywhere in the declarative or statement part and instructs the compiler to ensure that the named object(s) are available at that point for inspection by tools such as a debugger. No code should be generated for the inspection point, so it has no run-time penalty, but it should be possible to set break points on the pragma from within a debugger. In actuality this pragma instructs the compiler not to perform any optimization that might remove the object from the resulting code.

9.7.2 Restrictions

The pragma `Restrictions` is used by the developer to instruct the compiler and/or run-time to disallow certain features. In this annex 15 new parameters to the pragma are defined:

- `Immediate_Reclamation`
- `No_Access_Subprograms`
- `No_Allocators`
- `No_Delay`
- `No_Dispatch`
- `No_Exceptions`
- `No_Fixed_Point`
- `No_Floating_Point`
- `No_IO`
- `No_Local_Allocators`
- `No_Protected_Types`
- `No_Recursion`
- `No_Reentrancy`
- `No_Unchecked_Conversion`
- `No_Unchecked_Deallocation`

It can be seen that a large combination of these can provide a safe, efficient, and small subset of the run-time requirements for an application and without such facilities as unchecked programming a much safer program can be built.

9.8 Summary

This now concludes our tour of the Ada95 programming language. You should now understand the structure and concepts behind the language itself and the shape and size of the standard library.

Bibliography

Rather than simply presenting a numbered list of references I decided to produce a list grouped by primary subject and to include some of my own comments on them.

Ada books

1 International Organization for Standardization (1995). *Information Technology – Programming Languages – Ada. Ada Reference Manual*. ISO/IEC 8652.

2 Intermetrics Inc. (1995). *Annotated Ada95 Reference Manual, Version 6.0:* Cambridge MA.

3 Intermetrics Inc. (1995). *Ada95 Rationale:* Cambridge MA.

4 Software Productivity Consortium (1995). *Ada Quality and Style: Guidelines for Professional Programmers (Working Draft)*. SPC-94093-CMC.

5 Barnes J. G. P. (1989). *Programming in Ada* (3rd Edition). Harlow UK: Addison Wesley.

6 Barnes J. G. (1995). *Programming in Ada95*. Harlow UK: Addison Wesley.

7 Burns A. and Wellings A. (1995). *Concurrency in Ada*. Cambridge UK: Cambridge University Press.

8 Feldman M. B. and Koffman E. B. (1996). *Ada 95 Problem Solving and Program Design*. Reading MA: Addison Wesley.

9 Feldman M. B. (1996). *Software Construction and Data Structures with Ada*. Reading MA: Addison Wesley.

The first three texts above are standards documents and as such are the most vital reference material for all Ada programmers. It is important that if you do not have access to these documents then the companion CD contains either on-line or printable versions of these documents and they are also available on the Internet.

The fourth document is also found on many professional Ada programmers' bookshelves. It outlines good programming practice and is often used by organizations as their standard programming style guide.

The books by John Barnes are highly recommended reading. John's books were among the first texts available on Ada and have continued as one of the foremost teaching texts on the language. Many critics of the books point at the lack of large examples as a weakness but the book is aimed at first-time programmers or people with little background and as such large complex examples may seem daunting. I would recommend a copy of the new *Programming in Ada95* as the best thing to keep next to any machine you are developing Ada programs on.

The Burns and Wellings book is a very specialized and in-depth cover of one of the more complex and difficult areas in Ada, that of tasking. The book expects a degree of familiarity with the language but is *very* readable and does have good, clear, and concise examples. If you expect to program highly concurrent or real-time systems then you should have a copy of this book.

Finally in this section the two books by Michael Feldman are essential reading for those new to Ada or Ada95. The first is the best computer science textbook I have ever read, bar none. Both books work in a step-wise fashion and are easy to read, full of excellent well-described examples, and above all teach not only Ada programming but good technique as well.

C and C++ books

10 Stroustrup B. (1991). *The C++ Programming Language* (2nd Edition). Reading MA: Addison Wesley.

11 Stroustrup B. (1994). *Design and Evolution of C++*. Reading MA: Addison Wesley.

12 Ellis M. and Stroustrup B. (1991). *The Annotated C++ Reference Manual*. Reading MA: Addison Wesley.

13 American National Standards Institute (1995). *Working Paper for Draft Proposed International Standard for Information Systems – Programming Language C++* (*X3J16/95-0087WG21/N0687*).

14 Coplien J. O. (1993). *Advanced C++, Programming Styles and Idioms*. Reading MA: Addison Wesley.

15 Musser D. R. and Saini A. (1996). *STL Tutorial and Reference Guide*. Reading MA: Addison Wesley.

16 Sessions R. (1989). *Reusable Data Structures for C*. Englewood Cliffs NJ: Prentice Hall.

Reference 10 is the C++ programmer's bible. It contains Stroustrup's own discussion of the language and contains a copy of the language reference manual. For a more in-depth look at the language-lawyer issues then the *Annotated C++ Reference Manual* (or ARM as it is commonly known) is currently the best published material. Currently the new C++ standard is only available in draft form but is already a very weighty document covering both the language and the new extended library (including STL). I know this draft can be quite difficult to track down but I do not know many C++ programmers without access to [10] or [12].

James Coplien's book [14] is a very hard read, the examples are frequently complex and often take two reads before they sink in; however, the book is entitled *Advanced C++* and so expects a high level of C++ knowledge and if read with this in mind can be a very useful text. [16] is a somewhat dated text and although good in its day has been largely superseded. It is useful though to compare the style and content with more modern texts to see how the use of encapsulation techniques make a difference to the safety of software systems.

Last and not least [11] is a great book which although not introducing new features or new techniques to the professional programmer does give an insight into the way the language has evolved. For anyone who is working on a large project the information can be useful in evaluating language features and their performance/safety trade-offs. To Ada programmers it is roughly equivalent to [3] the language rationale.

Other programming languages

17   Reiser M. and Wirth N. (1992). *Programming in Oberon – Steps beyond Pascal and Modula*. Wokingham UK: Addison Wesley.

18   Harbison S. P. (1992). *Modula-3*. Englewood Cliffs NJ: Prentice Hall.

19   Ritchey T. (1995). *Java!* Indianapolis, IN: New Riders.

These three texts cover programming languages other than C++ and Ada. I have introduced a reference to what I consider to be a good book for each of these languages when I mention them in this book. It is frequently the case that books on other programming languages contain new or different examples and ideas, so always have a quick look when in the book store to see what else has been written.

Object oriented design

20   Rumbaugh J., Blaha M., Premerlani W., Eddy F. and Lorensen W. (1991). *Object-oriented Modeling and Design*. Englewood Cliffs NJ: Prentice Hall.

This text describes the OMT method for object oriented modeling. This technique has been used in my book where class hierarchies have been described.

Resources and papers on Ada

21   *Ada Programmers Frequently Asked Questions (FAQ)*.
      http://www.adahome.com/FAQ/programming.html

The last set of references are to on-line resources and published papers. [21] is always changing and is available from the web site shown. As this document is constantly updated it covers many problems found by new Ada programmers and is therefore worth checking.

22   Kempe M. (1994). Abstract data types are under full control with Ada9X. In *Proc. TRI-Ada '94*, ACM Press.

23   Barbey S. (1994). Working with Ada9X classes. In *Proc. TRI-Ada '94*, ACM Press.

These and other papers are linked to the same Internet site as [21] and make interesting reading even though their target audience is expected to be already Ada aware.

24   Wheeler D. Lovelace Ada95 tutorial.
      http://www.adahome.com/Tutorials/Lovelace/Lovelace.html.

This Internet site contains an interactive tutorial which takes you step by step through a structured learning process. Try it; hopefully this book will have taught you enough to work through the pages with success and confidence.

25   Comar C., Gasperoni F. and Schonberg E. The GNAT Project : A GNU Ada9X
      Compiler. http://www.gnat.com/
This paper describes the GNAT compiler and might make interesting reading for those who are familiar with the GNU GCC C/C++ compiler or who are thinking of using the GNAT compilers on the companion CD.

26   Erlingson U. and Konstaninou A. V. (1996). Implementing the C++ Standard
      Template Library in Ada95. Rensselaer Polytechnic Institute.
      ftp://ftp.rpi.edu/pub/stl2ada.ps.gz

This last paper is an attempt to implement a subset of the C++ STL [13,15] in Ada95. The subset is small enough to make the paper readable, yet large enough to cover many of the issues. It does highlight some of the features used within the STL which are either unavailable in Ada95 or are implemented in a different manner. On the FTP site there is also the Ada source of the work done so far (stlrefimp-1.0.tar.gz).

Index

Ada95 Library Packages